TO PRAY OR NOT TO PRAY!

CHARLES WESLEY LOWRY
Ph.D. (Oxon.), D.D.

TO PRAY

OR NOT TO PRAY!

A Handbook for Study of Recent Supreme Court Decisions and American Church-State Doctrine

With a Foreword by
THE RT. REV. ALFRED L. BANYARD, D.D., S.T.D.
Episcopal Bishop of New Jersey

THE UNIVERSITY PRESS OF WASHINGTON, D. C.

KATERINAE

Cum autem venerit

quod perfectum est,

evacuabitur quod ex parte est.

ACKNOWLEDGMENTS

Grateful acknowledgment is made

to The Rt. Rev. Alfred L. Banyard,
Episcopal Bishop of New Jersey,
for his generous interest and
encouragement—

to five distinguished scholars for
most valuable materials:

>Rev. Pres. Henry P. Van Dusen
>Dean Erwin R. Griswold
>Professor Will Herberg
>Rev. Maurice A. Kidder
>Rabbi Bernard Zlotowitz—

to Yale University Press for
permission to quote *Jefferson on
Religion in Public Education*
by Robert M. Healey (1962)—

to Miss Sheri Ann Small, Chaplain,
Honor Society, Seabreeze High School,
Daytona Beach, Florida,
who is a symbol of young America
at its best in religious commitment.

Foreword

By The Rt. Rev. Alfred L. Banyard, D.D., S.T.D.
Bishop of the Episcopal Diocese of New Jersey

I count it both a privilege and a duty to commend this book by Dr. Charles Wesley Lowry.

It is about Prayer—not how or what to pray but about the right to pray on National occasions and in public schools. It is a great pity that we have reached a point in American history where this right, which has been a proud and profound privilege, is called in question, in part at least, by the august tribunal which all of us have been trained to reverence—the Supreme Court of the United States.

We must pray and hope that the recent words of our highest Court on prayer and Bible-reading are not its final word, but that, as has often happened in the past, the honorable Justices will have second thoughts and recover themselves and our country before we have cast away a priceless inheritance— reverence as a Nation and a United People for Almighty God, our Father in Heaven.

I note from its full title and from examining it that this is a Handbook for study. This is good. Dr. Lowry, the author, is noted for being a fearless man. Setting himself against the massive conformity complex of the time, he is not afraid to be unpopular and even lonely. This is why he has proven himself to be a true prophet, leader, and statesman, both in Church and in State. But he is not a rabble-rouser. He is, above all, a scholar and a thinker. His appeal is to right reason.

At the same time, this is not a stiff, technical treatise but a highly varied work of absorbing interest. The reader will find in it a helpful combination of subject matter. He will find closely reasoned discussions and arguments by Dr. Lowry and others. He will find some unusual human documents. And he will encounter a veritable treasure house of the most fascinating materials drawn from American history, including our greatest State Papers and the principal decisions of the Supreme Court involving religious issues over a hundred and fifty year period.

There is one special feature of the book which I have found exciting. I am sure it is going to thrill many Americans. I do not know where Dr. Lowry gets the time to do all he does, but he has brought together in this book a superb collection of religious passages drawn from literally dozens of the Inaugural Addresses of our Presidents. These form a precious testament of faith as well as a matchless document of State, and should be in every home library, every Church library, and every school library in the Nation.

This book is out at a most timely moment in history. We are in an age of exceedingly rapid change in every department of life. I in no way decry this. It is the destiny of our generation and, I am certain, is of Divine Providence.

But we have a responsibility to be sure that we do not lose, in the era of the jet plane, the rocket, the atom, and the exploration of outer space, the permanent truths on which the highest civilizations of man have been built. There are wild and lawless forces abroad in our world which are indifferent to the past and reject with hostility the permanent and the eternal. It will be a calamity of the first order if these forces get entrenched in high places in this country.

I do not expect this to happen. I refuse to join in the chorus of the Cassandras who are legion in some ecclesiastical circles and who sometimes seem to hail the coming of the post-Christian era. I think it is time for all soldiers of the Cross, all members of the Church Militant here on earth, all men and women of faith whate'er their name or sign, to rouse themselves and to give battle against the evil powers which presently seek with blatancy to undermine and take over this Nation and the whole world.

Under God, a counteroffensive in the Spirit is possible and is commanded. I believe that this volume, *To Pray or not to Pray!*, can be an instrument of enlightenment and power as we grapple with the spiritual hosts of wickedness in high places, and as we seek to strike strong blows in our generation for God and His Kingdom of righteousness and truth.

Preface

The United States, in the period between the great World Wars and in continuing Cold War, has emerged as a consciously pluralistic society.

This is not as new as we perhaps tend to think. We have always been a nation of immigrants. In the nineteenth century we espoused the role of the melting pot. Already in every distinctive cultural and sociological segment of the Nation there was in process a notable melding and fusion of many tongues, nationalities, races, and religious backgrounds.

Actually in the present century we have undertaken through restraint and control upon immigration to direct in some degree the national crucible known as the melting pot. The resultant unity and solidarity, whatever the full explanation, as manifest in an era of unprecedented peril, conflict, disunity, and worldwide social revolution, has been most impressive.

With respect to religion, we are likely to look back on the seed-time of the Republic and the period of winning our Independence and a durable Constitution as to a Golden Age. In truth, there is no evidence that the older America was more religious than the new, consciously pluralistic United States. On the contrary, the conclusion of World War II, with the descent and extinction of Hitler and the Nazi racial myth, and the era of Cold War, marked by a transference of conflict from one brand of absolutistic totalitarianism to another, were marked by a unique wave of religiousness and churchianity.

It is most interesting and important that this phenomenon was confined, among the nations of the West, to the United States. It did not appear anywhere in Latin America and it was arrestingly absent in the older and far more sorely tried nations of Europe. Perhaps only in captive Poland, with its 90 or 95 per cent Catholic population, and in enslaved East Germany, which is 85 per cent Protestant in background, was there a religious

7

quickening in any way comparable to the church situation in the United States.

Without getting into questions of valuation or qualitative theological judgment, it is evident that religion in America is not dead and is not sleeping. The spirit that moved in the Declaration of Independence, in the Great Seal of the United States, in the Northwest Ordinance, in President George Washington's First Inaugural and Farewell Address, in our spontaneously chosen National Motto, in the songs that won the patriotic assent of the People, and in the mind and heart and Biblical figure of Abraham Lincoln, is very much alive.

Tradition is not something inert and wooden, of the past merely. It is the living stream of the life of an institution, a family, the Church, the Nation. In the case of the American religious tradition, we can see it continued in three Actions of the Congress prompted by the feelings and will of a united People. In 1954, 1955, and 1956 respectively, Lincoln's phrase "under God" was added to the pledge of allegiance; it was ordered that "In God We Trust" should be inscribed on all coins and paper money; and these words were made officially the National Motto.

Unfortunately, there is a strong counter trend. It is a spirit widely and powerfully, even frighteningly, manifest in the world of our time. This impulse is the spirit of irreligion and nonreligion. It is not only doctrine but the practice of the absence and the nonexistence of God. It is atheism, not in the form of mere intellectual doubt or a Victorian agnosticism of mood, but crusading, militant, and intolerant, the negative erected into an anti-religious orthodoxy.

This aspect of twentieth-century atheism has been too much neglected by American intellectuals, including Churchmen of various faiths. We have tended to obscure it or ignore it, despite the fact that in Communism, which has undeniably tilted the world to a leaning position, even if it has not turned it upside down, we have a system of militant atheism and idolatrous humanism organized as a missionary secular church.

That great Russian and Christian, Fyodor Dostoevsky, understood this prophetically and long in advance of events. The problem of Communism, he said, "is not the problem of economics. The problem of Communism is the problem of atheism."

A Dostoevskian figure of America, a Communist who recovered his soul and became a profound Christian as well as a selfless patriot, had a similar insight. Communism, he said, is man's second oldest faith. "Like all great faiths, its force derives from a simple vision. Other ages have had great visions. They have always been different versions of the same vision: the vision of God and man's relationship to God. The Communist vision is the vision of Man without God . . . of man's mind displacing God as the creative intelligence of the world."[1]

The counter force to religion, the dread spirit of negation, is present everywhere. But so far in the United States it expresses itself in the main as a secularizing tendency, a disposition to practical but unconfessed atheism, an impulse to immersion in science and the sensate while religion is relegated to the temple and the closet. The ancient Western framework of free rational inquiry remains intact. There is real hope in this, provided responsible religious intellectuals stand their ground and insist on dialogue and debate.

This is the task of some of us in the generation of an "establishment" predominantly though not wholly radical. This is the task of many in the rising generation. This book is written out of faith in the younger generation—the generation whom many now in the seats of the mighty would deprive of the full right to believe and to know.

I have very great faith in our young people. They have special problems and must endure and master unusual strains, inherent in premature freedom of the sexes and withholding of thorough moral knowledge and training. But anyone who has addressed high school assemblies, as I have, in many states and invariably seen devotions freely led by a student, and who has corresponded with gifted leaders of our high schools over the seeming implications of recent decisions by our highest Court, cannot but feel confidence in the future of America.

It is thus that the Lord God reigns principally by grace and

---

[1] Whittaker Chambers, *Witness*, p. 9.

persuasion, and forever renews the world and mankind whom He has made.

> And for all this, nature is never spent;
> There lives the dearest freshness deep down things;
> And though the last lights off the black West went
> Oh, morning, at the brown brink eastward, springs—
> Because the Holy Ghost over the bent
> World broods with warm breast and with ah! bright wings.

The great question before this Nation, aware of and rightly seeking to assimilate its pluralism, including a special situation of racial diversity rooted deeply in our history, is whether freedom, including religious liberty, is our principal or only essential attribute; or whether we are truly a religious people whose institutions, rituals, and abiding aspirations presuppose a Supreme Being and involve an unbidden outreach to God, the Creator of all nature and the Redeemer of mankind.

A neglected but significant aspect of the public stir first raised by the New York School Prayer case is the degree to which prominent Negro leaders in Church and education in Washington have staunchly favored prayer and Bible-reading in our public schools. When it is remembered that the Supreme Court is for other reasons highly emotive as a symbol, this speaks well for the integrity and independence of these leaders. They are undoubtedly aware, more than many in high and privileged places seem to be, that there are innumerable children who, if they do not learn in school elementary lessons of morality and religion, will never learn them.

This question is immeasurably grave from the angle of the welfare of our People and the health and safety of the State, internally considered. It is also from another standpoint an issue of national and international destiny. There is something august and awe-inspiring, not only in the fact of the unending grapple of the two colossi of modern nations, but in the character and head-on clash of their respective ideologies. I do not believe that the United States at this supreme moment of mission is going to abandon her sacred heritage and accept secularity as enough. I feel that our underlying spiritual resources are great and that as a Nation and People we will hold fast by the vision of an order and a will transcending time and the frailty and finitude of man.

> O God, we have heard with our ears, and our
> fathers have declared unto us, the noble works
> that Thou didst in their days, and
> in the old time before them.

> Far-called, our navies melt away;
> On dune and headland sinks the fire:
> Lo, all our pomp of yesterday
> Is one with Nineveh and Tyre!
> Lord God of hosts, be with us yet,
> Lest we forget—lest we forget!

In His will is our peace.

Charles Wesley Lowry

"Laurusknoll"
McLean, Virginia
St. Augustine, Bp., C., D.
August 28, 1963

The rubrics of a society are an indication of its values. Only the superficial miss the significance of symbols.

—Rev. Joseph N. Moody

Oyez, Oyez, Oyez. All persons having business before the Honorable, the Supreme Court of the United States, are admonished to draw near and give their attention, for the Court is now sitting. God save the United States and this Honorable Court.
—Opening of each session since John Marshall

The future lasts a long time.

—General Charles de Gaulle
in *Salvation* (War Memoirs III)

Contents

Foreword   By The Rt. Rev. Alfred L. Banyard, D.D.,S.T.D.   5
              Bishop of the Episcopal Diocese of New Jersey

Preface   7

Chapter   1. Introduction   15

Chapter   2. Open Letter to Bishop Angus Dun   21

Appendix A   Article by Bishop Dun   29

Chapter   3. Brief of a Theologian, *Amicus Curiae*   33

Chapter   4. The Supreme Court on Prayer and the Bible   45

Chapter   5. Some Unofficial Dissents   105

Chapter   6. Thomas Jefferson as Authority and Witness   131

Appendix B   First Thanksgiving Day Proclamation by a
              President   148

Chapter   7. The Heart of Earlier Church-State Decisions   151

Chapter   8. Religion in American State Papers   179

Appendix C   Franklin's Plea for Prayer   226

Chapter   9. What Is the Remedy?   227

Epilogue: Two Witnesses   239

Appendix D   A Creed for Americans   245

A Select Bibliography   249

Chapter 1

Introduction

The years 1962 and 1963 will appear to posterity as years of revolution in the relations of Church and State, religion and government in the United States.

The revolution was not one which proceeded from or was accomplished by the American people. It was a revolution from above. It was imposed on the people in two stages through edicts handed down by the Supreme Court in deciding cases brought before it and which the Court felt it should accept for trial and decision.

The first edict, the decision of the highest Court in June, 1962, striking down the strictly nonsectarian School Prayer worked out by the Board of Regents of New York State, created a furore. There was a tremendous outburst of indignation throughout the country. People were genuinely aroused. Influential members of Congress in both Houses expressed themselves strongly, and there was much talk of a Constitutional Amendment to straighten out this issue once and for all.

Then something quite singular occurred. A combination educational and public relations campaign was initiated, aimed at explaining the Court, quieting the fears of the people, developing support for an extreme liberal outlook on issues of religion in the public schools, and preparing Americans for a further and more decisive action by the highest Court.

Among the first to speak out publicly were some of the Justices of the Court. In itself this was highly unusual. The ball was carried next by an unusual number of Protestant clergymen. It had been evident at the time of the New York decision that there was a decided split in the ranks of Protestant preachers and moulders of opinion. But activity somehow continued among those favorable to the trend of the Court and by the time of the hearings in the new Pennsylvania and Maryland cases, in March 1963, it was evident that a high-powered movement of thought-formation was in full swing.

The National Council of Churches had a study under way. So did the General Assembly of the United Presbyterian Church, U. S. A. The National Conference of Christians and Jews gave high priority to the general problem in its first National Institute held in Washington, D. C., November 18-21, 1962, and three prominent representatives of Protestantism, Catholicism, and Judaism got out a prophylactic volume under the curious title *The Outbursts That Await Us.* The American Civil Liberties Union never disguised its continuing aggressive intentions with respect to the public role of religion and in the Nation's Capital it was able to enlist the leadership of a distinguished, newly retired Episcopal Bishop, the Rt. Rev. Angus Dun, in the preparation of a study which fully anticipated the still forthcoming decision of the Supreme Court.

We do not suggest that there was anything necessarily improper in these activities. We are merely impressed by their energy, purposiveness, and success. On the negative side in the debate, which to a degree did take place after the New York decision, Bishop James A. Pike played an outstanding role. The writer made an effort to persuade him that a group undertaking of an educational and informative character was necessary if the battle was not going to be lost in the next round by default. I got the distinct impression however that the Bishop was not alarmed and even thought too highly of the legal knowledge and good judgment of the Justices of the highest Court to give credence to the fears I expressed.

Finally, there was a mild flutter in Washington when on the eve of the hearings in March already referred to there was a wide publicizing of a lecture at the University of Utah by Dean Erwin M. Griswold of the Harvard Law School. In this lecture, one of the ablest and most mature pronouncements of recent times on Religion in the American tradition, the eminent law Dean questioned current trends toward absolutism in the Supreme Court and strongly criticized the ban on the New York School Prayer.

This unexpected break was a transient comfort and perhaps

revived the hopes of a few hearts in the common sense of the members of our highest Court. Unfortunately it was too little and too late. It is clear that the climactic outcome in the Pennsylvania and Maryland Cases was preordained, given the prevailing mentality in the Court, ruling circles in the Capital, and influential ministerial elites.

One aspect of what I have called a campaign, whether or not there was much coordinated planning behind it, was rather peculiar. At the outset, following the loud clamor at the end of June, 1962, attention was directed to the proper point that any decision in a court of law is binding only on the litigants in that case and that the decision in *Engel v. Vitale* (the New York case) was a very narrow one. What Associate Justice Black had stressed in his majority opinion, we were told over and over, was that a group of public officials could not compose a prayer. *It was that which constituted an establishment of religion.*

I remember this well, for it seemed to me that the logic of Mr. Black's opinion was sweeping in its implications and I clearly foresaw that the next step would be to strike down the Lord's Prayer, or any prayer, and Bible-reading in the public school. When I stated as much, I was met by the propaganda of the narrow base of the decision in the case of the Regents' prayer. This refrain was taken up very widely by lawyers, clergy, and even average laymen in the churches. It is hard, in retrospect, not to think that the point was used very deliberately as a means, and an effective one, of assuaging public anxiety and putting the Supreme Court in a more constructive light at that particular moment.

When the cases involving reading from the Bible and praying in unison the Lord's Prayer came up, there was no issue about state officials composing a prayer or usurping the role of a church. But this did not stay the reformatory broom of the Justices. They again invoked, by a majority of 8 to 1, the establishment clause and forbade such exercises. Though the rule of confinement to this case alone undoubtedly applies from a technical standpoint, the Justices appeared to sweep with broad strokes and to say in no uncertain tones: "There is no place under the American constitutional system for prayer, reverent Bible reading, or devotional exercises of any kind in the public school. The business of the school is education not religion, the mind not the soul."

This, we repeat, is a very radical decision. It marks a turning point in our history. It adds up to a major revolution. A tradition is dead that began as early as 1684 when the rules of the New Haven Hopkins Grammar School required "that the Scholars being called together, the Mr. shall every morning begin his work with a short prayer for a blessing on his Laboures and their learning."

Can it be said that what has happened is the result of changing public opinion and is therefore a true expression of American democracy? The answer would seem to be clearly in the negative. All the evidence is that the overwhelming majority of our people accepted and approved the practices that have been struck down. Once again it is the Supreme Court that is ahead of the people and seeks to direct them, not in accordance with legal precedents but in obedience to current philosophical judgments. Opinion in the Court is, of course, not isolated. It exists among elite groups in the country as a whole and is expressive of an ideology that has been gaining adherents among American intellectuals, in varying degrees of intensity, for at least two generations. It has however picked up real speed only in the last generation. It is an ideology and its name is secular liberalism.

In the pages which follow we shall have a good deal to say about secularism. The reason why we are concerned about the recent decisions of the Supreme Court is that they symbolize much more than they enact. They may well represent a turning point that is irreversible in the process of the secularization not only of the public schools but of America. This is a very serious matter. It is not a minor happening of no great consequence but means that for 175 years we believed and did certain things and now the Ship of State has been turned in an opposite direction.

To return to the interesting question of how and why such a revolutionary development has come upon our Republic, we repeat that it is the work of a minority or a combination of minorities. Most normal lay people favor what had been the status quo in the matter of religion in public education. It is the clergy within the ranks of Protestantism who for their own reasons, some of them theological and reflective of the combined pessimism and inverted perfectionism of Neo-orthodoxy, have spoken with diverse and conflicting voices.

Along with the majority, though by no means all, of America's five million Jews and a small minority of religious radicals and free-thinkers, a weighty sector of Protestant clerical leadership has turned away from its own tradition and from the central stream of our American religious heritage in church and state. At the Requiem Mass for Pope John XXIII in Washington on June 6 I could not forbear saying to a prominent Presbyterian by whom I was seated: "Did the General Assembly feel it the other day when John Calvin turned over twice in his grave?"

The result is a most interesting reversal of historic roles in American religion. In the 19th century it was the dominant Protestant culture, embracing many disagreements but united on the public role of religion in a fundamental and nonsectarian form, which grafted on to the new public school system the older American tradition that took for granted the intimate alliance of religion, morality, and knowledge.

Today it is principally the Roman Catholic Church which is able to make the distinction between simple religious verities and fullblown creed and which champions valiantly the lost cause of traditional Americanism in the sphere of religion and the state. Father Joseph N. Moody has recently written a most apropos word: "It may appear curious to posterity that at this central point in history the three great religious bodies in America spent their time wrangling about a children's morning prayer. Maimonides, Aquinas, and Calvin would have been puzzled."

The most important thing now is for Americans to reject conformity and indifference and to do some basic thinking about church and state, religion and government, God and the nation, ultimate values and education. What we need to do is to scrutinize cliches such as, religion is the business of home and church but has no place in school, and decide what we really think about God and the civil order.

The crucial word in the opinion of the Court in the Prayer

and Bible-reading cases is neutrality. The question is, Is "religious neutrality," not as between churches and sects, but as between religion and irreligion, God and no-God, the American position? Is our nation's motto—"In God We Trust"—valid and compelling in some definite sense? Is our ancient, instinctive connection of reverence with great and special occasions as well as the daily round sound and still binding? If so, what are the implications for the training of youth, the Americans of the future?

It is here that I feel we have fallen into a morass of deep contradiction. But this is for Americans as a whole to say. They can either say Amen to what has now happened or—since the power is in the people—they can insist that the Supreme Court look more steadily at our tradition; or, if necessary, that the Constitution state precisely what the American position is.

I write not to criticize or denounce our highest Justices, who are sincere men and have done their best as they saw it, but to be a humble gadfly in a Socratic spirit and to urge on Americans deeper and more strenuous thinking.

Chapter 2

Open Letter to
Bishop Angus Dun

This is a reply to your article written for the United Press International and published in The Washington Post of May 4, 1963. The Editor of the Post notes that since your retirement you have conducted an extensive study of the religion-in-schools problem as chairman of a special committee appointed by the Civil Liberties Union of the National Capital Area.

As my old Theology teacher and spiritual mentor at Cambridge, it is with hesitancy that I take issue with you. Also, there is, as usual, much that is true and commanding in your pronouncement. Indeed, I am concerned especially by the combination in it of persuasiveness with oversimplification and omission of bristling related considerations.

Let me mention as a reminder that I have been concerned for many years with the question of religion and the American Republic. I regard this as the primary issue and see the problem of religious observances and teaching in the public schools as only one part of the larger subject, albeit an especially sensitive part. I am sure that we are agreed in fundamental concern, and I would like to emphasize my enthusiastic concurrence in a seminal portion of your statement, as follows:

> From the standpoint of any serious faith, religion has a central place in the total educational curriculum. There is an empty place in any scheme of education which fails to offer a faith to live by, a central devotion and an object of final trust.

> For Christians and for Jews, God as apprehended by faith is the object of central devotion and the object of

final trust. To leave God out of any total educational experience is to teach effectively that He does not count.

This is a masterly and most responsible theological and philosophical declaration. I am grateful for it. Where then do we
differ? What do I object to in your position as a whole?

The answer is fourfold: 1. Your position is simplistic and un-
balanced from the standpoint of the total problem. 2. You appear to accept an unhistorical view of the relations of religion
and the state in the American tradition, and you strangely
ignore, for a theologian, the reality of the unwritten and un-
legislated but well established in our tradition as a Nation and
People. 3. You give no clue as to how you interpret the Lincolnian and Biblical concept of "one Nation, under God" and
how this bears on the issue of public reverence and recognition
of Deity in prayer and otherwise. 4. Your position is set forth
without any reference to the most momentous general trend of
the age, namely—to adapt the phrase of another—the great advancing Leviathan of world-wide secularism.

It will be convenient and conducive to the avoidance of
digressions if I deal with these critical assertions one by one.

1. You conclude, on the basis of a summary analysis of the
"establishment" and "free exercise" clauses of the First Amendment, laid out without reference to historical background, legal
precedents, or principles of hermeneutics, that the Supreme
Court has no choice, in adjudicating the school cases now before it, but to strike down prayer and Bible-reading in the
public schools of the Nation.

You are undoubtedly aware that Bishop James A. Pike, a
distinguished jurist as well as a theologian, takes an opposite
view. And it is most interesting to you and me as Cambridge
men that early in the Spring (1963) Dean Erwin N. Griswold
of the Harvard Law School came out with a strong defense of
the constitutionality of religious observances in our public
schools.

In theology we accept the necessity, as a first law of
hermeneutics, of taking into account the historical background
and reference of a passage of Scripture in expounding its meaning and truth. I think it is self-evident that we must do this

carefully and thoroughly in exegeting for our time the force of the First Amendment.

Here we run into some problems, but also much solid factuality. James Madison, who wrote the first proposed draft of the Bill of Rights and took part in the debates on them in the first Congress assembled under the Federal Constitution, strongly favored the wording "an establishment of national religion." He expressed in the Congressional discussion apprehension that "one sect might obtain a preeminence and establish a religion."

This language reflects the background of the Church of England by law established in the pre-Revolutionary period and the fact that subsequent to 1776 various States established either specific churches or "the Christian religion." What the First Amendment did was to interdict the Congress from getting into such business, on the one hand, or from interfering with the free exercise of religion by individuals, sects, and churches, on the other.

The position of Thomas Jefferson can now be summarized with some degree of certainty, thanks to the publication of a Yale Ph.D. thesis entitled *Jefferson on Religion in Public Education* by Robert M. Healey (Yale University Press, 1962). This great man, of course, intended to construe the First Amendment strictly. With respect to Federal Government actions that reached into the religious field but did not involve establishment of a church or religion, he was not consistent. He did not like national Thanksgivings or Fastings and, unlike his predecessors, declined to proclaim them. On the other hand, President Jefferson did not hesitate to sign bills appropriating money for the salaries of Chaplains in both Houses of Congress and in the Armed Forces. He did the same with appropriations for the support of religion, religious education, and a priest among the Kaskaskia Indians, who were dominantly Roman Catholics.

But it is on the question of religion in public education that the most interesting Jeffersonian material is now available and clearly analyzed in the masterly monograph of Dr. Healey. Here it will be sufficient to note that Jefferson has every right to be regarded as the father of the American public school system and to quote Healey's highly informed summary of Jefferson's position. Incidentally it may be remarked that Healey rejects, on the one hand, the interpretation of the Catholic educator J. M. O'Neill, and, on the other, that of R. F. Butts, C. H. Moehlman, and Leo Pfeffer. He commends while slightly correcting the intermediate interpretation of the late Canon A. P. Stokes. This is the summary:

> The inclusion in public education of what he (Jefferson) held to be the common core of religious belief would, as he saw it, result neither in an establishment of religion nor prevent the free exercise thereof, and, even more important, it would make public education sound.

Dr. Healey brings out the profound concern of Jefferson for morality and religion as fundamentally necessary to a good society and a sound nation. This is the doctrine of Washington's *Farewell Address* and is the unanimous consensus of the Founding Fathers. It never occurred to them to doubt that this was a prime concern of the state.

You, Bishop Dun, appear to have joined the contemporary secularists in saying that religion is no business of government and in desiring to see it turned over exclusively to the home and the church. This, I feel sure, cannot be your full view, but your article leaves this vital and burning issue up in the air.

2. Many Supreme Court decisions over several decades and including Justice Douglas' just and comprehensive summation of the American tradition in *Zorach v. Clauson* (1952) have recognized the rich range of American religious practices and institutions that are public and national in character. These rituals and institutions along with such a rich strand of tradition as the religious emphasis in great State Papers and the pertinent church-state decisions of the Supreme Court make up the total tradition that we commonly call by the phrase "the American religious heritage." It is closely related to but is distinct from the various denominational and churchly traditions which cannot be said to be specifically national.

It has always seemed to me that it was illogical to pick out the public school and purify it from a secularist standpoint while electing to retain all manner of public religious observances in other areas and in some cases adding new ones. Examples are Acts of Congress in 1954, 1955, and 1956 which inserted the words "under God" into the Pledge of Allegiance to the Flag, ordered the inscription *In God We Trust* to be placed on all paper money and coins, and designated these words as the U. S. National Motto.

I acknowledge that I am a traditionalist in this matter, feeling with pride that the United States under Divine Providence had found a synthesis in the relations of church and state which stands well in between the twin extremes of an intermixture or identification of the two and the radically lay or secular state which was foreshadowed by the French Revolution but found complete expression for the first time in the Soviet Russian State. I fear that what the radical liberals of our day are doing, no doubt unintentionally and perhaps like sleepwalkers, is to open the sluice gates and let in a tide which will sweep us far from our ancestral moorings.

In any case, I question the validity of taking up the position you have on religion in public education without making clear your stand on related issues in national life and our whole public tradition.

3. Tradition is always evolving. It is the living stream of the life of a church or a nation. A vital climax of this evolution in the case of our Republic came with the prophetic work and mission of Abraham Lincoln. This President without being aware of it was a great Biblical theologian, and Fate cast him in the role of a central reinterpreter of the place and meaning of the Nation. This has been perceived in a brilliant manner by your pupil and former colleague Professor William J. Wolf in his volume on Lincoln's religion entitled *The Almost Chosen People*.

Lincoln saw the Republic of the United States as related to the God who is Living Word and Almighty Will in a manner as real as the relation of Israel to Jehovah God in the Old Testament. He saw the Bible as addressed in a living way to the American Nation and People and took for granted the propriety of Prayer, Thanksgiving, Repentance and Fasting in a national context. For him in the crisis and beyond it, we were a People whose God is the Lord.

This magnificent development, unique in modern annals, perhaps in all history, which I call *the Lincolnian concept of the Nation,* may be of everlasting significance. It may be an unrepealable aspect of our nature and destiny as a People. I am convinced that it is. Of course, I may be mistaken. It may be that this was of a time only and has no permanent meaning. But in any case this is a question for discussion. It is the question which underlies all the lesser discussions about prayer and reading of the Bible in school and religious reverence and recognition of Deity in public life. It is a grave disservice to ignore the larger issue or to stand by vacantly while it is obscured. This is especially true from a Biblical standpoint. At stake is the precious unique core of our history, consciousness, and destiny as a people.

4. The background issue of secularism has been stressed especially by Bishop Pike in relation to the New York School Prayer case, *Engel v. Vitale.* He views secularism as a form of faith, rivalling what we normally call religion. Recent Supreme Court decisions in the religion-school field he sees as having begun "the secularization and deconsecration of the Nation." In every precise agreement with Bishop Pike is His Eminence Francis Cardinal Spellman. The latter sees as abroad in our land a new spirit which seeks to change the religious tradition of America, to interpret the Constitution in a novel manner, and in effect to bring about "the establishment of a new religion of secularism." Professor Reinhold Niebuhr, whose forthright criticism of the same decision, surprised many, expressed apprehension lest we are heading toward a "consistently secular education that the Founding Fathers certainly did not intend." Another eminent theologian, the Roman Catholic Father Gustave Weigel, in a neutral context, speaks of naturalistic secularism as "the privileged theology of our land." Actually, he says, "our action as a nation rests" on this "amalgam of skepticism, empiricism and pragmatism."

My personal view is that these gentlemen are right. The overriding philosophical and spiritual issue of the present age is presented by the rise and growth of secularism. In the area of power, which is the sphere of politics, the big issue is Communism versus Freedom. In the political, economic, social and scientific field, regarded as a single field for practical purposes, the supreme problem is presented by the population explosion. But even if these issues are resolved, there is still the question, Whither the mind and soul of man? What will he worship? Whom will he serve? Whence are the sources of his values?

Secularism as a cultural distemper is not new. It has however never before been reenforced by so many powerful currents of thought and social dynamism as in our immediate time. In the United States it is not necessary that we should simply accept this tide, lying down and letting it roll over us. There is much in our society and in the intuitive assumptions of the masses of our people which is opposed to the counter-faith of secularism. I have long said that the problem was that there was a dangerous schism between the education that the elites of the Nation have been getting during the course of this century and the persisting traditionalism of the plain people amid a great variety of churches and sects. I note with keen interest that Father Weigel in his new book *The Modern God* speaks of America's theology as *double*.

> Two entirely different theologies intermingle in our people. One has the advantage of being preferred, but the other stubbornly survives without being able to suffocate its neighbor. One is the faith of the literati and the other, oblivious of criticism, is at home in the hearts of a large sector of our population.[1]

The big surprise in the public and national reaction to the 6 to 1 decision of the Supreme Court in *Engel v. Vitale* (the New York School Prayer case) and to the arguments as far as published in two suits now before the Court involving the Lord's Prayer and Bible-reading in classrooms at the opening of school, is the divided attitude of the Protestant clergy. At first it seemed that the countrywide response was one of anger and dismay, with a determination to amend the First Amendment if necessary to make it clear that we are a religious people

[1] *The Modern God: Faith in a Secular Culture* (Macmillan, 1963), p. 31. In Weigel's thinking every culture rests on a theology and the theology on a faith. The theology is religious only if the ultimate in reality is conceived as the holy.

and a Nation under God. This came out in the Congress, the reaction of Governors and Attorney Generals in almost all the States, the press, the response of the Roman Catholic hierarchy and clergy, and many Protestant pronouncements. But gradually it was revealed that Protestantism, once unanimous in this land on such issues and sure of the rightfulness of public prayer and the recognition of our deep roots as a people in the Bible, had become a house divided. Many voices from the tradition of Protestant "independency" were raised in approval of the decision in *Engel v. Vitale.* The Liberals and the Neo-orthodox, also, proved to be split. A good many younger clergy, the second generation brought up under Neo-orthodoxy, were either indifferent or inclined to be happy over a good clean-cut recognition with or without an assist from the Supreme Court that we were in a post-Christian situation. Finally, as I write, the General Assembly of the United Presbyterian Church, U. S. A., has issued what appears to be the most ringing declaration yet put forward of emancipation of church from state, and state from church.

In the face of this and because you, Bishop Dun, and I belong to a communion that has understood historically with particular clarity the interrootedness of the sacred and the secular, the eternal and the temporal, the religious and the political in human civilization, I draw your attention to these questions raised in my mind by your statement and especially to the great unanswered query raised by the threatened dominance of the spirit of secularism.

This query is, Shall responsible churchmen and conscientious religious-minded Americans accept secularism as an irresistible tide so far as state and government are concerned, or shall they hold fast to the *Lincolnian* intuition of a *Nation under God* and insist that in our system the State, equally with the Church an ordinance of God, must be as genuinely concerned as the Church for the moral education and spiritual formation of the youth of this country?

Appendix A (*From* The Washington Post)

Bishop Dun Sees Reduced Role of Religion in Schools

(Editor's Note: The U. S. Supreme Court soon will hand down a decision on the constitutionality of prayer and Bible reading in public schools. In the following dispatch, the Rt. Rev. Angus Dun discusses what the Court is likely to rule and why.

(Bishop Dun retired last year after 18 years as Episcopal Bishop of Washington. Since, he has conducted an extensive study of the religion-in-schools problem as chairman of a special committee appointed by the National Capital Area Civil Liberties Union.)

By the Rt. Rev. Angus Dun
Retired Episcopal Bishop of Washington
Written for United Press International

The decision of the U. S. Supreme Court in the New York Regents' prayer case and the cases having to do with Bible readings and the use of the Lord's Prayer in public schools, now awaiting decision, have focused attention on fundamental questions regarding the place of religion in American education.

Our society is committed by the Constitution to two principles of church-state relations.

On the one hand there is the negative principle which provides that Congress and the authorities of states shall make no laws or binding decisions respecting an establishment of religion. This principle bars our Federal Government and state authorities from giving special privileges or support to any particular religion or religious institutions.

On the other hand there is the positive principle which provides that Congress and the states shall make no laws prohibiting the free exercise of religion. This principle is designed to guard the freedom of all individuals and groups to profess and witness to their religious faith or lack of it; to worship according to their convictions and allegiances; to provide for the religious education of their children and youth, and to carry on other activities and good works expressive of their faith.

We accept these principles as fundamental to the maintenance of justice and freedom. But it does not require much reflection to conclude that they

29

cannot work themselves out without presenting difficult problems and real conflicts of interest.

Education is our most deliberate undertaking as a society to pass on to our children what we consider most important in our cultural inheritance. From the standpoint of any serious faith, religion has a central place in the total educational process. There is an empty place in any scheme of education which fails to offer a faith to live by, a central devotion and an object of final trust.

For Christians and for Jews, God as apprehended by faith is the object of central devotion and the object of final trust. To leave God out of any total educational experience is to teach effectively that He does not count.

The family has a primary role in education, particularly in the areas of religion and morality. Humanly speaking, parents determine for good or ill the intimate exposures and contagions shaping a child's life in the earlier years. In this sense, religion and morality are generally "home made."

Although religious education begins in the family, it does not end there. Few parents have the knowledge and skill to provide for their children a religious education which will keep step with their education in science, history, literature, etc., as given in their schools.

If a child's religious and moral education is to be carried forward outside the family, the primary responsibility rests with the churches and synagogues. Churches and synogogues have sought to carry out their distinctive educational role by Sunday schools and in other ways, with markedly varying educational effectiveness.

Some 85 per cent of American children attend our public schools. We must acknowledge that as things are now, the time in the lives of youth which most of the churches and synagogues can command, and the educational skills and resources they muster, are heavily outweighed by our public educational system.

It is this situation which has led the Roman Catholic Church in a massive way, and synagogues in a substantial way, to set up systems of parochial and synagogue schools, parallel to our public school system. These provide over-all elementary and secondary education under religious auspices and pervaded with religious beliefs and influences.

So we come to the particular issues brought into focus by recent and anticipated decisions of our Supreme Court.

Can or should we expect our public schools to take any part in the religious teaching and nurture of the children of religiously committed parents?

The question would not arise if it were not for the fact that some modest religious observances have been widely included in public school practice in the past.

The churches had a large part in the beginnings of American schooling. Despite the fact that our country has from the beginning been a land of many denominations, there were in the past many areas where Evangelical Protestantism was heavily dominant. In that situation it was quite natural for Bible readings and Christian prayers to be an acceptable part of public school practice.

By the middle of the last century, the number of Roman Catholics and Jews in our population had greatly increased. Questions began to be raised as to what translation of the Bible might be used in public schools.

In the past twenty years, problems arising from religious practices in the public schools have been steadily mounting. Obviously, these problems do not arise in the courts. They arise out of the American community in which people of many religious beliefs and of none have been increasingly mingled.

It is surely understandable that faithful Jewish parents do not wish their children to be asked to listen to a religious reading of Christian scriptures or to take part in a religious or semi-religious observance of the birth of Christ. It is understandable that parents who are conscientious agnostics or atheists do not want their children to be asked to join in or even listen to a prayer to the God of Christian faith, or be put in the position of publicizing their dissent.

Once these questions have been raised, it is difficult to see what decisions the Supreme Court could make save the ones it has made or seems likely to make.

Those of us who are believing Christians have mixed feelings concerning the direction in which these court decisions have been moving. Many Christians have welcomed for their children in their public school experience even a small reference to God and to Christ. Some believe that even a relatively external act can in time come to have inner meaning.

But we know that faith cannot be enforced. It is free. We know that the Bible was written from faith to faith, and can only be read religiously in a setting of faith. We know that public prayer belongs in a community of faith. And a public school cannot provide that setting. The same can be said with equal force of the religious reading of Jewish scriptures and the offerings of Jewish prayers.

Most of us who have reflected on these issues, and not simply reacted emotionally, conclude that in common justice and in conformity with the principles of our Constitution we must accept the elimination of the vestigial remains of religion from our public schools. We do this with some sense of loss but likewise with a sense of liberation.

If this be the outcome, it will be all the more important that our public schools, in their task of providing our children an understanding and appreciation of our American heritage, do full justice to the large place of the Jewish and Christian tradition in that heritage.

Our history and our political and social thought cannot be dealt with faithfully without an objective interpretation of the part played by religious convictions, motives, movements and institutions. Our literature and music and art and communal observances cannot be understood apart from the religious content and leaven found in them.

We hope that with the elimination of official religious observances from our public schools there may be a generous and imaginative exploration of ways in which young people in our public schools, especially at the high school level, might be encouraged to express voluntarily their religious interests and concerns, outside regular school hours.

Their school associations are a major part of their experience, and offer a natural framework for such activities. Such voluntary activities would help to offset the impression that this period in their lives is one from which religion is rigorously excluded.

The exclusion of religious observances from public schools will have the advantage of clearly placing responsibility for religious education where it belongs, on parents and on the churches and synagogues.

It is likely that this will stimulate further the establishment of church-controlled schools, to the possible detriment of the public schools and perhaps to the detriment of the quality of all education. We hope that continuing study and experimentation may go forward in the direction of cooperative relations between the religious communities and the public schools.

For example, the type of arrangement commonly called "shared time" might free parochial schools from the heavy financial burden of teaching subjects of only remote religious significance, and at the same time enable the churches and the synagogues to provide a far more substantial religious and moral education for children whose parents desire this for them.

(The Washington Post, May 4, 1963)

Chapter 3

Brief of a Theologian, Amicus Curiae

in

School District v. Schempp

and

Murray v. Curlett

On Lincoln's Birthday, 1963, I fell into conversation with a Justice of the Supreme Court, a splendid Christian gentleman with whom I have been pleasantly acquainted over a period of years. I told him how concerned I was with the cases before the Court on Prayer and Bible-reading and asked whether there was any way in which I could properly register my opinion, with whatever weight of knowledge and conviction it might have. He was very cordial and said that if I would draw up a statement of my views he would gladly receive it as an *Amicus Curiae* Brief and see that it was circulated among all the Justices of the Court. I produced the document printed below and carried it to the Justice in question. I have no precise knowledge as to what happened to it, but assume that my friend did as he promised. It obviously had little effect, but I want to take this opportunity to express most cordial thanks to Mr. Justice _____ for his generous courtesy.

The Supreme Court of the United States is not only unique as an institution in the governmental annals of men. It is unique in the brilliance and creativity of intellect called forth in the discharge of the grave and weighty tasks of final judicial review under the American constitutional system.

I am not sufficiently learned in the law or widely enough read to judge of the total output of Supreme Court opinions. I am however convinced, after reading and re-reading the decisions in "church-state" cases since the *United States v. Macintosh* in 1931, that the learned Justices over the past generation compare favorably in fertility of thought and dialectical

33

skill, with the theologians of Paris at the time of Thomas Aquinas or the philosophers of Germany from Kant to Hegel.

This is said with the utmost respect and entire seriousness. There is furthermore a precise application of the comparisons thus made. For the great problem with which our Justices continue to be confronted is the same as the initial, deeply determinative problem of theology and philosophy. From what premises does one set out? Where does one derive true and reliable criteria of deliberation?

A recent documentary volume *The Supreme Court on Church and State,* edited by Joseph Tussman, begins with the following sentence:

> Preoccupation by our people with the constitutionality, instead of with the wisdom, of legislation or executive action is preoccupation with a false value.

This daring dictum of former Associate Justice Felix Frankfurter would if followed to its logical implications have one of two results. It would either reduce the highest Court to the humble estate originally envisioned for it and persistently advocated all his life by Thomas Jefferson[1] or it would convert the Justices into unabashed Guardians of the State on a quasi-Platonic model. Doubtless it was Justice Frankfurter's keen perception into the complexities of the demand for wisdom, the mandate of philosophy, alongside the oh! so solid fact of a

[1] Quotations from Jefferson, which sound however sharp and excessively critical of the Court to modern American ears, could easily be multiplied. Recently Professor Sidney Hook in lectures before the University of California has championed a Jeffersonian view of the Supreme Court in relation to democratic self-government by a people (*The Paradoxes of Freedom,* University of California Press, 1962). I do not espouse Jefferson's fundamental position here save for its continuing value as a corrective and a point of anchorage for objective historical perspective. The eminent authority on constitutions, Sir Henry Maine, was right in acclaiming the American Constitution as the most successful bulwark in history against majority tyranny and mass radicalism and in protection of received liberties and basic governmental continuity. In this achievement the Supreme Court has played a decisive role. But keen sensitivity, steadfast disinterestedness, and a flexible empiricism are to the Court what vigilance is to liberty. Ever present is the danger to the most powerful judiciary in history of overplaying its hand.

written constitutional instrument that made him the contemporary champion of judicial self-restraint.

The cases before the Court at this time involving not churches or sects in any ordinary sense but persistent, deeply rooted American traditions of the public acknowledgment of God and reverence toward Him in all relationships including the public schools, have brought our republic to a decisive parting of the ways.

Every student of our national traditions—and they are beautifully spread before us in opinion after opinion of recent and present Supreme Court Justices—must acknowledge that this is so. No one thoroughly familiar with the ideas and settled convictions of George Washington, John Adams, Samuel Adams, Patrick Henry, Thomas Jefferson, James Madison, and the greatest Jeffersonian of them all though he was so much more, Abraham Lincoln, can deny the imminent possibility of the abandonment of the faith and public practice of a religious people.

Because the issues are so serious, because the youth of our country are so centrally involved, because of the peculiar configuration of religious circumstances at the present dread climax of international destiny, the search for wisdom is in a peculiar way incumbent on the Court. More than ever "this means pertinacious pursuit of the processes of Reason in the disposition of the controversies . . . before the Court."[2]

For these reasons, with profound respect and out of a compelling sense of duty on the part of one individual, this Brief is presented and the following specific considerations are adduced.

How is it with the youth of America, for which we are all responsible, and with the education of this youth, in the middle of the twentieth century? Are we sure that there is sense and wisdom in officially divorcing public education from morality and religion, and thereby flying in the face of the most definitive injunctions of our forefathers?

In the summer of 1787, while the architects of the Constitution labored at Philadelphia in travail and in pain, the Congress of the United States passed as one of its last acts, under the old

[2] Another quotation from Justice Frankfurter, from his letter to the Chief Justice and Associate Justices of September 28, 1962.

Confederation and after three readings, with only one dissenting vote, the Northwest Ordinance. This great charter of government and development for the vast Territory of the United States "northwest of the River Ohio" was reenacted by the new Congress elected and convened under the Constitution—the very same body that hammered out and submitted to the States the Bill of Rights in the form of Ten Amendments.

Article 3 of the Northwest Ordinance begins with this sentence: "Religion, morality and knowledge being necessary to good government and the happiness of mankind, schools and the means of education shall for ever be encouraged."

These words found their way into the Constitutions of many States as they were later formed, and they are carved on the stone gate of entrance to the campus of Ohio University at Athens. It cannot be fanciful to conclude dogmatically that the Northwest Ordinance embodies with an impressive unanimity on the part of the American legislators who enacted it the central conviction respecting government, society, religion, and morality which President George Washington enunciated classically in the testament of his *Farewell Address*.

The strongest historical argument those who take a broadly prohibitive view of the Establishment clause have, is one body of facts derived from the words and acts of Thomas Jefferson. Madison followed Jefferson, despite his earlier, precocious and creative originality in 1787, though as President he was less rigorous than Jefferson in upholding absolute separation of the *Federal* Government from religion. The two men are properly bracketed together.

We cannot, in my judgment, be certain of the precise meaning given to the phrase "an establishment of religion" by Madison, the original proposer of the first ten Amendments on June 8, 1789 and a member of the select House Committee to which his draft was referred, and later by Jefferson. Madison, it is true, had as his original wording: "nor shall any national religion be established." In the debate in the House on the version worked up by the select committee, he moved to re-insert the word "national" but was persuaded by Elbridge Gerry to withdraw the motion on the ground that the word had certain political overtones in contrast to "federal." Jefferson, on the other hand, was to use while he was President the fateful phrase "a wall of separation between church and state" as a description of the American system, despite the abundant certainty from many words and acts that this did not mean to him what it has come to mean to Bill of Rights absolutists today.

My own view is that what both Virginians feared was organized religious activity by churchmen, not religious influence or profession or worship within the limits of natural religion as understood by all educated men of the time. Jefferson's "wall of separation" really meant to keep church and state apart, not to isolate religion from government or education or public life.

But even if argument on the central text is bound to continue, there are undeniable facts available on Jefferson's point of view and practice which should require revision of quite a lot that has been written in opinions of the Supreme Court and that is commonly held and taught in contemporary academic circles. These facts are especially relevant to public school issues for they involve education and schools supported in the time of Jefferson by public taxation.

The most important field of facts is Jefferson's policy and outlook as Rector of the University of Virginia. This University was the crown of the life and work of the Sage of Monticello, and its founding was one of the three things for which he wished especially to be remembered by posterity. It was from its establishment in 1819 wholly controlled and supported by the State of Virginia. In 1822 Jefferson as Rector set forth his views on religious education in this public institution at considerable length. He wrote:

> In the same report of the commissioners of 1818 it was stated by them that in conformity with the principles of constitution which place all sects of religion on an equal footing . . . they had not proposed that any professorship of divinity should be established in the university. . . .
> It was not, however, to be understood that instruction in religious opinion and duties was meant to be precluded by the public authorities, as indifferent to the interests of society. On the contrary, the relations which exist between man and his maker, and the duties resulting from these relations, are the most interesting and

important to every human being, and the most incumbent on his study and investigation.

Jefferson goes on to say that a promising remedy has been proposed, and that the Visitors, of whom Madison was one, look favorably upon it. This solution was to invite the various churches or sects to establish their own religious schools "on the confines of the university" and to offer them every accommodation and cooperation, including library facilities, instruction in other sciences than theology, and the use of a room in the library for worship according to whatever rite was preferred by a given group of worshippers. Mutual independence as between these schools and the university was understood and was to be maintained. "Such an arrangement," he concludes, "would complete the circle of the useful sciences embraced by this institution, and would fill the chasm now existing, on principles which would leave inviolate the constitutional freedom of religion, the most inalienable and sacred of all human rights."

Such was the "high and impregnable" wall between Church and State erected by the First Amendment according to the understanding of Thomas Jefferson.

It seems that a great but unnecessary gulf exists between this outlook and the understanding of Jefferson's doctrine current among today's liberals, including some honorable Justices past and present. Actually it would seem that Mr. Justice Douglas in *Zorach v. Clauson* came close to enunciating the real views of Jefferson as disclosed in his acts. The one exception would be that the latter was untroubled by the expenditure of some public funds for religious purposes. In fact this clearly is not even an issue in his mind. Whereas for Mr. Douglas this is *the* issue in *Engel v. Vitale.* In his concurring opinion he wrote: "The question presented by this case is therefore an extremely narrow one. It is whether New York oversteps the bounds when it finances a religious exercise."

For the sake of completeness and because so much has been made in decisions of the Court of Jefferson's precept and example, the following additional facts are noted:

(a) Jefferson advocated the maintenance by the tax-supported College of William and Mary of "a perpetual mission among the Indian tribes" which among other things would "instruct them in the principles of Christianity." (See Healey, Robert M., *Jefferson on Religion in Public Education,* Yale University Press, 1962.)

(b) In a proposed curriculum for the University of Virginia which was drawn substantially as he had drafted it, Jefferson proposed a "professor of ethics" who would present "the Proofs of the being of a God, the Creator, Preserver, and Supreme Ruler of the universe, the Author of all the relations of morality, and of the laws and obligations these infer. . . ." (See Healey, ibid.)

(c) In 1803 as President Jefferson sent to the Senate a treaty with the Kaskaskia Indians containing this passage: "And whereas the greater part of the said tribe have been baptized and received into the Catholic Church, to which they are much attached, the United States will give, annually for 7 years, $100 toward the support of a priest of that religion, who will engage to perform for said tribe the duties of his office, and also to instruct as many of their children as possible, in the rudiments of literature. And the United States will further give the sum of $300, to assist the said tribe in the erection of a church."

Moving from the historical to the contemporary aspect of religion in education, we may helpfully focus on the reasons for the big shift in outlook on the part of many Americans and in constitutional concern. There are two main reasons. As the nineteenth century ended and the twentieth began, education in this country was undergoing a process of steady and ever increasing secularization. The impact of science was an important factor, along with high optimism about evolution interpreted— I believe erroneously—as a universal philosophical truth as applicable to society as to the biological origin of species. Another element was the backwardness of much religion in coming to terms with scientific progress.

A second reason is the twentieth century plant of slow but impressive steady growth—the concept of a plural society. This was the result directly of massive immigration, population growth, and cultural development of minorities and subsequent interfusion among themselves and older American stocks. Indirectly, the American system including the Bill of Rights and the strongest implications respecting freedom of religion and tolerance of divergent doctrines, played an indispensable role.

Secularization coming to flower and a more radical and pressing concept of tolerance explain the changed outlook of the recent past and the present generation respecting religion in society, education, and public affairs and concerns. Despite the apparent phenomenal growth of religiousness in the United States since World War II, which Professor Will Herberg has interpreted as expressive of the search of Catholic, Jew, and Protestant[3] for identity in a prosperous yet insecure America, there is probably among intellectuals less strong conviction about God, His providence and purpose, and a Divine moral law than there was in the seed-time of the Republic or in the nineteenth century. This expresses itself in a noticeable growth of uncertainty, apathy, and even hostility in respect to religious exercises once taken for granted in our public schools.

In addition, we must in all honesty note the ambivalent role of Protestantism caught between a Catholicism motivated toward earlier American church-state patterns and a Judaism dominantly though not universally inclined to desire and press harder for complete secularization in public education. Many Protestant leaders are, consciously or unconsciously, troubled by fears of an ultimate Catholic majority. They welcome therefore the erection while there is time of the strongest barricades in the form of complete church-state separation, irrespective of the traditional position of Protestants, including Congregationalism in New England, and the dominant part played by Protestants in the persistence of numerous social and governmental institutions involving the interplay of religion and the state. I believe personally as a Protestant that we must look not to our fears but to our faith and ask what is right for our Nation.

This brings us, in conclusion, to the crux of the controversy now before the Court and before the American people. This is the place of religion in the life of the Nation and in our Nation's understanding of itself. Mr. Justice Douglas was pre-occupied with this in his *Zorach* opinion. "We are a religious people whose institutions presuppose a Supreme Being." Many of his illustrious predecessors had voiced a similar view. Mr. Justice

[3] See the book *Protestant-Catholic-Jew,* Doubleday, 1955.

Story in *Vidal v. Girard's Executors* (1844) declared: "It is also said, and truly, that the Christian religion is a part of the common law of Pennsylvania." Mr. Justice Brewer in *Trinity Church v. United States* (1892) opined: "These, and many other matters which might be noted, add a volume of unofficial declarations to the mass of organic utterances that this is a Christian nation." Mr. Justice Sutherland in *United States v. Macintosh* (1931) wrote: "We are a Christian people, according to one another the equal right of religious freedom, and acknowledging with reverence the duty of obedience to the will of God." Mr. Justice Hughes in the same case in a dissenting opinion said: "One cannot speak of religious liberty, with proper appreciation of its essential and historic significance, without assuming the existence of a belief in supreme allegiance to the will of God."

Not a one of these eminent jurists doubted the interdiction of an establishment of religion or of interference with the free exercise of religion. No good American does. But do these principles taken with the impressive mass of organic utterances, prescriptions, customs, institutions, and laws in which religion and politics are intermingled according to the instincts still largely prevailing of our people, require the elimination of prayer and Bible-reading from the public schools of the Nation?

Clearly from the angle of precedents and the understanding of the Constitution through most of our history, the answer is in the negative. This is true from the standpoint of regarding prayer as a religious act, which it always is in sincere intent or it is blasphemy and mockery. One of the most threatening developments that has occurred is the supine and confused attitude of some spokesmen even before the Court who are willing to drain all religiousness out of the actions in question and settle for acknowledging in them some obscure moral value.

The readiness to compromise may be due to the seeming trend of the Court in the post-World War II period and the tendency, in our opinion a symptom of conformism and loss of individual conviction, to accept as a fact of life the progressive elimination of religion from national and public life. It is therefore to be hoped that the Court will use the present opportunity to clarify the American constitutional position on religious expressions in national life.

It should not be thought a shameful or a questionable thing to pray under government auspices. It might be very useful and a service to reverence to diminish the volume of prayer at the inauguration of a President. That of course is a problem for the President. But the point of praying is a religious point. Prayer in all ages is the soul of religion. Let all accept this, be the consequences what they may.

Prayer does not have to be spoken out loud in words. There is the prayer of silence and there is prayer in silence. But a period of quiet for silent meditation and prayer, if it is to be meaningful, is also a religious act. It might from a constitutional standpoint be an alleviation of problems connected with diverse religious faiths. But the atheist's complaint would logically remain the same.

The wisest and most truly American and constitutional decision would be an authoritative recognition of the valid place of prayer and the Bible without commentary and public reverence before God coupled with the illegality of sectarian or creedal exploitation of this or exercising compulsion on individuals as parents or otherwise in a religious context.

To illustrate, it has long seemed to me that the part of wisdom and equity would be for schools where Protestant and Catholic pupils are well intermixed to have a policy of alternation between the Catholic form of the Lord's Prayer, which follows the oldest extant manuscript, the Codex Vaticanus, and the King James and Protestant usage which continues the Jewish-Christian doxology appended to the original prayer at a very early time, no doubt for liturgical reasons. This could be both educational and a beneficial practical exercise in tolerance.

Similarly I see no reason why a rabbinically authorized, short and simple prayer, taken from an ancient Hebrew use, should not be welcomed as a further alternative where an appreciable number of scholars in the classroom are Jewish. Were Buddhists to desire and to merit because of numbers of children the use in turn of a similarly authenticated Buddhist prayer, as might conceivably be the case in Hawaii, I see no reason for hesitation in accepting such an enrichment of America in its totality.

The Nation has come a long way in the recognition of tolerance and plurality as implicates of the dignity of the individual and as foundation stones of democratic society. If relieved from continuous apprehension as to what the American and constitutional position is and if encouraged to work for the highest good of all their pupils, I believe that our state and local authorities could be trusted to work out all problems in this sphere constructively and generously. The pupils would benefit accordingly and be prepared for real, appreciative tolerance and not mere toleration as adults.

Thus, also, our precious and unique American religious heritage in its fulness may be preserved and our path as a Nation continue along the fruitful middle way, elected by our forefathers, between establishmentarianism and the dismissal of religion from public status and significance.

Chapter 4

The Supreme Court
On Prayer and the Bible

This book is both forensic and documentary. It is both a think piece and a work book.

It is obviously necessary for us to know what our highest Court says and why, before we can pass any judgment on it or form an opinion about its decisions. If we undertake this seriously and really work at it, striving to consider the issues rationally rather than merely emotionally, we shall certainly benefit both educationally and as Americans. We shall also be showing proper respect to the Supreme Court of our land, which after all is a division of government under the Constitution and has a job to do on behalf of us all.

The highest Court does not claim infallibility or exemption from criticism. I am sure that the eminent Justices would unanimously agree that the Court profits in the long run from criticism and that it desires to be related in a proper manner to reasoned public opinion, and not merely to be instrumental in forming it. Certainly over the decades, and over more than a century and a half, the Court has changed often and reversed itself in varying degrees numerous times. This will undoubtedly continue.

Dean Erwin M. Griswold has stated exceptionally well and in a critical context—with respect to the New York School Prayer decision reproduced below—what our attitude toward the highest Court should be. He said, before the University of Utah Law School:

> An institution charged with the role which the Supreme Court has successfully filled for so many years is entitled to our respect and understanding. If one criticizes the court (as people have always done in the past, and should continue to do so in the future), it should be essentially for the purpose of trying to contribute to that respect and to that understanding. The debt which we all owe to the court is far greater than any individual can repay. Criticism of decisions of the court or opinions of its members should be offered as an effort to repay that debt, and with the thought that conscientious criticism may be an aid to the court in carrying out its difficult and essential task.

Two recent and highly controversial decisions of the Supreme Court are presented now in full and with all footnotes intact. This is seldom if ever done in a nonlegal work. The opinion of the Court is given in each case, followed by the dissenting opinion. The concurring opinions are not included. In a later chapter, an attempt is made to skim the cream off the most important Church-State decisions of the highest Court from the beginning.

Chapter Contents

(Internal Pagination for Reference)

THE TWO CONTROVERSIAL DECISIONS

1. *Engel vs. Vitale*

(June 25, 1962)

OPINION OF THE COURT

Mr. Justice Black 47

DISSENTING OPINION

Mr. Justice Stewart 62

2. *Abingdon School District vs. Schempp*
and
Murray vs. Curlett
(June 17, 1963)

OPINION OF THE COURT

Mr. Justice Clark 68

DISSENTING OPINION

Mr. Justice Stewart 91

SUPREME COURT OF THE UNITED STATES

No. 468.—October Term, 1961.

| Steven I. Engel et al., Petitioners, *v.* William J. Vitale, Jr., et al. | On Writ of Certiorari to the Court of Appeals of New York. |

[June 25, 1962.]

Mr. Justice Black delivered the opinion of the Court.

The respondent Board of Education of Union Free School District No. 9, New Hyde Park, New York, acting in its official capacity under state law, directed the School District's principal to cause the following prayer to be said aloud by each class in the presence of a teacher at the beginning of each school day:

> "Almighty God, we acknowledge our dependence upon Thee, and we beg Thy blessings upon us, our parents, our teachers and our country."

This daily procedure was adopted on the recommendation of the State Board of Regents, a governmental agency created by the State Constitution to which the New York Legislature has granted broad supervisory, executive, and legislative powers over the State's public school system.[1] These state officials composed the prayer which they recommended and published as a part of their "Statement on Moral and Spiritual Training in the Schools," saying: "We believe that this Statement will be subscribed to by all men and women of good will, and we call upon all of them to aid in giving life to our program."

---

[1] See New York Constitution, Art. V, § 4; New York Education Law, §§ 101, 120 *et seq.*, 202, 214–219, 224, 245 *et seq.*, 704, and 801 *et seq.*

Shortly after the practice of reciting the Regents'
prayer was adopted by the School District, the parents of
ten pupils brought this action in a New York State Court
insisting that use of this official prayer in the public
schools was contrary to the beliefs, religions, or religious
practices of both themselves and their children.   Among
other things, these parents challenged the constitutionality of both the state law authorizing the School District
to direct the use of prayer in public schools and the School
District's regulation ordering the recitation of this particular prayer on the ground that these actions of official
governmental agencies violate that part of the First
Amendment of the Federal Constitution which commands
that "Congress shall make no law respecting an establishment of religion"—a command which was "made applicable to the State of New York by the Fourteenth
Amendment of the said Constitution."   The New York
Court of Appeals, over the dissents of Judges Dye and
Fuld, sustained an order of the lower state courts which
had upheld the power of New York to use the Regents'
prayer as a part of the daily procedures of its public
schools so long as the schools did not compel any pupil
to join in the prayer over his or his parents' objection.[2]
We granted certiorari to review this important decision

---

[2] 10 N. Y. 2d 174, 176 N. E. 2d 579. The trial court's opinion,
which is reported at 18 Misc. 2d 659, 191 N. Y. S. 2d 453, had
made it clear that the Board of Education must set up some sort
of procedures to protect those who objected to reciting the prayer:
"This is not to say that the rights accorded petitioners and their
children under the 'free exercise' clause do not mandate safeguards
against such embarrassments and pressures. It is enough on this
score, however, that regulations, such as were adopted by New
York City's Board of Education in connection with its released time
program, be adopted, making clear that neither teachers nor any
other school authority may comment on participation or nonparticipation in the exercise nor suggest or require that any posture or

involving rights protected by the First and Fourteenth Amendments.[3]

We think that by using its public school system to encourage recitation of the Regents' prayer, the State of New York has adopted a practice wholly inconsistent with the Establishment Clause. There can, of course, be no doubt that New York's program of daily classroom invocation of God's blessings as prescribed in the Regents' prayer is a religious activity. It is a solemn avowal of divine faith and supplication for the blessings of the Almighty. The nature of such a prayer has always been religious, none of the respondents has denied this and the trial court expressly so found:

> "The religious nature of prayer was recognized by Jefferson and has been concurred in by theological writers, the United States Supreme Court and State courts and administrative officials, including New York's Commissioner of Education. A committee of the New York Legislature has agreed.

> "The Board of Regents as *amicus curiae*, the respondents and intervenors all concede the religious

---

language be used or dress be worn or be not used or not worn. Nonparticipation may take the form either of remaining silent during the exercise, or if the parent or child so desires, of being excused entirely from the exercise. Such regulations must also make provision for those nonparticipants who are to be excused from the prayer exercise. The exact provision to be made is a matter for decision by the board, rather than the court, within the framework of constitutional requirements. Within that framework would fall a provision that prayer participants proceed to a common assembly while nonparticipants attend other rooms, or that nonparticipants be permitted to arrive at school a few minutes late or to attend separate opening exercises, or any other method which treats with equality both participants and nonparticipants." 18 Misc. 2d, at 696, 191 N. Y. S. 2d, at 492–493. See also the opinion of the Appellate Division affirming that of the trial court, reported at 11 App. Div. 2d 340, 206 N. Y. S. 2d 183.

[3] 368 U. S. 924.

nature of prayer, but seek to distinguish this prayer because it is based on our spiritual heritage. . . ." [4]

The petitioners contend among other things that the state laws requiring or permitting use of the Regents' prayer must be struck down as a violation of the Establishment Clause because that prayer was composed by governmental officials as a part of a governmental program to further religious beliefs. For this reason, petitioners argue, the State's use of the Regents' prayer in its public school system breaches the constitutional wall of separation between Church and State. We agree with that contention since we think that the constitutional prohibition against laws respecting an establishment of religion must at least mean that in this country it is no part of the business of government to compose official prayers for any group of the American people to recite as a part of a religious program carried on by government.

It is a matter of history that this very practice of establishing governmentally composed prayers for religious services was one of the reasons which caused many of our early colonists to leave England and seek religious freedom in America. The Book of Common Prayer, which was created under governmental direction and which was approved by Acts of Parliament in 1548 and 1549,[5] set out in minute detail the accepted form and content of prayer and other religious ceremonies to be used in the established, tax-supported Church of England.[6] The controversies over the Book and what should

---

[4] 18 Misc. 2d, at 671–672, 191 N. Y. S. 2d, at 468–469.

[5] 2 & 3 Edward VI, c. 1, entitled "An Act for Uniformity of Service and Administration of the Sacraments throughout the Realm"; 3 & 4 Edward VI, c. 10, entitled "An Act for the abolishing and putting away of divers Books and Images."

[6] The provisions of the various versions of the Book of Common Prayer are set out in broad outline in the Encyclopedia Britannica, Vol. 18 (1957 ed.), pp. 420–423. For a more complete description, see Pullan, The History of the Book of Common Prayer (1900).

be its content repeatedly threatened to disrupt the peace of that country as the accepted forms of prayer in the established church changed with the views of the particular ruler that happened to be in control at the time.[7] Powerful groups representing some of the varying religious views of the people struggled among themselves to impress their particular views upon the Government and obtain amendments of the Book more suitable to their respective notions of how religious services should be conducted in order that the official religious establishment would advance their particular religious beliefs.[8] Other

---

[7] The first major revision of the Book of Common Prayer was made in 1552 during the reign of Edward VI. 5 & 6 Edward VI, c. 1. In 1553, Edward VI died and was succeeded by Mary who abolished the Book of Common Prayer entirely. 1 Mary, c. 2. But upon the accession of Elizabeth in 1558, the Book was restored with important alterations from the form it had been given by Edward VI. 1 Elizabeth, c. 2. The resentment to this amended form of the Book was kept firmly under control during the reign of Elizabeth but, upon her death in 1603, a petition signed by more than 1,000 Puritan ministers was presented to King James I asking for further alterations in the Book. Some alterations were made and the Book retained substantially this form until it was completely suppressed again in 1645 as a result of the successful Puritan Revolution. Shortly after the restoration in 1660 of Charles II, the Book was again reintroduced, 13 & 14 Charles II, c. 4, and again with alterations. Rather than accept this form of the Book some 2,000 Puritan ministers vacated their benefices. See generally Pullan, The History of the Book of Common Prayer (1900), pp. vii–xvi; Encyclopedia Britannica (1957 ed.), Vol. 18, pp. 421–422.

[8] For example, the Puritans twice attempted to modify the Book of Common Prayer and once attempted to destroy it. The story of their struggle to modify the Book in the reign of Charles I is vividly summarized in Pullan, History of the Book of Common Prayer, at p. xiii: "The King actively supported those members of the Church of England who were anxious to vindicate its Catholic character and maintain the ceremonial which Elizabeth had approved. Laud, Archbishop of Canterbury, was the leader of this school. Equally resolute in his opposition to the distinctive tenets of Rome and of Geneva, he enjoyed the hatred of both Jesuit and Calvinist. He helped the Scottish bishops, who had made large concessions to the

groups, lacking the necessary political power to influence the Government on the matter, decided to leave England and its established church and seek freedom in America from England's governmentally ordained and supported religion.

It is an unfortunate fact of history that when some of the very groups which had most strenuously opposed the established Church of England found themselves sufficiently in control of colonial governments in this country to write their own prayers into law, they passed laws making their own religion the official religion of their respective colonies.[9]   Indeed, as late as the time of the Revolutionary War, there were established churches in at least eight of the thirteen former colonies and established religions in at least four of the other five.[10]   But the success-

---

uncouth habits of Presbyterian worship, to draw up a Book of Common Prayer for Scotland. It contained a Communion Office resembling that of the book of 1549. It came into use in 1637, and met with a bitter and barbarous opposition. The vigour of the Scottish Protestants strengthened the hands of their English sympathisers. Laud and Charles were executed, Episcopacy was abolished, the use of the Book of Common Prayer was prohibited."

[9] For a description of some of the laws enacted by early theocratic governments in New England, see Parrington, Main Currents in American Thought (1930), Vol. 1, pp. 5–50; Whipple, Our Ancient Liberties (1927), pp. 63–78; Wertenbaker, The Puritan Oligarchy (1947).

[10] The Church of England was the established church of at least five colonies: Maryland, Virginia, North Carolina, South Carolina and Georgia. There seems to be some controversy as to whether that church was officially established in New York and New Jersey but there is no doubt that it received substantial support from those states. See Cobb, The Rise of Religious Liberty in America (1902), pp. 338, 408. In Massachusetts, New Hampshire and Connecticut, the Congregationalist Church was officially established. In Pennsylvania and Delaware, all Christian sects were treated equally in most situations but Catholics were discriminated against in some respects. See generally Cobb, The Rise of Religious Liberty in America (1902). In Rhode Island all Protestants enjoyed equal privileges but it is not

ful Revolution against English political domination was shortly followed by intense opposition to the practice of establishing religion by law. This opposition crystallized rapidly into an effective political force in Virginia where the minority religious groups such as Presbyterians, Lutherans, Quakers and Baptists had gained such strength that the adherents to the established Episcopal Church were actually a minority themselves. In 1785–1786, those opposed to the established Church, led by James Madison and Thomas Jefferson, who, though themselves not members of any of these dissenting religious groups, opposed all religious establishments by law on grounds of principle, obtained the enactment of the famous "Virginia Bill for Religious Liberty" by which all religious groups were placed on an equal footing so far as the State was concerned.[11] Similar though less far-reaching legislation was being considered and passed in other States.[12]

By the time of the adoption of the Constitution, our history shows that there was a widespread awareness among many Americans of the dangers of a union of Church and State. These people knew, some of them from bitter personal experience, that one of the greatest

---

clear whether Catholics were allowed to vote. Compare Fiske, The Critical Period in American History (1899), p. 76 with Cobb, The Rise of Religious Liberty in America (1902), pp. 437–438.

[11] 12 Hening, Statutes of Virginia (1823), 84, entitled "An Act for establishing religious freedom." The story of the events surrounding the enactment of this law was reviewed in *Everson* v. *Board of Education*, 330 U. S. 1, both by the Court, at pp. 11–13, and in the dissenting opinion of Mr. Justice Rutledge, at pp. 33–42. See also Fiske, The Critical Period in American History (1899), pp. 78–82; James, The Struggle for Religious Liberty in Virginia (1900); Thom, The Struggle for Religious Freedom in Virginia: The Baptists (1900); Cobb, The Rise of Religious Liberty in America (1902), pp. 74–115, 482–499.

[12] See Cobb, The Rise of Religious Liberty in America (1902), pp. 482–509.

dangers to the freedom of the individual to worship in his own way lay in the Government's placing its official stamp of approval upon one particular kind of prayer or one particular form of religious services. They knew the anguish, hardship and bitter strife that could come when zealous religious groups struggled with one another to obtain the Government's stamp of approval from each King, Queen, or Protector that came to temporary power. The Constitution was intended to avert a part of this danger by leaving the government of this country in the hands of the people rather than in the hands of any monarch. But this safeguard was not enough. Our Founders were no more willing to let the content of their prayers and their privilege of praying whenever they pleased be influenced by the ballot box than they were to let these vital matters of personal conscience depend upon the succession of monarchs. The First Amendment was added to the Constitution to stand as a guarantee that neither the power nor the prestige of the Federal Government would be used to control, support or influence the kinds of prayer the American people can say— that the people's religions must not be subjected to the pressures of government for change each time a new political administration is elected to office. Under that Amendment's prohibition against governmental establishment of religion, as reinforced by the provisions of the Fourteenth Amendment, government in this country, be it state or federal, is without power to prescribe by law any particular form of prayer which is to be used as an official prayer in carrying on any program of governmentally sponsored religious activity.

There can be no doubt that New York's state prayer program officially establishes the religious beliefs embodied in the Regents' prayer. The respondents' argument to the contrary, which is largely based upon the

contention that the Regents' prayer is "non-denominational" and the fact that the program, as modified and
approved by state courts, does not require all pupils to
recite the prayer but permits those who wish to do so
to remain silent or be excused from the room, ignores the
essential nature of the program's constitutional defects.
Neither the fact that the prayer may be denominationally neutral, nor the fact that its observance on the
part of the students is voluntary can serve to free it from
the limitations of the Establishment Clause, as it might
from the Free Exercise Clause, of the First Amendment,
both of which are operative against the States by virtue
of the Fourteenth Amendment. Although these two
clauses may in certain instances overlap, they forbid two
quite different kinds of governmental encroachment upon
religious freedom. The Establishment Clause, unlike the
Free Exercise Clause, does not depend upon any showing
of direct governmental compulsion and is violated by the
enactment of laws which establish an official religion
whether those laws operate directly to coerce nonobserv-
ing individuals or not. This is not to say, of course, that
laws officially prescribing a particular form of religious
worship do not involve coercion of such individuals.
When the power, prestige and financial support of government is placed behind a particular religious belief, the
indirect coercive pressure upon religious minorities to conform to the prevailing officially approved religion is plain.
But the purposes underlying the Establishment Clause
go much further than that. Its first and most immediate purpose rested on the belief that a union of government and religion tends to destroy government and to
degrade religion. The history of governmentally established religion, both in England and in this country,
showed that whenever government had allied itself with
one particular form of religion, the inevitable result had

been that it had incurred the hatred, disrespect and even contempt of those who held contrary beliefs.[13] That same history showed that many people had lost their respect for any religion that had relied upon the support of government to spread its faith.[14] The Establishment Clause thus stands as an expression of principle on the part of the Founders of our Constitution that religion is too personal, too sacred, too holy, to permit its "unhallowed perversion" by a civil magistrate.[15] Another purpose of the Establishment Clause rested upon an awareness of the historical fact that governmentally established religions and religious persecutions go hand in hand.[16] The Founders

---

[13] "[A]ttempts to enforce by legal sanctions, acts obnoxious to so great a proportion of Citizens, tend to enervate the laws in general, and to slacken the bands of Society. If it be difficult to execute any law which is not generally deemed necessary or salutary, what must be the case where it is deemed invalid and dangerous? and what may be the effect of so striking an example of impotency in the Government, on its general authority." Memorial and Remonstrance against Religious Assessments, II Writings of Madison 183, 190.

[14] "It is moreover to weaken in those who profess this Religion a pious confidence in its innate excellence, and the patronage of its Author; and to foster in those who still reject it, a suspicion that its friends are too conscious of its fallacies, to trust it to its own merits. . . . [E]xperience witnesseth that ecclesiastical establishments, instead of maintaining the purity and efficacy of Religion, have had a contrary operation. During almost fifteen centuries, has the legal establishment of Christianity been on trial. What have been its fruits? More or less in all places, pride and indolence in the Clergy; ignorance and servility in the laity; in both, superstition, bigotry and persecution. Enquire of the Teachers of Christianity for the ages in which it appeared in its greatest lustre; those of every sect, point to the ages prior to its incorporation with Civil policy." *Id.*, at 187.

[15] Memorial and Remonstrance against Religious Assessments, II Writings of Madison, at 187.

[16] "[T]he proposed establishment is a departure from that generous policy, which, offering an asylum to the persecuted and oppressed of every Nation and Religion, promised a lustre to our country, and

knew that only a few years after the Book of Common Prayer became the only accepted form of religious services in the established Church of England, an Act of Uniformity was passed to compel all Englishmen to attend those services and to make it a criminal offense to conduct or attend religious gatherings of any other kind [17]—a law which was consistently flouted by dissenting religious groups in England and which contributed to widespread

---

an accession to the number of its citizens. What a melancholy mark is the Bill of sudden degeneracy? Instead of holding forth an asylum to the persecuted, it is itself a signal of persecution. . . . Distant as it may be, in its present form, from the Inquisition it differs from it only in degree. The one is the first step, the other the last in the career of intolerance. The magnanimous sufferer under this cruel scourge in foreign Regions, must view the Bill as a Beacon on our Coast, warning him to seek some other haven, where liberty and philanthropy in their due extent may offer a more certain repose from his troubles." *Id.*, at 188.

[17] 5 & 6 Edward VI, c. 1, entitled "An Act for the Uniformity of Service and Administration of Sacraments throughout the Realm." This Act was repealed during the reign of Mary but revived upon the accession of Elizabeth. See note 7, *supra*. The reasons which led to the enactment of this statute were set out in its preamble: "Where there hath been a very godly Order set forth by the Authority of Parliament, for Common Prayer and Administration of Sacraments to be used in the Mother Tongue within the Church of *England*, agreeable to the Word of God and the Primitive Church, very comfortable to all good People desiring to live in Christian Conversation, and most profitable to the Estate of this Realm, upon the which the Mercy, Favour and Blessing of Almighty God is in no wise so readily and plenteously poured as by Common Prayers, due using of the Sacraments, and often preaching of the Gospel, with the Devotion of the Hearers: (1) And yet this notwithstanding, a great Number of People in divers Parts of this Realm, following their own Sensuality, and living either without Knowledge or due Fear of God, do wilfully and damnably before Almighty God abstain and refuse to come to their Parish Churches and other Places where Common Prayer, Administration of the Sacraments, and Preaching of the Word of God, is used upon *Sundays* and other Days ordained to be Holydays."

persecutions of people like John Bunyan who persisted in
holding "unlawful [religious] meetings . . . to the great
disturbance and distraction of the good subjects of this
kingdom. . . ." [18] And they knew that similar persecutions had received the sanction of law in several of the
colonies in this country soon after the establishment of
official religions in those colonies.[19] It was in large part
to get completely away from this sort of systematic religious persecution that the Founders brought into being
our Nation, our Constitution, and our Bill of Rights with
its prohibition against any governmental establishment
of religion. The New York laws officially prescribing the
Regents' prayer are inconsistent with both the purposes
of the Establishment Clause and with the Establishment
Clause itself.

It has been argued that to apply the Constitution in
such a way as to prohibit state laws respecting an
establishment of religious services in public schools is
to indicate a hostility toward religion or toward prayer.
Nothing, of course, could be more wrong. The history
of man is inseparable from the history of religion. And
perhaps it is not too much to say that since the beginning
of that history many people have devoutly believed that
"More things are wrought by prayer than this world
dreams of." It was doubtless largely due to men who
believed this that there grew up a sentiment that caused
men to leave the cross-currents of officially established
state religions and religious persecution in Europe and
come to this country filled with the hope that they
could find a place in which they could pray when they

---

[18] Bunyan's own account of his trial is set forth in A Relation of
the Imprisonment of Mr. John Bunyan, reprinted in Grace Abound-
ing and The Pilgrim's Progress (Brown ed. 1907), at 103–132.

[19] For a vivid account of some of these persecutions, see Wertenbaker, The Puritan Oligarchy (1947).

pleased to the God of their faith in the language they chose.[20]   And there were men of this same faith in the power of prayer who led the fight for adoption of our Constitution and also for our Bill of Rights with the very guarantees of religious freedom that forbid the sort of governmental activity which New York has attempted here.   These men knew that the First Amendment, which tried to put an end to governmental control of religion and

---

[20] Perhaps the best example of the sort of men who came to this country for precisely that reason is Roger Williams, the founder of Rhode Island, who has been described as "the truest Christian amongst many who sincerely desired to be Christian."   Parrington, Main Currents of American Thought (1930), Vol. 1, at p. 74.   Williams, who was one of the earliest exponents of the doctrine of separation of church and state, believed that separation was necessary in order to protect the church from the danger of destruction which he thought inevitably flowed from control by even the best-intentioned civil authorities: "The unknowing zeale of *Constantine* and other Emperours, did more hurt to *Christ Jesus* his Crowne and Kingdome, then the raging fury of the most bloody *Neroes*.   In the *persecutions* of the later, *Christians* were sweet and fragrant, like spice pounded and beaten in morters: But those *good* Emperours, persecuting some erroneous persons, *Arrius, &c.* and advancing the professours of some Truths of Christ (for there was no small number of *Truths* lost in those times) and maintaining their *Religion* by the materiall Sword, I say by this meanes *Christianity* was *ecclipsed,* and the Professors of it fell asleep . . . ."   Williams, The Bloudy Tenent, of Persecution, for cause of Conscience, discussed, in A Conference betweene Truth and Peace (London, 1644), reprinted in Naragansett Club Publications, Vol. III, p. 184.   To Williams, it was no part of the business or competence of a civil magistrate to interfere in religious matters: "[W]hat imprudence and *indiscretion* is it in the most common affaires of Life, to conceive that *Emperours, Kings* and *Rulers* of the earth must not only be qualified with *politicall* and *state abilities* to *make* and *execute* such *Civill Lawes* which may concerne the common *rights, peace* and *safety* (which is worke and businesse, load and burthen enough for the ablest shoulders in the Commonweal) but also furnished with such *Spirituall* and heavenly *abilities* to governe the *Spirituall* and *Christian Commonweale.* . . ."   *Id.,* at 366.   See also *id.,* at 136–137.

of prayer, was not written to destroy either. They knew rather that it was written to quiet well-justified fears which nearly all of them felt arising out of an awareness that governments of the past had shackled men's tongues to make them speak only the religious thoughts that government wanted them to speak and to pray only to the God that government wanted them to pray to. It is neither sacrilegious nor antireligious to say that each separate government in this country should stay out of the business of writing or sanctioning official prayers and leave that purely religious function to the people themselves and to those the people choose to look to for religious guidance.[21]

It is true that New York's establishment of its Regents' prayer as an officially approved religious doctrine of that State does not amount to a total establishment of one particular religious sect to the exclusion of all others— that, indeed, the governmental endorsement of that prayer seems relatively insignificant when compared to the governmental encroachments upon religion which were commonplace 200 years ago. To those who may subscribe to the view that because the Regents' official prayer is so brief and general there can be no danger to religious freedom in its governmental establishment, however, it may be appropriate to say in the words of James Madison, the author of the First Amendment:

---

[21] There is of course nothing in the decision reached here that is inconsistent with the fact that school children and others are officially encouraged to express love for our country by reciting historical documents such as the Declaration of Independence which contain references to the Deity or by singing officially espoused anthems which include the composer's professions of faith in a Supreme Being, or with the fact that there are many manifestations in our public life of belief in God. Such patriotic or ceremonial occasions bear no true resemblance to the unquestioned religious exercise that the State of New York has sponsored in this instance.

"[I]t is proper to take alarm at the first experiment on our liberties. . . . Who does not see that the same authority which can establish Christianity, in exclusion of all other Religions, may establish with the same ease any particular sect of Christians, in exclusion of all other Sects? That the same authority which can force a citizen to contribute three pence only of his property for the support of any one establishment, may force him to conform to any other establishment in all cases whatsoever?" [22]

The judgment of the Court of Appeals of New York is reversed and the cause remanded for further proceedings not inconsistent with this opinion.

Reversed and remanded.

Mr. Justice Frankfurter took no part in the decision of this case.

Mr. Justice White took no part in the consideration or decision of this case.

---

[22] Memorial and Remonstrance against Religious Assessments, II Writings of Madison 183, at 185–186.

SUPREME COURT OF THE UNITED STATES

No. 468.—OCTOBER TERM, 1961.

Steven I. Engel et al., Petitioners, v. William J. Vitale, Jr., et al.

On Writ of Certiorari to the Court of Appeals of New York.

[June 25, 1962.]

MR. JUSTICE STEWART, dissenting.

A local school board in New York has provided that those pupils who wish to do so may join in a brief prayer at the beginning of each school day, acknowledging their dependence upon God and asking His blessing upon them and upon their parents, their teachers, and their country. The Court today decides that in permitting this brief non-denominational prayer the school board has violated the Constitution of the United States. I think this decision is wrong.

The Court does not hold, nor could it, that New York has interfered with the free exercise of anybody's religion. For the state courts have made clear that those who object to reciting the prayer must be entirely free of any compulsion to do so, including any "embarrassments and pressures." Cf. *West Virginia State Board of Education* v. *Barnette,* 319 U. S. 624. But the Court says that in permitting school children to say this simple prayer, the New York authorities have established "an official religion."

With all respect, I think the Court has misapplied a great constitutional principle. I cannot see how an "official religion" is established by letting those who want to say a prayer say it. On the contrary, I think that to deny the wish of these school children to join in reciting this prayer is to deny them the opportunity of sharing in the spiritual heritage of our Nation.

The Court's historical review of the quarrels over the Book of Common Prayer in England throws no light for me on the issue before us in this case. England had then and has now an established church. Equally unenlightening, I think, is the history of the early establishment and later rejection of an official church in our own States. For we deal here not with the establishment of a state church, which would, of course, be constitutionally impermissible, but with whether school children who want to begin their day by joining in prayer must be prohibited from doing so. Moreover, I think that the Court's task, in this as in all areas of constitutional adjudication, is not responsibly aided by the uncritical invocation of metaphors like the "wall of separation," a phrase nowhere to be found in the Constitution. What is relevant to the issue here is not the history of an established church in sixteenth century England or in eighteenth century America, but the history of the religious traditions of our people, reflected in countless practices of the institutions and officials of our government.

At the opening of each day's Session of this Court we stand, while one of our officials invokes the protection of God. Since the days of John Marshall our Crier has said, "God save the United States and this Honorable Court." [1] Both the Senate and the House of Representatives open their daily Sessions with prayer.[2] Each of our Presidents, from George Washington to John F. Kennedy, has upon assuming his Office asked the protection and help of God.[3]

---

[1] See Warren, The Supreme Court in United States History, Vol. 1, p. 469.

[2] See Rule III, Senate Manual, S. Doc. No. 2, 87th Cong., 1st Sess. See Rule VII, Rules of the House of Representatives, H. R. Doc. No. 459, 86th Cong., 2d Sess.

[3] For example:

On April 30, 1789, President George Washington said:

". . . it would be peculiarly improper to omit in this first official act my fervent supplications to that Almighty Being who

Footnote 3—Continued.

rules over the universe, who presides in the councils of nations, and whose providential aids can supply every human defect, that His benediction may consecrate to the liberties and happiness of the people of the United States a Government instituted by themselves for these essential purposes, and may enable every instrument employed in its administration to execute with success the functions allotted to His charge. In tendering this homage to the Great Author of every public and private good, I assure myself that it expresses your sentiments not less than my own, nor those of my fellow-citizens at large less than either. No people can be bound to acknowledge and adore the Invisible Hand which conducts the affairs of men more than those of the United States.

.   .   .   .   .

"Having thus imparted to you my sentiments as they have been awakened by the occasion which brings us together, I shall take my present leave; but not without resorting once more to the benign Parent of the Human Race in humble supplication that, since He has been pleased to favor the American people with opportunities for deliberating in perfect tranquillity, and dispositions for deciding with unparalleled unanimity on a form of government for the security of their union and the advancement of their happiness, so His divine blessing may be equally *conspicuous* in the enlarged views, the temperate consultations, and the wise measures on which the success of this Government must depend."

On March 4, 1797, President John Adams said:

"And may that Being who is supreme over all, the Patron of Order, the Fountain of Justice, and the Protector in all ages of the world of virtuous liberty, continue His blessing upon this nation and its Government and give it all possible success and duration consistent with the ends of His providence."

On March 4, 1805, President Thomas Jefferson said:

"I shall need, too, the favor of that Being in whose hands we are, who led our fathers, as Israel of old, from their native land and planted them in a country flowing with all the necessaries and comforts of life; who has covered our infancy with His providence and our riper years with His wisdom and power, and to whose goodness I ask you to join in supplications with me

Footnote 3—Continued.

that He will so enlighten the minds of your servants, guide their councils, and prosper their measures that whatsoever they do shall result in your good, and shall secure to you the peace, friendship, and approbation of all nations."

On March 4, 1809, President James Madison said:

"But the source to which I look . . . is in . . . my fellow-citizens, and in the counsels of those representing them in the other departments associated in the care of the national interests. In these my confidence will under every difficulty be best placed, next to that which we have all been encouraged to feel in the guardianship and guidance of that Almighty Being whose power regulates the destiny of nations, whose blessings have been so conspicuously dispensed to this rising Republic, and to whom we are bound to address our devout gratitude for the past, as well as our fervent supplications and best hopes for the future."

On March 4, 1865, President Abraham Lincoln said:

"Fondly do we hope, fervently do we pray, that this mighty scourge of war may speedily pass away. Yet, if God wills that it continue until all the wealth piled by the bondsman's two hundred and fifty years of unrequited toil shall be sunk, and until every drop of blood drawn with the lash shall be paid by another drawn with the sword, as was said three thousand years ago, so still it must be said 'the judgments of the Lord are true and righteous altogether.'

"With malice toward none, with charity for all, with firmness in the right as God gives us to see the right, let us strive on to finish the work we are in, to bind up the nation's wounds, to care for him who shall have borne the battle and for his widow and his orphan, to do all which may achieve and cherish a just and lasting peace among ourselves and with all nations."

On March 4, 1885, President Grover Cleveland said:

"And let us not trust to human effort alone, but humbly acknowledging the power and goodness of Almighty God, who presides over the destiny of nations, and who has at all times been revealed in our country's history, let us invoke His aid and His blessing upon our labors."

On March 5, 1917, President Woodrow Wilson said:

"I pray God I may be given the wisdom and the prudence to do my duty in the true spirit of this great people."

The Court today says that the state and federal governments are without constitutional power to prescribe any particular form of words to be recited by any group of the American people on any subject touching religion.[4] The third stanza of "The Star-Spangled Banner," made our National Anthem by Act of Congress in 1931,[5] contains these verses:

> "Blest with victory and peace, may the heav'n rescued land
>> Praise the Pow'r that hath made and preserved us a nation!
> Then conquer we must, when our cause it is just,
>> And this be our motto 'In God is our Trust.' "

In 1954 Congress added a phrase to the Pledge of Allegiance to the Flag so that it now contains the words "one Nation *under God,* indivisible, with liberty and justice

---

On March 4, 1933, President Franklin D. Roosevelt said:
"In this dedication of a Nation we humbly ask the blessing of God. May He protect each and every one of us. May He guide me in the days to come."

On January 21, 1957, President Dwight D. Eisenhower said:
"Before all else, we seek, upon our common labor as a nation, the blessings of Almighty God. And the hopes in our hearts fashion the deepest prayers of our whole people."

On January 20, 1961, President John F. Kennedy said:
"The world is very different now. . . . And yet the same revolutionary beliefs for which our forebears fought are still at issue around the globe—the belief that the rights of man come not from the generosity of the state, but from the hand of God.

.   .   .   .   .

"With a good conscience our only sure reward, with history the final judge of our deeds, let us go forth to lead the land we love, asking His blessing and His help, but knowing that here on earth God's work must truly be our own."

[4] My brother DOUGLAS says that the only question before us is whether government "can constitutionally finance a religious exercise." The official chaplains of Congress are paid with public money. So are military chaplains. So are state and federal prison chaplains.

[5] 36 U. S. C. § 170.

for all." [6]   In 1952 Congress enacted legislation calling upon the President each year to proclaim a National Day of Prayer.[7] Since 1865 the words "IN GOD WE TRUST" have been impressed on our coins.[8]

Countless similar examples could be listed, but there is no need to belabor the obvious.[9] It was all summed up by this Court just ten years ago in a single sentence: "We are a religious people whose institutions presuppose a Supreme Being." *Zorach* v. *Clauson,* 343 U. S. 306, 313.

I do not believe that this Court, or the Congress, or the President has by the actions and practices I have mentioned established an "official religion" in violation of the Constitution. And I do not believe the State of New York has done so in this case. What each has done has been to recognize and to follow the deeply entrenched and highly cherished spiritual traditions of our Nation— traditions which come down to us from those who almost two hundred years ago avowed their "firm reliance on the Protection of Divine Providence" when they proclaimed the freedom and independence of this brave new world.[10]

I dissent.

---

[6] 36 U. S. C. § 172.   [7] 36 U. S. C. § 185.

[8] 13 Stat. 517, 518; 17 Stat. 427; 35 Stat. 164; 69 Stat. 290. The current provisions are embodied in 31 U. S. C. §§ 324, 324a.

[9] I am at a loss to understand the Court's unsupported *ipse dixit* that these official expressions of religious faith in and reliance upon a Supreme Being "bear no true resemblance to the unquestioned religious exercise that the State of New York has sponsored in this instance." See p. ——, *supra,* n. 21. I can hardly think that the Court means to say that the First Amendment imposes a lesser restriction upon the Federal Government than does the Fourteenth Amendment upon the States. Or is the Court suggesting that the Constitution permits judges and Congressmen and Presidents to join in prayer, but prohibits school children from doing so?

[10] The Declaration of Independence ends with this sentence: "And for the support of this Declaration, with a firm reliance on the Protection of Divine Providence, we mutually pledge to each other our Lives, our Fortunes and our sacred Honor."

SUPREME COURT OF THE UNITED STATES

Nos. 142 AND 119.—OCTOBER TERM, 1962.

School District of Abington Township, Pennsylvania, et al., Appellants, 142 *v.* Edward Lewis Schempp et al.	On Appeal From the United States District Court for the Eastern District of Pennsylvania.
William J. Murray III, etc., et al., Petitioners, 119 *v.* John N. Curlett, President, et al., Individually, and Constituting the Board of School Commissioners of Baltimore City.	On Writ of Certiorari to the Court of Appeals of Maryland.

[June 17, 1963.]

MR. JUSTICE CLARK delivered the opinion of the Court.

Once again we are called upon to consider the scope of the provision of the First Amendment to the United States Constitution which declares that "Congress shall make no law respecting an establishment of religion or prohibiting the free exercise thereof . . . ." These companion cases present the issues in the context of state action requiring that schools begin each day with readings from the Bible. While raising the basic questions under slightly different factual situations, the cases permit of joint treatment. In light of the history of the First Amendment and of our cases interpreting and applying its requirements, we hold that the practices at issue and the laws requiring them are unconstitutional under the Establishment Clause, as applied to the states through the Fourteenth Amendment.

I.

The Facts in Each Case: No. 142. The Commonwealth of Pennsylvania by law, 24 Pa. Stat. § 15–1516, as amended, Pub. Law 1928 (Supp. 1960) Dec. 17, 1959, requires that "At least ten verses from the Holy Bible shall be read, without comment, at the opening of each public school on each school day. Any child shall be excused from such Bible reading, or attending such Bible reading, upon the written request of his parent or guardian." The Schempp family, husband and wife and two of their three children, brought suit to enjoin enforcement of the statute, contending that their rights under the Fourteenth Amendment to the Constitution of the United States are, have been, and will continue to be violated unless this statute be declared unconstitutional as violative of these provisions of the First Amendment. They sought to enjoin the appellant school district, wherein the Schempp children attend school, and its officers and the Superintendent of Public Instruction of the Commonwealth from continuing to conduct such readings and recitation of the Lord's Prayer in the public schools of the district pursuant to the statute. A three-judge statutory District Court for the Eastern District of Pennsylvania held that the statute is violative of the Establishment Clause of the First Amendment as applied to the States by the Due Process Clause of the Fourteenth Amendment and directed that appropriate injunctive relief issue. 201 F. Supp. 815.[1] On appeal by the District, its officials and

---

[1] The action was brought in 1958, prior to the 1959 amendment of § 15–1516 authorizing a child's nonattendance at the exercises upon parental request. The three-judge court held the statute and the practices complained of unconstitutional under both the Establishment Clause and the Free Exercise Clause. 177 F. Supp. 398. Pending appeal to this Court by the school district, the statute was so amended, and we vacated the judgment and remanded for further

the Superintendent, under 28 U. S. C. § 1253, we noted probable jurisdiction. 371 U. S. 807.

The appellees Edward Lewis Schempp, his wife Sidney, and their children, Roger and Donna, are of the Unitarian faith and are members of the Unitarian Church in Germantown, Philadelphia, Pennsylvania, where they, as well as another son, Ellory, regularly attend religious services. The latter was originally a party but having graduated from the school system *pendente lite* was voluntarily dismissed from the action. The other children attend the Abington Senior High School, which is a public school operated by appellant district.

On each school day at the Abington Senior High School between 8:15 and 8:30 a. m., while the pupils are attending their home rooms or advisory sections, opening exercises are conducted pursuant to the statute. The exercises are broadcast into each room in the school building through an intercommunications system and are conducted under the supervision of a teacher by students attending the school's radio and television workshop. Selected students from this course gather each morning in the school's workshop studio for the exercises, which include readings by one of the students of 10 verses of the Holy Bible, broadcast to each room in the building. This is followed by the recitation of the Lord's Prayer, likewise over the intercommunications system, but also by the students in the various classrooms, who are asked to stand and join in repeating the prayer in unison. The exercises are closed with the flag salute and such pertinent announcements as are of interest to the students. Participation in the opening exercises, as directed by the statute, is voluntary. The student reading the verses

---

proceedings. 364 U. S. 298. The same three-judge court granted appellees' motion to amend the pleadings, 195 F. Supp. 518, held a hearing on the amended pleadings and rendered the judgment, 201 F. Supp. 815, from which appeal is now taken.

from the Bible may select the passages and read from any
version he chooses, although the only copies furnished by
the school are the King James version, copies of which
were circulated to each teacher by the school district.
During the period in which the exercises have been conducted the King James, the Douay and the Revised
Standard versions of the Bible have been used, as well as
the Jewish Holy Scriptures. There are no prefatory
statements, no questions asked or solicited, no comments
or explanations made and no interpretations given at or
during the exercises. The students and parents are ad-
vised that the student may absent himself from the classroom or, should he elect to remain, not participate in the
exercises.

It appears from the record that in schools not having an
intercommunications system the Bible reading and the
recitation of the Lord's Prayer were conducted by the
home-room teacher,[2] who chose the text of the verses and
read them herself or had students read them in rotation
or by volunteers. This was followed by a standing recitation of the Lord's Prayer, together with the Pledge of
Allegiance to the flag by the class in unison and a closing
announcement of routine school items of interest.

At the first trial Edward Schempp and the children
testified as to specific religious doctrines purveyed by a
literal reading of the Bible "which were contrary to the
religious beliefs which they held and to their familial
teaching." 177 F. Supp. 398, 400. The children testified that all of the doctrines to which they referred were
read to them at various times as part of the exercises.
Edward Schempp testified at the second trial that he had
considered having Roger and Donna excused from at-

---

[2] The statute as amended imposes no penalty upon a teacher refusing to obey its mandate. However, it remains to be seen whether
one refusing could have his contract of employment terminated for
"wilful violation of the school laws." 24 Pa. Stat. (Supp. 1960)
§ 11–1122.

tendance at the exercises but decided against it for several reasons, including his belief that the children's relationships with their teachers and classmates would be adversely affected.[3]

Expert testimony was introduced by both appellants and appellees at the first trial, which testimony was summarized by the trial court as follows:

"Dr. Solomon Grayzel testified that there were marked differences between the Jewish Holy Scriptures and the Christian Holy Bible, the most obvious of which was the absence of the New Testament in the Jewish Holy Scriptures. Dr. Grayzel testified that portions of the New Testament were offensive to Jewish tradition and that, from the standpoint of Jewish faith, the concept of Jesus Christ as the Son of God was 'practically blasphemous.' He cited instances in the New Testament which, assertedly, were not only sectarian in nature but tended to bring the Jews into ridicule or scorn. Dr. Grayzel gave

---

[3] The trial court summarized his testimony as follows:

"Edward Schempp, the children's father, testified that after careful consideration he had decided that he should not have Roger or Donna excused from attendance at these morning ceremonies. Among his reasons were the following. He said that he thought his children would be 'labeled as "odd balls" ' before their teachers and classmates every school day; that children, like Roger's and Donna's classmates, were liable 'to lump all particular religious difference[s] or religious objections [together] as "atheism" ' and that today the word 'atheism' is often connected with 'atheistic communism,' and has 'very bad' connotations, such as 'un-American' or 'anti-Red,' with overtones of possible immorality. Mr. Schempp pointed out that due to the events of the morning exercises following in rapid succession, the Bible reading, the Lord's Prayer, the Flag Salute, and the announcements, excusing his children from the Bible reading would mean that probably they would miss hearing the announcements so important to children. He testified also that if Roger and Donna were excused from Bible reading they would have to stand in the hall outside their 'homeroom' and that this carried with it the imputation of punishment for bad conduct." 201 F. Supp., at 818.

as his expert opinion that such material from the New Testament could be explained to Jewish children in such a way as to do no harm to them. But if portions of the New Testament were read without explanation, they could be, and in his specific experience with children Dr. Grayzel observed, had been, psychologically harmful to the child and had caused a divisive force within the social media of the school.

"Dr. Grayzel also testified that there was significant difference in attitude with regard to the respective Books of the Jewish and Christian Religions in that Judaism attaches no special significance to the reading of the Bible *per se* and that the Jewish Holy Scriptures are source materials to be studied. But Dr. Grayzel did state that many portions of the New, as well as of the Old, Testament contained passages of great literary and moral value.

"Dr. Luther A. Weigle, an expert witness for the defense, testified in some detail as to the reasons for and the methods employed in developing the King James and the Revised Standard Versions of the Bible. On direct examination, Dr. Weigle stated that the Bible was non-sectarian. He later stated that the phrase 'non-sectarian' meant to him non-sectarian within the Christian faiths. Dr. Weigle stated that his definition of the Holy Bible would include the Jewish Holy Scriptures, but also stated that the 'Holy Bible' would not be complete without the New Testament. He stated that the New Testament 'conveyed the message of Christians.' In his opinion, reading of the Holy Scriptures to the exclusion of the New Testament would be a sectarian practice. Dr. Weigle stated that the Bible was of great moral, historical and literary value. This is conceded by all the parties and is also the view of the court." 177 F. Supp. 398, 401–402.

The trial court, in striking down the practices and the statute requiring them, made specific findings of fact that the children's attendance at Abington Senior High School is compulsory and that the practice of reading 10 verses from the Bible is also compelled by law. It also found that:

> "The reading of the verses, even without comment, possesses a devotional and religious character and constitutes in effect a religious observance. The devotional and religious nature of the morning exercises is made all the more apparent by the fact that the Bible reading is followed immediately by a recital in unison by the pupils of the Lord's Prayer. The fact that some pupils, or theoretically all pupils, might be excused from attendance at the exercises does not mitigate the obligatory nature of the ceremony for . . . Section 1516 . . . unequivocally requires the exercises to be held every school day in every school in the Commonwealth. The exercises are held in the school buildings and perforce are conducted by and under the authority of the local school authorities and during school sessions. Since the statute requires the reading of the 'Holy Bible,' a Christian document, the practice . . . prefers the Christian religion. The record demonstrates that it was the intention of . . . the Commonwealth . . . to introduce a religious ceremony into the public schools of the Commonwealth." 201 F. Supp., at 819.

No. 119. In 1905 the Board of School Commissioners of Baltimore City adopted a rule pursuant to Art. 77, § 202 of the Annotated Code of Maryland. The rule provided for the holding of opening exercises in the schools of the city consisting primarily of the "reading, without comment, of a chapter in the Holy Bible and/or the use of the Lord's Prayer." The petitioners, Mrs. Madalyn Murray and her son, William J. Murray, III, are both professed atheists. Following unsuccessful attempts to have the respondent school board rescind the rule this suit was filed for mandamus to compel its rescission and cancellation. It was alleged that William was a student in a public school of the city and Mrs. Murray, his mother, was a taxpayer therein; that it was the practice under the rule to have a reading on each school morning from the King James version of the Bible; that at petitioners' insistence the rule was amended [4] to permit children to be excused from the exercise on request of the parent and that William had been excused pursuant thereto; that nevertheless the rule as amended was in violation of the petitioners' rights "to freedom of religion under the First and Fourteenth Amendments" and in violation of "the principle of separation between church and state, contained therein. . . ." The petition particularized the petitioners' atheistic beliefs and stated that the rule, as practiced, violated their rights

> "in that it threatens their religious liberty by placing a premium on belief as against non-belief and subjects their freedom of conscience to the rule of the majority; it pronounces belief in God as the source of all moral and spiritual values, equating these values with religious values, and thereby renders sinister,

---

[4] The rule as amended provides as follows:

"Opening Exercise. Each school, either collectively or in classes, shall be opened by the reading, without comment, of a chapter in the Holy Bible and/or the use of the Lord's Prayer. The Douay version may be used by those pupils who prefer it. Appropriate patriotic exercises should be held as a part of the general opening exercise of the school or class. Any child shall be excused from participating in the opening exercises or from attending the opening exercises upon written request of his parent or guardian."

alien and suspect the beliefs and ideals of . . . . Petitioners, promoting doubt and question of their morality, good citizenship and good faith."

The respondents demurred and the trial court, recognizing that the demurrer admitted all facts well pleaded, sustained it without leave to amend. The Maryland Court of Appeals affirmed, the majority of four justices holding the exercise not in violation of the First and Fourteenth Amendments, with three justices dissenting. 228 Md. 239, 179 A. 2d 698. We granted certiorari. 371 U. S. 809.

II.

It is true that religion has been closely identified with our history and government. As we said in *Engel* v. *Vitale,* 370 U. S. 421, 434 (1962), "The history of man is inseparable from the history of religion. And . . . since the beginning of that history many people have devoutly believed that 'More things are wrought by prayer than this world dreams of.' " In *Zorach* v. *Clauson,* 343 U. S. 306, 313 (1952), we gave specific recognition to the proposition that "[w]e are a religious people whose institutions presuppose a Supreme Being." The fact that the Founding Fathers believed devotedly that there was a God and that the unalienable rights of man were rooted in Him is clearly evidenced in their writings, from the Mayflower Compact to the Constitution itself. This background is evidenced today in our public life through the continuance in our oaths of office from the Presidency to the Alderman of the final supplication, "So help me God." Likewise each House of the Congress provides through its Chaplain an opening prayer, and the sessions of this Court are declared open by the crier in a short ceremony, the final phrase of which invokes the grace of God. Again, there are such manifestations in our military forces, where those of our citizens who are under the restrictions of military service wish to engage in voluntary worship. Indeed, only last year an official survey of the country indicated that 64% of our people have church membership, Bureau of Census, U. S. Department of Commerce, Statistical Abstract of the United States, 48 (83d ed. 1962), while less than 3% profess no religion whatever. *Id.,* at p. 46. It can be truly said, therefore, that today, as in the beginning, our national life reflects a religious people who, in the words of Madison, are "earnestly praying, as . . . in duty bound, that the Supreme Lawgiver of the Universe . . . guide them into every measure which may be worthy of his . . . blessing . . . ." Memorial and Remonstrance Against Religious Assessments, quoted in *Everson* v. *Board of Education,* 330 U. S. 1, 71–72 (1947) (Appendix to dissenting opinion of Rutledge, J.).

This is not to say, however, that religion has been so identified with our history and government that religious freedom is not likewise as strongly imbedded in our public and private life. Nothing but the most telling of personal experiences in religious persecution suffered by our forebears, see *Everson* v. *Board of Education, supra,* at 8–11, could have planted our belief in liberty of religious opinion any more deeply in our heritage. It is true that this liberty frequently was not realized by the colonists, but this is readily accountable to their close ties to the Mother Country.[5] However, the views of Madison and Jefferson, preceded by Roger Williams,[6] came to be incor-

---

[5] There were established churches in at least eight of the original colonies, and various degrees of religious support in others as late as the Revolutionary War. See *Engel* v. *Vitale, supra,* at 428, n. 10.

[6] "There goes many a ship to sea, with many hundred souls in one ship, whose weal and woe is common, and is a true picture of a commonwealth, or human combination, or society. It hath fallen out sometimes, that both Papists and Protestants, Jews and Turks, may be embarked in one ship; upon which supposal, I affirm that all the liberty of conscience I ever pleaded for, turns upon these two

porated not only in the Federal Constitution but likewise in those of most of our States. This freedom to worship was indispensable in a country whose people came from the four quarters of the earth and brought with them a diversity of religious opinion. Today authorities list 83 separate religious bodies, each with memberships exceeding 50,000, existing among our people, as well as innumerable smaller groups. Bureau of Census, *op. cit., supra,* at 46–47.

III.

Almost a hundred years ago in *Minor* v. *Board of Education of Cincinnati,*[7] Judge Alphonzo Taft, father of the revered Chief Justice, in an unpublished opinion stated the ideal of our people as to religious freedom as one of

"absolute equality before the law of all religious opinions and sects . . . ."

.   .   .   .   .

"The government is neutral, and, while protecting all, it prefers none, and it disparages none."

Before examining this "neutral" position in which the Establishment and Free Exercise Clauses of the First Amendment place our government it is well that we discuss the reach of the Amendment under the cases of this Court.

---

hinges, that none of the Papists, Protestants, Jews, or Turks be forced to come to the ship's prayers or worship, nor compelled from their own particular prayers or worship, if they practice any."

[7] Superior Court of Cincinnati, February 1870. The opinion is not reported but is published under the title, The Bible in the Common Schools (Cincinnati: Robert Clarke & Co. 1870). Judge Taft's views, expressed in dissent, prevailed on appeal. See *Board of Education of Cincinnati* v. *Minor,* 23 Ohio St. 211, 253 (1872), in which the Ohio Supreme Court held that:

"The great bulk of human affairs and human interests is left by any free government to individual enterprise and individual action. Religion is eminently one of these interests, lying outside the true and legitimate province of government."

First, this Court has decisively settled that the First Amendment's mandate that "Congress shall make no law respecting an establishment of religion, or prohibiting the free exercise thereof" has been made wholly applicable to the states by the Fourteenth Amendment. Twenty-three years ago in *Cantwell* v. *Connecticut,* 310 U. S. 296, 303 (1940), this Court, through Mr. Justice Roberts, said:

> "The fundamental concept of liberty embodied in that [Fourteenth] Amendment embraces the liberties guaranteed by the First Amendment. The First Amendment declares that Congress shall make no law respecting an establishment of religion or prohibiting the free exercise thereof. The Fourteenth Amendment has rendered the legislatures of the states as incompetent as Congress to enact such laws . . . ." [8]

In a series of cases since *Cantwell* the Court has repeatedly reaffirmed that doctrine, and we do so now. *Murdock* v. *Pennsylvania,* 319 U. S. 105, 108 (1943); *Everson* v. *Board of Education, supra; Illinois ex rel. McCollum* v. *Board of Education,* 333 U. S. 203, 210–211 (1948); *Zorach* v. *Clauson, supra; McGowan* v. *Maryland,* 366 U. S. 420 (1961); *Torcaso* v. *Watkins,* 367 U. S. 488 (1961); and *Engel* v. *Vitale, supra.*

Second, this Court has rejected unequivocally the contention that the establishment clause forbids only governmental preference of one religion over another. Al-

---

[8] Application to the States of other clauses of the First Amendment obtained even before *Cantwell.* Almost 40 years ago in the opinion of the Court in *Gitlow* v. *New York,* 268 U. S. 652, 666 (1925), Mr. Justice Sanford said: "For present purposes we may and do assume that freedom of speech and of the press—which are protected by the First Amendment from abridgement by Congress—are among the fundamental personal rights and 'liberties' protected by the Due Process Clause of the Fourteenth Amendment from impairment by the States."

most 20 years ago in *Everson, supra,* at 15, the Court said that "[n]either a state nor the Federal government can set up a church. Neither can pass laws which aid one religion, aid all religions, or prefer one religion over another." And Mr. Justice Jackson, dissenting, agreed:

> "There is no answer to the proposition . . . that the effect of the religious freedom Amendment to our Constitution was to take every form of propagation of religion out of the realm of things which could directly or indirectly be made public business and thereby be supported in whole or in part at taxpayers' expense . . . . This freedom was first in the Bill of Rights because it was first in the forefathers' minds; it was set forth in absolute terms, and its strength is its rigidity." *Id.,* at 26.

Further, Mr. Justice Rutledge, joined by Justices Frankfurter, Jackson and Burton, declared:

> "The [First] Amendment's purpose was not to strike merely at the official establishment of a single sect, creed or religion, outlawing only a formal relation such as had prevailed in England and some of the Colonies. Necessarily it was to uproot all such relationships. But the object was broader than separating church and state in this narrow sense. It was to create a complete and permanent separation of the spheres of religious activity and civil authority by comprehensively forbidding every form of public aid or support for religion." *Id.,* at 31–32.

The same conclusion has been firmly maintained ever since that time, see *Illinois ex rel. McCollum, supra,* at pp. 210–211; *McGowan* v. *Maryland, supra,* at 442–443; *Torcaso* v. *Watkins, supra,* at 492–493, 495, and we reaffirm it now.

While none of the parties to either of these cases has questioned these basic conclusions of the Court, both of which have been long established, recognized and consistently reaffirmed, others continue to question their history, logic and efficacy. Such contentions, in the light of the consistent interpretation in cases of this Court, seem entirely untenable and of value only as academic exercises.

IV.

The interrelationship of the Establishment and the Free Exercise Clauses was first touched upon by Mr. Justice Roberts for the Court in *Cantwell* v. *Connecticut, supra,* at 303, where it was said that their "inhibition of legislation" had

> "a double aspect. On the one hand, it forestalls compulsion by law of the acceptance of any creed or the practice of any form of worship. Freedom of conscience and freedom to adhere to such religious organization or form of worship as the individual may choose cannot be restricted by law. On the other hand, it safeguards the free exercise of the chosen form of religion. Thus the Amendment embraces two concepts—freedom to believe and freedom to act. The first is absolute but, in the nature of things, the second cannot be."

A half dozen years later in *Everson* v. *Board of Education, supra,* at 14–15, this Court, through MR. JUSTICE BLACK, stated that the "scope of the First Amendment . . . was designed forever to suppress" the establishment of religion or the prohibition of the free exercise thereof. In short, the Court held that the Amendment

> "requires the state to be a neutral in its relations with groups of religious believers and non-believers; it does not require the state to be their adversary. State power is no more to be used so as to handicap religions than it is to favor them." *Id.,* at 18.

And Mr. Justice Jackson, in dissent, declared that public schools are organized

> "on the premise that secular education can be isolated from all religious teaching so that the school can inculcate all needed temporal knowledge and also maintain a strict and lofty neutrality as to religion. The assumption is that after the individual has been instructed in worldly wisdom he will be better fitted to choose his religion." *Id.*, at 23–24.

Moreover, all of the four dissenters, speaking through Mr. Justice Rutledge, agreed that

> "Our constitutional policy . . . . [D]oes not deny the value or necessity for religious training, teaching or observance. Rather it secures their free exercise. But to that end it does deny that the state can undertake or sustain them in any form or degree. For this reason the sphere of religious activity, as distinguished from the secular intellectual liberties, has been given the two-fold protection and, as the state cannot forbid, neither can it perform or aid in performing the religious function. The dual prohibition makes that function altogether private." *Id.*, at 52.

Only one year later the Court was asked to reconsider and repudiate the doctrine of these cases in *McCollum* v. *Board of Education*. It was argued that "historically the First Amendment was intended to forbid only government preference of one religion over another . . . . In addition they ask that we distinguish or overrule our holding in the *Everson* case that the Fourteenth Amendment made the 'establishment of religion' clause of the First Amendment applicable as a prohibition against the States." 333 U. S., at 211. The Court, with Mr. Justice Reed alone dissenting, was unable to "accept either of these contentions." *Ibid.* Mr. Justice Frankfurter, joined by Justices Jackson, Rutledge and Burton, wrote a very comprehensive and scholarly concurrence in which he said that "[s]eparation is a requirement to abstain from fusing functions of government and of religious sects, not merely to treat them all equally." *Id.*, at 227. Continuing, he stated that:

> "the Constitution . . . prohibited the government common to all from becoming embroiled, however innocently, in the destructive religious conflicts of which the history of even this country records some dark pages." *Id.*, at 228.

In 1952 in *Zorach* v. *Clauson, supra,* MR. JUSTICE DOUGLAS for the Court reiterated:

> "There cannot be the slightest doubt that the First Amendment reflects the philosophy that Church and State should be separated. And so far as interference with the 'free exercise' of religion and an 'establishment' of religion are concerned, the separation must be complete and unequivocal. The First Amendment within the scope of its coverage permits no exception; the prohibition is absolute. The First Amendment, however, does not say that in every and all respects there shall be a separation of Church and State. Rather, it studiously defines the manner, the specific ways, in which there shall be no concert or union or dependency one on the other. That is the common sense of the matter." 343 U. S., at 312.

And then in 1961 in *McGowan* v. *Maryland* and in *Torcaso* v. *Watkins* each of these cases was discussed and approved. CHIEF JUSTICE WARREN in *McGowan*, for a unanimous Court on this point, said:

> "But, the First Amendment, in its final form, did not simply bar a congressional enactment *establishing a church*; it forbade all laws *respecting an estab-*

lishment of religion. Thus this Court has given the Amendment a 'broad interpretation . . . in the light of its history and the evils it was designed forever to suppress. . . .' " 366 U. S., at 441–442.

And MR. JUSTICE BLACK for the Court in *Torcaso,* without dissent but with Justices Frankfurter and HARLAN concurring in the result, used this language:

"We repeat and again reaffirm that neither a State nor the Federal Government can constitutionally force a person 'to profess a belief or disbelief in any religion.' Neither can constitutionally pass laws or impose requirements which aid all religions as against non-believers, and neither can aid those religions based on a belief in the existence of God as against those religions founded on different beliefs." 367 U. S., at 495.

Finally, in *Engel* v. *Vitale,* only last year, these principles were so universally recognized that the Court without the citation of a single case and over the sole dissent of MR. JUSTICE STEWART reaffirmed them. The Court found the 22-word prayer used in "New York's program of daily classroom invocation of God's blessings as prescribed in the Regents' prayer . . . [to be] a religious activity." 370 U. S., at 424. It held that "it is no part of the business of government to compose official prayers for any group of the American people to recite as a part of a religious program carried on by the government." *Id.,* at 425. In discussing the reach of the Establishment and Free Exercise Clauses of the First Amendment the Court said:

"Although these two clauses may in certain instances overlap, they forbid two quite different kinds of governmental encroachment upon religious freedom. The Establishment Clause, unlike the Free Exercise

Clause, does not depend upon any showing of direct governmental compulsion and is violated by the enactment of laws which establish an official religion whether those laws operate directly to coerce non-observing individuals or not. This is not to say, of course, that laws officially prescribing a particular form of religious worship do not involve coercion of such individuals. When the power, prestige and financial support of government is placed behind a particular religious belief, the indirect coercive pressure upon religious minorities to conform to the prevailing officially approved religion is plain." *Id., at* 430–431.

And in further elaboration the Court found that the "first and most immediate purpose [of the Establishment Clause] rested on a belief that a union of government and religion tends to destroy government and to degrade religion." *Id.,* at 431. When government, the Court said, allies itself with one particular form of religion, the inevitable result is that it incurs "the hatred, disrespect and even contempt of those who held contrary beliefs." *Ibid.*

V.

The wholesome "neutrality" of which this Court's cases speak thus stems from a recognition of the teachings of history that powerful sects or groups might bring about a fusion of governmental and religious functions or a concert or dependency of one upon the other to the end that official support of the State or Federal Government would be placed behind the tenets of one or of all orthodoxies. This the Establishment Clause prohibits. And a further reason for neutrality is found in the Free Exercise Clause, which recognizes the value of religious training, teaching and observance and, more particularly, the right of every person to freely choose his own course with reference thereto, free of any compulsion from the state. This the Free Exercise Clause guarantees. Thus, as we have seen, the two clauses may overlap. As we have indicated, the Establishment Clause has been directly considered by this Court eight times in the past score of years and, with only one Justice dissenting on the point, it has consistently held that the clause withdrew all legislative power respecting religious belief or the expression thereof. The test may be stated as follows: what are the purpose and the primary effect of the enactment? If either is the advancement or inhibition of religion then the enactment exceeds the scope of legislative power as circumscribed by the Constitution. That is to say that to withstand the strictures of the Establishment Clause there must be a secular legislative purpose and a primary effect that neither advances nor inhibits religion. *Everson* v. *Board of Education, supra; McGowan* v. *Maryland, supra,* at 442. The Free Exercise Clause, likewise considered many times here, withdraws from legislative power, state and federal, the exertion of any restraint on the free exercise of religion. Its purpose is to secure religious liberty in the individual by prohibiting any invasions thereof by civil authority. Hence it is necessary in a free exercise case for one to show the coercive effect of the enactment as it operates against him in the practice of his religion. The distinction between the two clauses is apparent—a violation of the Free Exercise Clause is predicated on coercion while the Establishment Clause violation need not be so attended.

Applying the Establishment Clause principles to the cases at bar we find that the States are requiring the selection and reading at the opening of the school day of verses from the Holy Bible and the recitation of the Lord's Prayer by the students in unison. These exercises are prescribed as part of the curricular activities of students who are required by law to attend school. They are held in the school buildings under the supervision and with the participation of teachers employed in those schools. None of these factors, other than compulsory school attendance, was present in the program upheld in *Zorach* v. *Clauson*. The trial court in No. 142 has found that such an opening exercise is a religious ceremony and was intended by the State to be so. We agree with the trial court's finding is to the religious character of the exercises. Given that finding the exercises and the law requiring them are in violation of the Establishment Clause.

There is no such specific finding as to the religious character of the exercises in No. 119, and the State contends (as does the State in No. 142) that the program is an effort to extend its benefits to all public school children without regard to their religious belief. Included within its secular purposes, it says, are the promotion of moral values, the contradiction to the materialistic trends of our times, the perpetuation of our institutions and the teaching of literature. The case came up on demurrer, of course, to a petition which alleged that the uniform practice under the rule had been to read from the King James version of the Bible and that the exercise was sectarian. The short answer, therefore, is that the religious character of the exercise was admitted by the State. But even if its purpose is not strictly religious, it is sought to be accomplished through readings, without comment, from the Bible. Surely the place of the Bible as an instrument of religion cannot be gainsaid, and the State's recognition of the pervading religious character of the ceremony is evident from the rule's specific permission of the alternative use of the Catholic Douay version as well as the recent amendment permitting nonattendance at the exercises. None of these factors is consistent with the contention that the Bible is here used either as an instrument for nonreligious moral inspiration or as a reference for the teaching of secular subjects.

The conclusion follows that in both cases the laws require religious exercises and such exercises are being conducted in direct violation of the rights of the appellees and petitioners.[9] Nor are these required exercises mitigated by the fact that individual students may absent themselves upon parental request, for that fact furnishes no defense to a claim of unconstitutionality under the Establishment Clause. See *Engel* v. *Vitale, supra,* at 430. Further, it is no defense to urge that the religious practices here may be relatively minor encroachments on the First Amendment. The breach of neutrality that is today a trickling stream may all too soon become a raging torrent and, in the words of Madison, "it is proper to take alarm at the first experiment on our liberties." Memorial and Remonstrance Against Religious Assessments, quoted in *Everson, supra,* at 65.

It is insisted that unless these religious exercises are permitted a "religion of secularism" is established in the

---

[9] It goes without saying that the laws and practices involved here can be challenged only by persons having standing to complain. But the requirements for standing to challenge state action under the Establishment Clause, unlike those relating to the Free Exercise Clause, do not include proof that particular religious freedoms are infringed. *McGowan* v. *Maryland, supra,* at 429–430. The parties here are school children and their parents, who are directly affected by the laws and practices against which their complaints are directed. These interests surely suffice to give the parties standing to complain. See *Engle* v. *Vitale, supra.* Cf. *McCollum* v. *Board of Education, supra; Everson* v. *Board of Education, supra.* Compare *Doremus* v. *Board of Education,* 342 U. S. 429 (1952), which involved the same substantive issues presented here. The appeal was there dismissed upon the graduation of the school child involved and because of the appellants' failure to establish standing as taxpayers.

schools. We agree of course that the State may not establish a "religion of secularism" in the sense of affirmatively opposing or showing hostility to religion, thus "preferring those who believe in no religion over those who do believe." *Zorach* v. *Clauson, supra,* at 314. We do not agree, however, that this decision in any sense has that effect. In addition, it might well be said that one's education is not complete without a study of comparative religion or the history of religion and its relationship to the advancement of civilization. It certainly may be said that the Bible is worthy of study for its literary and historic qualities. Nothing we have said here indicates that such study of the Bible or of religion, when presented objectively as part of a secular program of education, may not be effected consistent with the First Amendment. But the exercises here do not fall into those categories. They are religious exercises, required by the States in violation of the command of the First Amendment that the Government maintain strict neutrality, neither aiding nor opposing religion.

Finally, we cannot accept that the concept of neutrality, which does not permit a State to require a religious exercise even with the consent of the majority of those affected, collides with the majority's right to free exercise of religion.[10] While the Free Exercise Clause clearly prohibits the use of state action to deny the rights of free exercise to *anyone,* it has never meant that a majority could use the machinery of the State to practice its beliefs. Such a contention was effectively answered by Mr.

---

[10] We are not of course presented with and therefore do not pass upon a situation such as military service, where the Government regulates the temporal and geographic environment of individuals to a point that, unless it permits voluntary religious services to be conducted with the use of government facilities, military personnel would be unable to engage in the practice of their faiths.

Justice Jackson for the Court in *West Virginia Board of Education* v. *Barnette,* 319 U. S. 624, 638 (1943):

> "The very purpose of a Bill of Rights was to withdraw certain subjects from the vicissitudes of political controversy, to place them beyond the reach of majorities and officials and to establish them as legal principles to be applied by the courts. One's right to . . . freedom of worship . . . and other fundamental rights may not be submitted to vote; they depend on the outcome of no elections."

The place of religion in our society is an exalted one, achieved through a long tradition of reliance on the home, the church and the inviolable citadel of the individual heart and mind. We have come to recognize through bitter experience that it is not within the power of government to invade that citadel, whether its purpose or effect be to aid or oppose, to advance or retard. In the relationship between man and religion, the State is firmly committed to a position of neutrality. Though the application of that rule requires interpretation of a delicate sort, the rule itself is clearly and concisely stated in the words of the First Amendment. Applying that rule to the facts of these cases, we affirm the judgment in No. 142. In No. 119, the judgment is reversed and the cause remanded to the Maryland Court of Appeals for further proceedings consistent with this opinion.

It is so ordered.

SUPREME COURT OF THE UNITED STATES

Nos. 142 AND 119.—OCTOBER TERM, 1962.

School District of Abington Township, Pennsylvania, et al., Appellants,

142   *v.*

Edward Lewis Schempp et al.

On Appeal From the United States District Court for the Eastern District of Pennsylvania.

William J. Murray III, etc., et al., Petitioners,

119   *v.*

John N. Curlett, President, et al., Individually, and Constituting the Board of School Commissioners of Baltimore City.

On Writ of Certiorari to the Court of Appeals of Maryland.

[June 17, 1963.]

Mr. JUSTICE STEWART, dissenting.

I think the records in the two cases before us are so fundamentally deficient as to make impossible an informed or responsible determination of the constitutional issues presented. Specifically, I cannot agree that on these records we can say that the Establishment Clause has necessarily been violated.[1] But I think there exist serious questions under both that provision and the Free Exercise Clause—insofar as each is imbedded in the Fourteenth Amendment—which require the remand of these cases for the taking of additional evidence.

---

[1] It is instructive, in this connection, to examine the complaints in the two cases before us. Neither complaint attacks the challenged practices as "establishments." What both allege as the basis for their causes of actions are, rather, violations of religious liberty.

91

I.

The First Amendment declares that "Congress shall make no law respecting an establishment of religion, or prohibiting the free exercise thereof . . . ." It is, I think, a fallacious oversimplification to regard these two provisions as establishing a single constitutional standard of "separation of church and state," which can be mechanically applied in every case to delineate the required boundaries between government and religion. We err in the first place if we do not recognize, as a matter of history and as a matter of the imperatives of our free society, that religion and government must necessarily interact in countless ways. Secondly, the fact is that while in many contexts the Establishment Clause and the Free Exercise Clause fully complement each other, there are areas in which a doctrinaire reading of the Establishment Clause leads to irreconcilable conflict with the Free Exercise Clause.

A single obvious example should suffice to make the point. Spending federal funds to employ chaplains for the armed forces might be said to violate the Establishment Clause. Yet a lonely soldier stationed at some faraway outpost could surely complain that a government which did *not* provide him the opportunity for pastoral guidance was affirmatively prohibiting the free exercise of his religion. And such examples could readily be multiplied. The short of the matter is simply that the two relevant clauses of the First Amendment cannot accurately be reflected in a sterile metaphor which by its very nature may distort rather than illumine the problems involved in a particular case. Cf. *Sherbert* v. *Verner, post,* p. ——.

II.

As a matter of history, the First Amendment was adopted solely as a limitation upon the newly created National Government. The events leading to its adoption strongly suggest that the Establishment Clause was primarily an attempt to insure that Congress not only would be powerless to establish a national church, but would also be unable to interfere with existing state establishments. See *McGowan* v. *Maryland,* 366 U. S. 420, 440–441. Each State was left free to go its own way and pursue its own policy with respect to religion. Thus Virginia from the beginning pursued a policy of disestablishmentarianism. Massachusetts, by contrast, had an established church until well into the nineteenth century.

So matters stood until the adoption of the Fourteenth Amendment, or more accurately, until this Court's decision in *Cantwell* v. *Connecticut,* in 1940. 310 U. S. 296. In that case the Court said: "The First Amendment declares that Congress shall make no law respecting an establishment of religion or prohibiting the free exercise thereof. The Fourteenth Amendment has rendered the legislatures of the states as incompetent as Congress to enact such laws." [2]

I accept without question that the liberty guaranteed by the Fourteenth Amendment against impairment by the States embraces in full the right of free exercise of religion protected by the First Amendment, and I yield to no one in my conception of the breadth of that freedom. See *Braunfeld* v. *Brown,* 366 U. S. 599, 616 (dissenting opinion). I accept too the proposition that the Fourteenth Amendment has somehow absorbed the Establishment Clause, although it is not without irony that a constitutional provision evidently designed to leave the States free to go their own way should now have become a restriction upon their autonomy. But I cannot agree with what seems to me the insensitive definition of the Establishment Clause contained in the Court's opinion, nor

---

[2] 310 U. S., at 303. The Court's statement as to the Establishment Clause in *Cantwell* was dictum. The case was decided on free exercise grounds.

with the different but, I think, equally mechanistic definitions contained in the separate opinions which have been filed.

III.

Since the *Cantwell* pronouncement in 1940, this Court has only twice held invalid state laws on the ground that they were laws "respecting an establishment of religion" in violation of the Fourteenth Amendment. *McCollum* v. *Board of Education,* 333 U. S. 203; *Engel* v. *Vitale,* 370 U. S. 421. On the other hand, the Court has upheld against such a challenge laws establishing Sunday as a compulsory day of rest, *McGowan* v. *Maryland,* 366 U. S. 420, and a law authorizing reimbursement from public funds for the transportation of parochial school pupils. *Everson* v. *Board of Education,* 330 U. S. 1.

Unlike other First Amendment guarantees, there is an inherent limitation upon the applicability of the Establishment Clause's ban on state support to religion. That limitation was succinctly put in *Everson* v. *Board of Education,* 330 U. S. 1, 18: "State power is no more to be used so as to handicap religions than it is to favor them." [3] And in a later case, this Court recognized that the limitation was one which was itself compelled by the free exercise guarantee. "To hold that a state cannot consistently with the First and Fourteenth Amendments utilize its public school system to aid any or all religious faiths or sects in the dissemination of their doctrines and ideals does not . . . manifest a governmental hostility to reli-

---

[3] See also, in this connection, *Zorach* v. *Clauson,* 343 U. S. 306, 314: "Government may not finance religious groups nor undertake religious instruction nor blend secular and sectarian education nor use secular institutions to force one or some religion on any person. But we find no constitutional requirement which makes it necessary for government to be hostile to religion and to throw its weight against efforts to widen the effective scope of religious influence."

gion or religious teaching. A manifestation of such hostility would be at war with our national tradition as embodied in the First Amendment's guaranty of the free exercise of religion." *McCollum* v. *Board of Education,* 333 U. S. 203, 211–212.

That the central value embodied in the First Amendment—and, more particularly, in the guarantee of "liberty" contained in the Fourteenth—is the safeguarding of an individual's right to free exercise of his religion has been consistently recognized. Thus, in the case of *Hamilton* v. *Regents,* 293 U. S. 245, 265, Mr. Justice Cardozo, concurring, assumed that it was ". . . *the religious liberty* protected by the First Amendment against invasion by the nation [which] is protected by the Fourteenth Amendment against invasion by the states." (Emphasis added.) And in *Cantwell* v. *Connecticut, supra,* the purpose of those guarantees was described in the following terms: "On the one hand, it forestalls compulsion by law of the acceptance of any creed or the practice of any form of worship. Freedom of conscience and freedom to adhere to such religious organization or form of worship as the individual may choose cannot be restricted by law. On the other hand, it safeguards the free exercise of the chosen form of religion." 310 U. S., at 303.

It is this concept of constitutional protection embodied in our decisions which makes the cases before us such difficult ones for me. For there is involved in these cases a substantial free exercise claim on the part of those who affirmatively desire to have their children's school day open with the reading of passages from the Bible.

It has become accepted that the decision in *Pierce* v. *Society of Sisters,* 268 U. S. 510, upholding the right of parents to send their children to nonpublic schools, was ultimately based upon the recognition of the validity of the free exercise claim involved in that situation. It might be argued here that parents who wanted their children to be exposed to religious influences in school could, under *Pierce,* send their children to private or parochial schools. But the consideration which renders this contention too facile to be determinative has already been recognized by the Court: "Freedom of speech, freedom of the press, freedom of religion are available to all, not merely to those who can pay their own way." *Murdock* v. *Pennsylvania,* 319 U. S. 105, 111.

It might also be argued that parents who want their children exposed to religious influences can adequately fulfill that wish off school property and outside school time. With all its surface persuasiveness, however, this argument seriously misconceives the basic constitutional justification for permitting the exercises at issue in these cases. For a compulsory state educational system so structures a child's life that if religious exercises are held to be an impermissible activity in schools, religion is placed at an artificial and state-created disadvantage. Viewed in this light, permission of such exercises for those who want them is necessary if the schools are truly to be neutral in the matter of religion. And a refusal to permit religious exercises thus is seen, not as the realization of state neutrality, but rather as the establishment of a religion of secularism, or at the least, as government support of the beliefs of those who think that religious exercises should be conducted only in private.

What seems to me to be of paramount importance, then, is recognition of the fact that the claim advanced here in favor of Bible reading is sufficiently substantial to make simple reference to the constitutional phrase "establishment of religion" as inadequate an analysis of the cases before us as the ritualistic invocation of the nonconstitutional phrase "separation of church and state." What these cases compel, rather, is an analysis of just what the "neutrality" is which is required by the interplay of the Establishment and Free Exercise Clauses of the First Amendment, as imbedded in the Fourteenth.

IV.

Our decisions make clear that there is no constitutional bar to the use of government property for religious purposes. On the contrary, this Court has consistently held that the discriminatory barring of religious groups from public property is itself a violation of First and Fourteenth Amendment guarantees. *Fowler* v. *Rhode Island,* 345 U. S. 67; *Niemotko* v. *Maryland,* 340 U. S. 268. A different standard has been applied to public school property, because of the coercive effect which the use by religious sects of a compulsory school system would necessarily have upon the children involved. *McCollum* v. *Board of Education,* 333 U. S. 203. But insofar as the *McCollum* decision rests on the Establishment rather than the Free Exercise Clause, it is clear that its effect is limited to religious instruction—to government support of proselytizing activities of religious sects by throwing the weight of secular authority behind the dissemination of religious tenets.[4]

The dangers both to government and to religion inherent in official support of instruction in the tenets of various religious sects are absent in the present cases, which involve only a reading from the Bible unaccompanied by comments which might otherwise constitute instruction. Indeed, since, from all that appears in either record, any teacher who does not wish to do so is free

---

[4] "This is beyond all question a utilization of the tax-established and tax-supported public school system to aid religious groups *to spread their faith." McCollum* v. *Board of Education,* 333 U. S. 203, 210. (Emphasis added.)

not to participate,[5] it cannot even be contended that some infinitesimal part of the salaries paid by the State are made contingent upon the performance of a religious function.

In the absence of evidence that the legislature or school board intended to prohibit local schools from substituting a different set of readings where parents requested such a change, we should not assume that the provisions before us—as actually administered—may not be construed simply as authorizing religious exercises, nor that the designations may not be treated simply as indications of the promulgating body's view as to the community's preference. We are under a duty to interpret these provisions so as to render them constitutional if reasonably possible. Compare *Two Guys* v. *McGinley*, 366 U. S. 582, 592–595; *Everson* v. *Board of Education*, 330 U. S. 1, 4, and n. 2. In the *Schempp* case there is evidence which indicates that variations were in fact permitted by the very school there involved, and that further variations were not introduced only because of the absence of requests from parents. And in the *Murray* case the Baltimore rule itself contains a provision permitting another version of the Bible to be substituted for the King James version.

If the provisions are not so construed, I think that their validity under the Establishment Clause would be extremely doubtful, because of the designation of a particular religious book and a denominational prayer. But since, even if the provisions are construed as I believe they must be, I think that the cases before us must be re-

---

[5] The Pennsylvania statute was specifically amended to remove the compulsion upon teachers. Act of December 17, 1959, P. L. 1928, 24 Purdon's Pa. Stat. Ann. § 15–1516. Since the Maryland case is here on a demurrer, the issue of whether or not a teacher could be dismissed for refusal to participate seems, among many others, never to have been raised.

manded for further evidence on other issues—thus affording the plaintiffs an opportunity to prove that local
variations are not in fact permitted—I shall for the balance of this dissenting opinion treat the provisions before
us as making the variety and content of the exercises, as
well as a choice as to their implementation, matters which
ultimately reflect the concensus of each local school community.   In the absence of coercion upon those who do
not wish to participate—because they hold less strong
beliefs, other beliefs, or no beliefs at all— such provisions
cannot, in my view, be held to represent the type of
support of religion barred by the Establishment Clause.
For the only support which such rules provide for religion
is the withholding of state hostility—a simple acknowledgment on the part of secular authorities that the Constitution does not require extirpation of all expression of
religious belief.

V.

I have said that these provisions authorizing religious
exercises are properly to be regarded as measures making
possible the free exercise of religion.   But it is important
to stress that, strictly speaking, what is at issue here is a
privilege rather than a right.   In other words, the question presented is not whether exercises such as those at
issue here are constitutionally compelled, but rather
whether they are constitutionally invalid.   And that issue,
in my view, turns on the question of coercion.

It is clear that the dangers of coercion involved in the
holding of religious exercises in a schoolroom differ quali-
tatively from those presented by the use of similar exercises or affirmations in ceremonies attended by adults.
Even as to children, however, the duty laid upon government in connection with religious exercises in the public
schools is that of refraining from so structuring the school

environment as to put any kind of pressure on a child to participate in those exercises; it is not that of providing an atmosphere in which children are kept scrupulously insulated from any awareness that some of their fellows may want to open the school day with prayer, or of the fact that there exist in our pluralistic society differences of religious belief.

These are not, it must be stressed, cases like *Brown* v. *Board of Education,* 347 U. S. 483, in which this Court held that, in the sphere of public education, the Fourteenth Amendment's guarantee of equal protection of the laws required that race not be treated as a relevant factor. A segregated school system is not invalid because its operation is coercive; it is invalid simply because our Constitution presupposes that men are created equal, and that therefore racial differences cannot provide a valid basis for governmental action. Accommodation of religious differences on the part of the State, however, is not only permitted but required by that same Constitution.

The governmental neutrality which the First and Fourteenth Amendments require in the cases before us, in other words, is the extension of even-handed treatment to all who believe, doubt, or disbelieve—a refusal on the part of the State to weight the scales of private choice. In these cases, therefore, what is involved is not state action based on impermissible categories, but rather an attempt by the State to accommodate those differences which the existence in our society of a variety of religious beliefs make inevitable. The Constitution requires that such efforts be struck down only if they are proven to entail the use of the secular authority of government to coerce a preference among such beliefs.

It may well be, as has been argued to us, that even the supposed benefits to be derived from noncoercive religious exercises in public schools are incommensurate with the administrative problems which they would create. The choice involved, however, is one for each local community and its school board, and not for this Court. For, as I have said, religious exercises are not constitutionally invalid if they simply reflect differences which exist in the society from which the school draws its pupils. They become constitutionally invalid only if their administration places the sanction of secular authority behind one or more particular religious or irreligious beliefs.

To be specific, it seems to me clear that certain types of exercises would present situations in which no possibility of coercion on the part of secular officials could be claimed to exist. Thus, if such exercises were held either before or after the official school day, or if the school schedule were such that participation were merely one among a number of desirable alternatives,[6] it could hardly be contended that the exercises did anything more than to provide an opportunity for the voluntary expression of religious belief. On the other hand, a law which provided for religious exercises during the school day and which contained no excusal provision would obviously be unconstitutionally coercive upon those who did not wish to participate. And even under a law containing an excusal provision, if the exercises were held during the school day, and no equally desirable alternative were provided by the school authorities, the likelihood that children might be under at least some psychological compulsion to participate would be great. In a case such as the latter, however, I think we would err if we *assumed* such coercion in the absence of any evidence.[7]

---

[6] See, *e. g.*, the description of a plan permitting religious instruction off school property contained in *McCollum* v. *Board of Education*, 333 U. S. 203, 224 (separate opinion of Mr. Justice Frankfurter).

[7] Cf. "The task of separating the secular from the religious in education is one of magnitude, intricacy and delicacy. To lay down a sweeping constitutional doctrine as demanded by complainant and apparently approved by the Court, applicable alike to all school

VI.

Viewed in this light, it seems to me clear that the records in both of the cases before us are wholly inadequate to support an informed or responsible decision. Both cases involve provisions which explicitly permit any student who wishes, to be excused from participation in the exercises. There is no evidence in either case as to whether there would exist any coercion of any kind upon a student who did not want to participate. No evidence at all was adduced in the *Murray* case, because it was decided upon a demurrer. All that we have in that case, therefore, is the conclusory language of a pleading. While such conclusory allegations are acceptable for procedural purposes, I think that the nature of the constitutional problem involved here clearly demands that no decision be made except upon evidence. In the *Schempp* case the record shows no more than a subjective prophecy by a parent of what he thought would happen if a request were made to be excused from participation in the exercises under the amended statute. No such request was ever made, and there is no evidence whatever as to what might or would actually happen, nor of what administrative arrangements the school actually might or could make to free from pressure of any kind those who do not want to participate in the exercises. There were no District Court findings on this issue, since

---

boards of the nation, . . . is to decree a uniform, rigid and, if we are consistent, an unchanging standard for countless school boards representing and serving highly localized groups which not only differ from each other but which themselves from time to time change attitudes. It seems to me that to do so is to allow zeal for our own ideas of what is good in public instruction to induce us to accept the role of a super board of education for every school district in the nation." *McCollum* v. *Board of Education*, 333 U. S. 203, 237 (concurring opinion of Mr. Justice Jackson).

the case under the amended statute was decided exclusively on Establishment Clause grounds. 201 F. Supp. 815.

What our Constitution indispensably protects is the freedom of each of us, be he Jew or Agnostic, Christian or Atheist, Buddhist or Freethinker, to believe or disbelieve, to worship or not worship, to pray or keep silent, according to his own conscience, uncoerced and unrestrained by government. It is conceivable that these school boards, or even all school boards, might eventually find it impossible to administer a system of religious exercises during school hours in such a way as to meet this constitutional standard—in such a way as completely to free from any kind of official coercion those who do not affirmatively want to participate.[8] But I think we must not assume that school boards so lack the qualities of inventiveness and good will as to make impossible the achievement of that goal.

I would remand both cases for further hearings.

---

[8] For example, if the record in the *Schempp* case contained proof (rather than mere prophecy) that the timing of morning announcements by the school was such as to handicap children who did not want to listen to the Bible reading, or that the excusal provision was so administered as to carry any overtones of social inferiority, then impermissible coercion would clearly exist.

Chapter 5

Some Unofficial Dissents

In this chapter we bring together several opinions, editorial, religious, theological, and legal, though also unofficial, which represent considered dissents from the opinion of the Supreme Court in the landmark cases covered by the official verdicts and Court documents printed *in extenso* in the previous chapter. It is believed that these unofficial dissents typify the thought and sentiment of the overwhelming majority of the American people.

THE EVENING STAR

Washington, D. C.   June 18, 1963

The Court Bars the Lord's Prayer

The Supreme Court has spoken. Both the Lord's Prayer and Bible reading have been barred from the public schools. This comes not as a surprise. But in our view it is a shame.

It all seems so silly. Writing for the majority, Justice Clark conjured up dreadful prospects if the court should allow a prayer to be said in a public school. To permit such a thing, he argued, would depart from the concept of a government that must be "neutral" in religious matters. And he went on to say: "The breach of neutrality that is today a trickling stream may all too soon become a raging torrent." Perhaps there is something to be said for this as rhetoric. But it is nonsense when measured against the rise of secularism and materialism in this country since the Founding Fathers drafted the First Amendment. We mention this because it helps a little in understanding what Justice Clark must have had in mind when he said that the application of his concept of neutrality requires "interpretation of a delicate sort." Delicate indeed!

Justice Stewart, the lone dissenter, stated his understanding of what is meant by the First Amendment's guarantee of religious freedom. It is a forthright statement, and it appeals to us.

"What our Constitution indispensably protects," he said, "is the freedom of each of us, be he Jew or Agnostic, Christian or Atheist, Buddhist or Freethinker, to believe or disbelieve, to worship or not worship, to pray or to keep silent, according to his own conscience, uncoerced and unrestrained by government." To us, this is quite different from saying that the Constitution forbids one child, who may wish to do so, to recite the Lord's Prayer in a public school merely because some other child, who does not want to pray and who is not required to pray, objects.

Also interesting were some comments by Justice Goldberg in a concurring opinion, in which Justice Harlan joined.

Justice Goldberg, of course, agreed with the majority ruling. But he seemed a bit disturbed by Justice Clark's neutral concept. "Untutored devotion to the concept of neutrality," he said, "can lead . . . to a brooding and pervasive devotion to the secular and a passive, or even active, hostility to the religious." For our part, we think the court's school rulings in the area of religion, although certainly not so intended, have already led to a climate of passive and perhaps even active hostility to the religious. At another point, Justice Goldberg, in what we take to be a reference to Justice Clark's trickling stream and raging torrent, added: "It is of course true that great consequences can grow from small beginnings, but the measure of constitutional adjudication is the ability and willingness to distinguish between real threat and mere shadow."

If we may put our own interpretation on this, we think it is a comment which hits the nail squarely on the head. For in this ruling, and in some of those that preceded it, the court has done precisely what Justice Goldberg warned against—mistaken mere shadow for real threat.

In the process God and religion have all but been driven from the public schools. What remains? Will the baccalaureate service and Christmas carols be the next to go? Don't bet against it.

(Published June 28, 1963)

To the Editor of The Evening Star:

The American equivalent of the philosophers of Periclean Athens, the theologians of Paris at the time of Thomas Aquinas, and the German metaphysicians from Kant to Hegel is the Supreme Court of the United States.

This might sound like an ironical statement or one made with tongue-in-cheek, especially when I differ with the post-World War II trend of the Court in the field of Church and State and feel that in the banning of Bible-reading and the Lord's Prayer in public schools this trend, at first cautious, has reached a crescendo. A turning point has been taken which may be irreversible from the standpoint of the process of the secularization of the Republic.

Like you, in your forthright editorial in The Evening Star of June 18, I think that this most recent prohibition of the Court is a shame. I agree also that the learned and sincere justices have "mistaken mere shadow for real threat" and I would add that they are not as far from discussing how many angels can stand on the point of a needle, only in a transposed secular context, as one might suppose. Nevertheless, having recently gone through the Church-State opinions of the Supreme Court since 1931 and having just read the 121-page array of opinions in the *School District* and *Murray* decision, I cannot withhold my admiration for the learning, industry, logical brilliance, and patriotic commitment of our nine Guardians. To read all these opinions is better than a course in philosophy, to say nothing of constitutional law and government.

What then is wrong with the ban on prayer and Bible-reading? Why is it likely to be necessary for many Americans to support and work for a clarifying Constitutional Amendment?

The first reason is the inherent absurdity of a sudden revelation that a well established practice rooted in traditions going back to our beginnings and corresponding to the deep instincts of our people for generations is unconstitutional.

We have had a public school system for over a hundred years and there have been some state schools since early colonial times. Horace Mann, for example, firmly regarded the Bible as essentially nonsectarian. So did Abraham Lincoln. There is nothing more surely established in American society than prayer, not as a private but as a public expression. Suddenly we are called on to believe that this is improper as a school use and is contrary to the Constitution.

This is not only confusing; it strains credibility to the breaking point.

A second reason involves the relative rights and positions of religion and irreligion, theism and atheism under the American system. This is a delicate area but it must be looked at.

The crux of Mr. Justice Clark's opinion, representing the Court, is the concept of absolute neutrality. As you pointed out in your editorial, Mr. Justice Goldberg joined by Mr. Justice Harlan seemed a little worried at this point.

The American position here surely has been that the free exercise of religion should be as nearly absolute as possible for individuals. This freedom expressed through governmental neutrality extends to atheism and irreligion.

But public policy is another matter. Judgment of the good of society is another matter. So is the right education of young Americans. Traditional Americanism has not involved neutrality or false objectivity at these points. It has involved benevolence toward expressions of religious faith in civil life and public institutions so long as these did not approach establishmentarianism in the semantic and historical sense of legally preferring one church or denomination over another.

This is the middle way in Church and State elected by our forefathers.

The results of abandoning this way will be with us for a long time to come. The worst consequence, in my opinion, is that the American Establishment—for we do have one in our society, though it is not churchly and it has not yet embraced unconditional religious neutrality—seems to say to our young people in their time of maximum uncertainty and need: Religion is a private matter: it is all right for any one who wants it, but it is out of place in the main rushing stream of social and civil life.

Charles Wesley Lowry

THE WALL STREET JOURNAL
June 19, 1963

Imagined Dangers and Real Issues

Of all the dangers to a free society of which our forefathers were fearful, and against which they sought to safeguard the people in the Constitution, the one that time has proved of no danger is that the State would prescribe a religious belief.

In our history we have had many Constitutional crises, some of which nearly tore the country apart. We are torn today by a Constitutional issue, that of the treatment of our Negro citizens, which will require the utmost efforts of great minds to resolve without lasting political wounds.

But nowhere in our history will you find any serious threat by any church or sect to seize the State or to persuade the State to use its powers to establish it as the State religion.

This elementary fact of our history, quite apart from all of the philosophical arguments, seems to us to make absolute nonsense of the Supreme Court's decision about Bible readings in the public schools. A more ponderous effort upon a more trivial issue has rarely, if ever, emerged from the robed men who sit upon that bench.

This is not to say that the result of the decision is trivial, or that its consequences do not now raise grave questions. For what the Supreme Court has done, in the name of protecting us from the establishment of religion by the State, is to establish secularization—atheism, if you would have it bluntly—as the one belief to which the State's power will extend its protection.

Thus if you believe in the God of the Jews, the God of the Christians, or the God of Islam, you are denied absolutely any public expression of it in the schools which the public supports. Hereafter the views of the nonbeliever alone are sheltered by the full panoply of the State's police powers.

The legal and philosophical answer to this interpretation of the Constitution, it seems to us, has been well put by Mr. Justice Stewart. "We err . . . if we do not recognize, as a matter of history and as a matter of the imperatives of our free society, that religion and government must necessarily interact in countless ways." He cites example after example of the interaction—from the use of prayer in the opening of courts and Congress to the State support of chaplains to minister to those in the armed forces who, of their own choice, seek such ministry.

And he puts his finger surely upon the specious argument of Government "neutrality" about religion. The duty of the State is to "accommodate those differences" of belief which a free

110 / To Pray or Not to Pray

society makes inevitable, not to try to set up "impermissible categories" and so throw its weight against those who may desire public expression of their beliefs.

"A compulsory state educational system so structures a child's life," he observes, "that if religious exercises are held to be impermissible in schools, religion is placed at an artificial and State-created disadvantage." In short, not neutrality but State action against religion.

Yet much as we share Justice Stewart's views, it is not alone the philosophy of the Court majority that troubles us. Surely it is a distortion of the Constitution to suggest that when the Founding Fathers put into it the prohibition against "the establishment of religion" they were aiming even distantly at a prohibition against the reading of Scripture or of prayers in public bodies, including the schools. To them "establishment" meant literally setting up a State religion.

It is certainly a distortion of the views of such men as Madison and Jefferson and Roger Williams to suggest that their devotion to religious liberty is somehow the seed of the view to which this court has now come, depriving people of the liberty to express their religious views openly in the school.

And what are we to make of it when this court, in order to buttress this opinion, reminds us of the danger "that powerful sects . . . might bring about a fusion of governmental and religious functions"? Are we to suppose that this danger, rightly guarded against by the Constitution, is somehow now threatened because school children hear the Bible read?

Apparently so. For in warning us against this "minor encroachment" against the Constitution, the Court thunders that "the breach of neutrality that is today a trickling stream may all too soon become a raging torrent." Here, without doubt, is upside-down logic. For if there has been any consistent trend in our religious history, it is that what might once have been described as a raging torrent of religious intolerance has become by comparison a trickling stream.

It is this disparity between argument and reality, between cause and remedy, that troubles us in the Court's decision. Perhaps it is undesirable public policy—although we do not think so—to provide a moment of prayer, or a brief reading of the

Scriptures, in a school whose purpose is to teach the ideas upon which Western society is based.

But it is wholly ridiculous to argue that this practice, followed by generation after generation without injury to our institutions, is now suddenly become a thing to undermine the Republic and demand the most absolute prohibitions against it in the name of the Constitution.

And it does not augur well for the future to see our highest judges torture history and turn metaphysical handsprings to justify that which they wish to decide. In the real Constitutional issues which face the nation today we should not have to fear that small minds will be brought to great questions.

(Published July 22, 1963)

To the Editor of The Wall Street Journal:

You have grasped the common sense of the whole matter. The much ado of the Court is out of all proportion. Logic is wrenched and history is either ignored or handled selectively in a highly tendentious manner.

The opinion of the Court, written by Mr. Justice Clark, puts weight above all on neutrality. The state is to be above preferences, prejudices, or favorable presuppositions of any kind in the field of religion. This absolute neutrality principle applies to religion vs. irreligion, theism vs. atheism as much as to various churches or major denominations or denominational groupings.

The result of this, as my former pupil Bishop James A. Pike urged so ably a year ago after *Engel v. Vitale* and as you bring out most clearly in your editorial, is not neutrality but a reverse species of preference or establishment. The state actually gets behind freedom *from* religion, a result which is certainly the last thing the Founding Fathers of this Republic expected or desired.

This leads me to focus on the crux of the constitutional issue which the Court has sought to settle by the invocation of the neutrality principle. Is this the American position?

It may become, as the Court presently believes and intends, the new American position. Our people, out of a mixture of weariness, conformity, and the influence of shortsighted spiritual leadership, may accept what has been done, declining to get behind the remedy of a clarifying Amendment to the Constitution. Very ominous in this respect is the extraordinary reaction of powerful elements among the Protestant clergy who literally advanced to meet the decision of the Justices before it was handed down.

Be this as it may, the point on which thoughtful people should focus is the character of the historic American synthesis in the sphere of Church and State. There are two propositions set forth in the documents and actions which together make up the living stream of the Nation's life we usually call tradition.

The first proposition is that the Federal Government shall do nothing to interfere with the free exercise of religion by individuals. (This is now taken by the Court as extended to the State governments by the 14th Amendment.) Neutrality here is carried to the most nearly absolute point that is possible, given the complexities of social and civil life. It is applied to irreligion as much as to various forms of religion.

But there is a second proposition, implicit in our traditions from the beginning and bound to affect the American position to the extent that we are indeed a religious people—a fact admitted and even emphasized by the Court. This proposition is that from the standpoint of public policy, including education, the spirit of religion and reverence before God are to be encouraged.

The outstanding example of this second, nonneutral proposition is one that I believe none of the so-called liberals of the Court has made anything of in even their most exhaustive opinions. It has the unique distinction of passage in 1787 by the last Congress meeting under the Articles of Confederation and of reconfirmation in 1789 by the first Congress under the new Constitution which also drew up the Bill of Rights. I refer to Article 3 of the Northwest Ordinance: "Religion, morality and knowledge being necessary to good government and the happiness of mankind, schools and the means of education shall forever be encouraged."

This is the second proposition in the American synthesis of church and state. If we allow it to be annulled, the Republic will cease to be what it has been for 187 years.

Charles Wesley Lowry

LETTER BY HENRY P. VAN DUSEN

President, Union Theological Seminary, New York

(Published July 7, 1963)

To the Editor of The New York Times:

The Supreme Court's latest deliverance on religion in public education surprised no one. Its novelty lay in its consistency with the Court's last previous decision in this area, in the New York Regents' prayer case a year ago. This consistency stands in sharp contrast to the vacillation which had marked the sequence of earlier decisions over more than a decade on the legality of recognition of religion in public schools. These decisions have swung pendulum-like with almost monotonous alteration, if not from one extreme to its opposite, certainly from a negative to a positive judgment and back again—from the "McCollum case's" prohibition of classes in religion in school buildings through approval of state subsidies for school buses to transport children to sectarian schools and permission to "release" children during school hours to attend religious instruction in their own churches to the interdiction on the use of prayers composed and authorized by a state educational authority.

This succession of contrasted if not irreconcilable judgments has left not merely the lay public but the highest legal and judicial minds of the nation in baffled uncertainty as to what, if any, consistent viewpoint might be guiding the majority of the Supreme Court and as to whither the justices might be directing the law of the land in their free-wheeling reinterpretations of the First and Fourteenth Amendments to the Constitution.

Decision's Significance

Clearly, the significance of this new decision does not lie in its proscription of somewhat perfunctory exercises of prayer and Bible-reading of dubious spiritual value. It lies at a far deeper and more basic level and at two points, one retrospective, the other prospective: on the one hand, in its radical recasting of the intent and meaning of the Constitution; on the other hand, in its possible anticipation of far more drastic and fundamental reversal of the historic and established practices of national, state and local governments in this country with respect to religion.

Nothing more deeply disturbs well-informed American citizens than the present Supreme Court's use—one must say, misuse—of the First Amendment for purposes which, however valid they may be held to be in contemporary pluralistic American society, are almost directly contrary both to the intention of that amendment and to prevailing practice under the Constitution throughout the nation's history.

The First Amendment forbids Congress to make a law "respecting an establishment of religion" or "prohibiting the free exercise thereof." The Court's earlier decisions extended these two caveats to state as well as national governments. There is no ground for uncertainty as to what the authors of the amendment intended. "It was never intended by the Constitution that the Government should be prohibited from recognizing religion—where it might be done without drawing any invidious distinctions between different religious beliefs, organizations, or sects." (T. M. Cooley, *Principles of Constitutional Law*, pp. 224-5.) Since no particular religion or religious group has been seeking preferred status in any of the recent court cases, the "establishment" clause in its original meaning has no applicability whatever.

The Founding Fathers unfailingly recognized a clear and elemental distinction which appears to elude the mind of the present Court—between religion as a well-nigh universal concern of men and the several specific forms and institutions of "organized religion." Their policy was clear, consistent and readily comprehensible: to religion, recognition and respect as reiterated by the present Court, "We are a religious people whose institutions presuppose a Supreme Being"; between the specific religions in their differences and contentions, strict impartiality; toward "all religions" various forms of assistance.

This policy has continued to determine the practice of the Federal and most state and local governments through the nation's history to today. At the present time, that policy of aid to "all religions" without preference for "one religion over another" is in effect in a variety of ways, including tax-exemption for church properties, charitable deductions for contributions to churches, etc.

By no stretch of language can the actual relations of government to religious institutions be defined as "strict neutrality, neither aiding nor opposing religion."

The legendary "wall of separation" is most impervious in the judiciary, most porous in such executive departments as Defense, Treasury, Interior, and Health, Education and Welfare.

The corollary in both law and logic of the Supreme Court's recent interdictions is inescapable: prohibition of the affirmative recognition and collaboration by Government at all levels with all organs of religion in all relationships and circumstances. A consistent application of such a policy would involve a revolution in the nation's habitual practice in the matter of religion, established by the Founding Fathers, faithfully followed by their successors, and prevailingly prevalent at this hour. Nothing less than that is at stake. Is that the authentic will of the American people?

RELIGION AND PUBLIC LIFE

By WILL HERBERG
Professor in Drew Theological Seminary

This statement by a distinguished Jewish thinker and scholar is of particular value because of the tendency of a large number of Protestant clergy to stand with recent Supreme Court decisions, in the mistaken notion, we believe, that somehow the purging of the religious out of the secular will make for the purification and strengthening of Christianity in the present age.

With its decisions in the *Engel* case last year and the *Schempp* and *Murray* cases just a few weeks ago, the United States Supreme Court has precipitated the problem of religious symbols and ceremonies in public life into a compelling issue of public policy. I want to address myself to a point that seems to me to need more careful consideration than it has received, since it touches the theological evaluation of these Supreme Court decisions and the trend they represent.

Every newspaper reader will remember, perhaps to his bewilderment, that the Supreme Court actions outlawing the New York State Regents' prayer a year ago, and enjoining Bible readings and the Lord's Prayer in public schools earlier this year, were greeted with approval by a considerable number of Prot-

estant theologians, and by some Catholic publicists, mostly laymen. These were men of acute mind and deep religious faith,
men I know and respect. Yet they welcomed the "separationist"
decisions of the Supreme Court, and, in effect, asked for more.
What was their argument? What *is* their argument?—for they
are still pressing it in resolutions, articles, and books. . . .

Their argument, brushing aside certain irrelevancies, is essentially a *religious* one. Whatever may have been the case some
centuries ago, they say, religious symbols and ceremonies in
public life today, considering the advance of secularism in our
culture, are becoming a mockery, a travesty of religion, a superficial routinization that, in its tendency to trivialize faith, is
worse than an honest and outright secularism. Let the movement
toward the "dereligionization" of our public life, so powerfully
promoted by the recent Supreme Court decisions, go on, they
say, and go on to the bitter end. Then, perhaps, the real religious
situation in this country will become apparent; and seriously
concerned men and women will turn in the only direction in
which a renascence of authentic faith could be expected—to the
home and the church.

A Higher Majesty

There is some truth in this argument. After all, what can the
routine repetition of a prayer mean in the religious life of a
child when all the rest of what goes on in school is so utterly
religionless? Is not the child more likely to receive an impression
of the marginal place of religion in life than of its central importance? Perhaps. But the argument of these religious advocates
of a public secularism remains profoundly and dangerously
wrong; for, as we should understand from our theological and
political traditions, a society, and the state through which it is
organized politically, remain "legitimate," "righteous" and "lawful" *only insofar as they recognize a higher majesty beyond
themselves,* limiting and judging their pretensions. Once the
state forgets or denies this, once it sets itself up as its own
highest majesty, beyond which there is nothing, it becomes
totalitarian: in effect, it divinizes itself, and thereby ceases to
be a "legitimate" state in the theological understanding of the
term. Therefore the "established order"—the state, above all—

ought to include within itself signs, symbols, and ceremonials constantly reminding itself and the people that it *is* subject to a majesty beyond all earthly majesties. That is the indispensable function of religious symbols and ceremonials in public life, one that no responsible theologian, however resentful he may be of trivialization and superficiality in religion, can afford to forget.

Children in American schools, public and private, generally salute the flag every school day, and pledge their allegiance to the United States. This pledge now includes the Lincolnian phrase, "this nation, *under God*"; and the child who takes this pledge of allegiance, if he is encouraged to pay attention to what he is saying, will know that the American state and nation are not absolute; that they stand under the scrutiny and judgment of a higher power. With this phrase "under God" removed, as it might well be removed by a sequential Supreme Court decision pursuing the "separationist" line, the child repeating the pledge of allegiance every day at school would have no reminder of a majesty beyond all earthly majesties, and would naturally be prone to see the state and nation as the supreme reality demanding his highest allegiance. The Founding Fathers, whether "conservative" or "radical," well understood this principle as the presupposition of our constitutional system. "Before any man can be considered a member of civil society," James Madison once declared, "he must be considered a subject of the Governor of the universe." It is to remind us, and especially the rising generation, that we are, first and foremost, "subjects of the Governor of the universe," that we need religious symbols and ceremonials in public life.

The Protestant theologians who applaud the Supreme Court decision, and even want to go beyond, seem for the most part to have overlooked the consequences of the "de-religionizing" movement for our political order, a political order which makes no sense except in terms of a higher majesty, a higher allegiance, and a higher law. This appears to be a failure of responsibility. And it is a failure of responsibility not unconnected with a deficient understanding of the religious task in America today, pursuing, as it does, a kind of "back to the catacombs" outlook.

(National Review, July 30, 1963)

LETTER BY REV. MAURICE A. KIDDER

Vicar, All Saints' Church, South Hadley, Mass.

(Published July 21, 1963)

To the Editor of the Living Church:

American Faux Pas

There is an old New Hampshire story about a man whose recipe for rabbit pie was "equal parts of horse meat and rabbit —one horse to one rabbit!" I am afraid that the Supreme Court in its recent decision on the place of the Lord's Prayer and Bible in school opening exercises has a similar recipe for democracy— "one avowed atheist equals one thousand professed Christians."

Granted that we were the first officially pluralistic religious culture in human history, whose First Amendment is a compromise of the mutual suspicions of established Anglicans in the south and established New England Calvinists. Granted that the infant republic had enough economic and political problems to overcome in 1791 without perpetuating the religious wars of Europe. But not even free-thinking Benjamin Franklin was prepared to deny that "God rules in the affairs of men."

It is dispiriting, to say the least, to read in the press the off-the-cuff reactions to this decision by Episcopal bishops, presidents of rabbinical associations, and legal representatives of humanistic cults all saying the same things in their relief that an annoying barrier to their agreement on education has been removed. This shows the extent of the long, slow erosion of the Biblical doctrine of man which fashioned our equal division of governmental powers; no sinful man or group of men being trusted completely. When no sectarian group could officially speak for God it became increasingly more comfortable to ignore Him by mutual consent. This is the most evident and bitter fruit of our "sinful divisions" as Christians. But it was never agreed upon in any definitive document, political or religious. We fell into it as the easy way out in avoiding the agony of our separation from God and each other. It is the great American *faux pas.*

I am not insensitive to the claims of religious minorities. After every meeting of a Massachusetts Council committee on Church and state I discipline myself by a visit to a beloved Jewish rabbi friend who disagrees with me completely on every facet of this problem. But every time I conduct worship I say a Creed, and mean what I say. There is only one Source of all things in heaven and earth. He came among us and wrought deliverance from sin for all men, whether they know it or accept it. He goes before us in the awful opportunities and catastrophes of our days. What precondition to thought and action is more necessary than this in facing Birmingham, Moscow, or outer space? What education that consciously ignored this could be called "adjustment" to the past or present environment of Bethlehem, Pa., Mars Hill, N. C., or Corpus Christi, Texas?

Two words which the dissenting Episcopalian, Mr. Justice Stewart, used to describe the majority opinion are the nub of the whole matter. He said it was "insensitive" and "mechanical." When the Court had the responsibility of "rightly dividing" the waters of the Colorado River they "gave" here and "took" there. They *adjudicated* a delicate and complicated economic issue. But when it came to a matter which involved our very knowledge of ourselves as a developing nation, a people "brought hither out many kindreds and tongues," predominantly Christian, they handed over their whole concern to an infinitesimal segment of the citizens. This can only be described as "minoritarianism," the rule of the many by the few.

Mrs. Murray, the victorious atheistic appellant, in an infamous television interview, crowed that she had "just begun" her fight and that she would not stop until she had wiped out every vestige of religion in our government. The Court majority opinion lamely assured us that their dicta did not, nor ever could, threaten the ministrations of chaplains in the armed forces, oaths in court, and prayers in Congress—all officially sponsored acts of worship. But it did not spell out how these acts differed from those which had just been struck down. If there is *no definitive principle* to explain why the Court can say "yea" here and "nay" there then we are obliged to wait for a succession of other shoes to drop.

There is only one ray of light and hope in this decision, which otherwise is adequately responded to by the latter part of the Epistle for Ash Wednesday (Joel 2:15-18). Both the Court and

Mrs. Murray did say that we could teach the "objective" facts about our different religious traditions and the historical place of religion in our heritage as required subjects in the public schools. This, if intelligently done, could mean more than indifferent prayer and indiscriminate Bible reading. Let us initiate this growing practice throughout our country.

SERMON BY RABBI BERNARD ZLOTOWITZ

Union Reform Temple, Freeport, Long Island
April 20, 1962

This sermon, somewhat abridged, is taken from the *Hearings* before the Committee on the Judiciary, U. S. Senate, July 26 and August 2, 1962. It was read into the *Hearings* by Congressman Frank J. Becker. It should be noted that this sermon was preached two months before the Supreme Court handed down its decision in the *Engel* case. It indicates that Jewish opinion in this whole matter may well be far less uniform than often appears to be the case.

The purpose of the Passover holiday is to make us conscious of the importance of freedom and the worth of the individual. Passover cautions us not to take for granted the privilege we enjoy as free men and women. The seder and its ceremonial symbols serve to remind us that the bread of affliction and the shackles of slavery must once and for all be destroyed, so that the dignity of the human being will be raised to a godly level, and all the peoples of this earth, regardless of their color, race, or creed will be truly recognized as children of God, created in His image.

It is, therefore, fitting and proper at this season of our joy and gladness when we commemorate the exodus from Egypt and our redemption from slavery to examine once again the religious ideals of our faith and the high principles of our country.

To be more specific, let us consider whether prayers and Bible reading in the public schools, or for that matter any religious celebration, is in keeping and in harmony with our religious tradition and American heritage—or whether it is a violation of our Constitution and all that we hold dear and sacred.

Our religion has its roots in the belief in one God who taught us through His prophets and seers that freedom of the individual is paramount and is the ideal of mankind. God himself took us out of the land of Egypt—out of the house of bondage to make us a kingdom of priests and a holy nation—where brotherhood would reign supreme and godliness reach unprecedented heights.

Similarly, our own Nation was founded "in order to form a more perfect Union, establish justice, insure domestic tranquility, provide for the common defense, promote the general welfare, and secure the blessings of liberty to ourselves and our posterity." And in order to put teeth into this preamble, the first amendment to the Constitution which the States ratified was the declaration that "Congress shall make no law respecting an establishment of religion or prohibiting the free exercise thereof."

The Founding Fathers knew only too well the dangers inherent in an established church. The experiences of the countries of the European Continent were only too vivid in their minds.

They fully realized that the freedom of the individual could never be complete if there was an official church recognized by the state. This the Founding Fathers wanted to avoid at all costs. They wanted a separation of church and state; and this they achieved.

But by no stretch of the imagination did the founders of our country ever desire the separation of religion from government. The founders were a godly group of men and this was to be a godly country. Religion imbued them with a spirit of love and high ideals. The Bible inspired them.

The Liberty Bell bears the Biblical inscription: "Proclaim liberty throughout the land unto all the inhabitants thereof." The Declaration of Independence refers to the Deity as the source of liberty.

From these significant examples we can readily recognize that the founders of this Nation were a godly people and not a godless people. That they wanted a godly nation and not a godless nation. They always sought divine help in all their deliberations just as the Houses of Congress do today. In fact, there are official chaplains in the Government, who bring spiritual aid and comfort to the representatives of the Government.

The President of the United States takes a Bible, places his hand on it, and raises his other hand to God and swears under an oath to God that he will uphold the Constitution and the laws of the United States. Governors, mayors, judges, and all people who hold public office take an oath to God that they will fulfill the duties of their office to the best of their ability. A nonbeliever cannot hold a public office in our land. The wheels of justice would be at a standstill if witnesses were not sworn in.

The laws of perjury are based on swearing falsely. Our currency reads: "In God We Trust." Even the Pledge of Allegiance has been modified to read: "This Nation under God."

All this is in keeping with the spirit of our Founding Fathers. For they realized, as we do, that God and religion cannot be divorced from life. It is as much a part of us as the air we breathe. It was Justice Warren who pointed out, when he spoke at the biennial convention of the Union of American Congregations in Washington last November, that we are a religious country by virtue of the fact that there is separation of church and state. Thus, in the opinion of the Chief Justice of the United States, our country is a religious nation because we do not recognize one church as the official church, but rather we recognize all houses of worship, be they Protestant, Roman Catholic, Jewish, or any others.

We recognize the vital role that religion plays in making our life meaningful. Yet today in our community and in some other communities, a group has seen fit to challenge this concept of our American way of life and to undermine it. Today there is a movement afoot to attempt to suppress God in our schools, and to make the mention of God's name subversive in any public school.

In fact, the matter has gained such serious proportions that the Supreme Court of the United States heard arguments on this issue early this month, and I understand that sometime in the fall it will render its decision on whether public schools are permitted to have Bible readings and prayers.

It now behooves us to ask: What is the function of the public school? The purpose of the public school is to teach our young to grow into useful and responsible citizens by preparing them properly for life. This can only be accomplished by having schools transmit our culture and our heritage which in this country is Judeo-Christian. We Jews live in a country where we are a minority—a very small minority at that. The overwhelming majority of the citizens of this Nation are of the Christian faith—and as such, exert a great influence over us. I need only point out, as I have on numerous occasions in the past, that we are unduly influenced by Christians not only in our schools, which is minute as compared to the influence generated through the mass media of advertising, TV, radio, movies, newspapers, magazines, our business associations, and indeed our whole environment.

The emphasis on Christmas, for example, is so strong that we have tried to offset this in our homes by overemphasizing the importance of Hanukkah, and making of a minor holiday—one not mentioned in the Bible—a major festival. It seems today that we Jews observe three high holidays a year—Rosh Hashanah, Yom Kippur, and Hanukkah. . . .

In New York State, the following prayer is offered in the public schools:

Almighty God, we acknowledge our dependence upon Thee, and we beg Thy blessings upon us, our parents, our teachers, and our country.

Now what is wrong with this prayer? Yet some see great danger to our American way of life if the recitation of this prayer is permitted to continue. In fact, they have gone so far as to take this issue into the courts, and, thank God, the New York courts have sustained this prayer. It is now before the Supreme Court, where arguments, as I noted earlier, have already been heard, and a decision is to be rendered as to its constitutionality.

I wonder why these groups don't object to the teaching of the Golden Rule, and ethics and morals. After all, these are also religious teachings having their roots in the Bible.

I think the school would be derelict in its duty if it did not transmit our culture in its entirety. For this is its function and responsibility. I admit that there are abuses connected with religious practices in the schools, and they do at times seem to be sectarian in character rather than nondenominational. But the solution does not lie in eliminating these prayers or Bible reading or holiday celebrations, but rather in correcting these abuses. One does not tear down a house if the roof leaks. He merely repairs the roof. Let us do the same. Let us repair the damage where necessary, but, in doing so, let us not destroy the structure. Let us not throw out the baby with the bath water. And let us pray, that in the teachings of this holiday of Passover, we may yet find the truth that will guide us to a solution that will benefit ourselves, our community, and our country. Amen.

LECTURE BY DEAN ERWIN M. GRISWOLD

Harvard Law School
At University of Utah Law School
February 28, 1963

The following excerpt is taken from The Sunday Star, Washington, D. C., March 3, 1963. We regard Dean Griswold's "dissent" as combining common sense, massive legal learning, and religious perceptivity of a high order. We hope that multiplied thousands of young Americans will read his critique of The New York School Prayer decision and his magnificent defense of the main-line American religious tradition.

Absolutism in the Supreme Court

A Text Cited

A number of years ago I saw in the Saturday Review a little item which may serve as a text for my remarks.

It reads as follows:

> In the land of Absolute, where everyone and everything is perfect, there is no light at night.
> The annals of the Absolutians record that they once discovered the electric light, but as is known, the perfect electric light burns in a perfect vacuum.
> Absolute is in the dark.

Absolutes are likely to be phantoms, eluding our grasp. Even if we think we have embraced them, they are likely to be misleading. If we start from absolute premises, we may find that we only over-simplify our problems and thus reach unsound results. It may well be that absolutes are the greatest hindrance to sound and useful thought—in law, as in other fields of human knowledge. I would like to suggest that the Supreme Court has, in recent years, been engaged in certain types of cases, in a species of absolutism in its reasoning, which is more likely to lead us into darkness than to light. It is, I think, a thoroughly unsatisfactory form of judging. . . .

The New York Case

Within the last year, a case came before the Supreme Court which directly involved the interpretation and application of the First Amendment. This was the New York school prayer case. Its name is Engel v. Vitale. It involved a prayer formulated by the State board of regents in New York, and recommended by them for use in the schools of that State. The prayer, in its entirety, was as follows:

> Almighty God, we acknowledge our dependence upon Thee, and we beg Thy blessings upon us, our parents, our teachers and our country.

The court, in an opinion by Mr. Justice Black, held that the reciting of this prayer in the public schools of New York violated the Constitution. It was, the court held, an "establishment of religion," forbidden by the First Amendment. Five of his colleagues joined with him. Mr. Justice Stewart dissented. Justice Douglas wrote a concurring opinion which, though differing some in his reasoning, showed the absolutist approach. He recounted all of the ways in which governmental bodies now finance some activity with a religious element or overtone: "Chaplains in both Houses and in the armed services"; "compulsory chapel at the service academies, and religious services . . . in Federal hospitals and prisons"; "religious proclamations" by the President; " 'In God We Trust' " on our money; "Bible-reading in the schools of the District of Columbia"; and many other things, including exemption from "the Federal income tax" and "postal privileges" for "religious organizations." All of this is bad, according to Justice Douglas. After recognizing that "Our system at the Federal and State levels is presently honeycombed with" such things, he said, summarily, and absolutely: "Nevertheless, I think it is an unconstitutional undertaking whatever form it takes." It's as simple as that. They are all bad. And perhaps they are if the absolutist approach to such matters can be accepted as sound. These are the lengths to which absolutism takes us.

Look at the Wording

But is it all as clear as this? Do words convey such positive and overpowering meaning? Is there no room whatever for thought or consideration? Perhaps it would be worthwhile just to look carefully at the words of the First Amendment, in all its majesty. I will not yield to any Justice of the Supreme Court in my respect for those words, or in my conception of their importance not merely in our history but in their present function and worth in helping us to preserve a free Nation. But what do they say? "Congress shall make no law. . . ."

Congress had made no law in the Engel case; no law of Congress was in any way involved.

What is it that Congress can make no law about? It is "an establishment of religion." What does that term mean? That takes some construing, too. Certainly there was much history behind the phrase. Not only did England (and Scotland) have an established church, but there were established churches in a number of the States at the time the First Amendment was adopted. And they were something very different from a regents' recommended prayer. It takes a measure of construction to bring this prayer within the no-establishment clause. "No law" may well mean no law.

But "establishment of religion" might mean establishment of religion; and those who wrote the "establishment of religion" clause might be rather perplexed by the use which has been made of it in 1962. "No law" means no law. It is as simple as that—that is, if one ignores the other words which are involved in the task, such as "Congress," "establishment of religion," "the free exercise thereof," and "deprive any person of life, liberty, or property without due process of law." I do not say that these are meaningless words. I do suggest they are words which require construction, which are by no means absolute in form or content, and that to ignore them under the guise of the absolutist approach is to fail to recognize and perform the most significant and fundamental part of the task of judging.

Unfortunate Move

Let me now turn to another aspect of the matter. I think it was unfortunate that the question involved in the Engel case was ever thought of as a matter for judicial decision, that it was unfortunate that the court decided the case, one way or the other, and that this unhappy situation resulted solely from the absolutist position which the court has taken.

What do I mean by this? I have in mind at least two separate lines of thought. One is the fact that we have a tradition, a spiritual and cultural tradition, of which we ought not to be deprived by judges carrying into effect the logical implications of absolutist notions not expressed in the Constitution itself, and surely never contemplated by those who put the constitutional provisions into effect. The other is that there are some matters which are essentially local in nature, important matters, but nonetheless matters to be worked out by the people themselves in their own communities, when no basic rights of others are impaired.

First, as to the long tradition. Is it not clear as a matter of historical fact that this was a Christian Nation? Are the Mayflower Compact, Ann Hutchison, Cotton Mather, Jonathan Edwards, and William Penn, and many others, no part of our history? It is true that we were a rather remarkable Christian Nation, having developed a tolerance in matters of religion which was at once virtually unique and a tribute to the men of the 17th and 18th centuries who developed the type of thought which came to prevail here. But this was not a purely humanistic type of thought. Nor did it deny the importance and significance of religion.

Provisions of Sweep

It is perfectly true that the First Amendment forbade Congress to pass any law "respecting an establishment of religion or prohibiting the free exercise thereof." These are great provisions, of great sweep and basic importance. But to say that they require that all trace of religion be kept out of any sort of public activity is sheer invention. Our history is full of these traces: chaplains in Congress and in the armed forces, chapels in prisons, "In God We Trust" on our money, to mention only a few. Must all of these things be rigorously extirpated in order to satisfy a constitutional absolutism?

Does our deep-seated tolerance of all religions—or, to the same extent, of no religion—require that we give up all religious observance in public activities? Why should it? It certainly never occurred to the Founders that it would. It is hardly likely that it was entirely accidental that these questions did not even come before the court in the first 150 years of our constitutional history. I do not believe that the contentions now made would occur to any man who could free himself from an absolute approach to the problem.

Matters for Communities

Now let me turn to the other point—that there are some matters which should be settled on the local level, in each community, and should not become great Supreme Court cases. The prayer involved in the Engel case was not compulsory. As the Supreme Court itself recited, no pupil was compelled "to join in the prayer over his or his parents' objection." This, to me, is crucial. If any student was compelled to join against his conviction, this would present a serious and justifiable question, akin to that presented in the flag salute case. The Supreme Court did not give sufficient weight to this fact, in my opinion, and relied heavily on such things as the history of the Book of Common Prayer, which, under various acts of Parliament, was compulsory on all.

Community Determination

Where there is no compulsion, what happens if these matters are left to the determination of each community? In New York, this determination was made by the elected authorities of the school district. It was, indeed, a fact that a large number of the school districts in New York did not adopt the so-called regents' prayer. Where such a decision was reached, there can surely be no constitutional objection on the ground that it was a decision locally arrived at, or that it amounts to an "establishment" of "no religion." But, suppose that in a particular school district, as in New Hyde Park, it was determined that the prayer should be used as a part of the opening exercises of the school day. Remember that it is not compulsory. No pupil is compelled to participate. Must all refrain because one does not wish to join? This would suggest that no school can have a pledge of allegiance to the flag if any student does not wish to join.

This is a country of religious toleration. That is a great consequence of our history embodied in the First Amendment. But does religious toleration mean religious sterility? I wonder why it should be thought that it does. This is a Christian country, in origin, history, tradition and culture. It was out of Christian doctrine and ethics, I think it can be said, that it developed its notion of toleration. No one in this country can be required to have any particular form of religious belief, and no one can suffer legal discrimination because he has or does not have any particular religious belief. But does the fact that we have officially adopted toleration as our standard mean that we must give up our history and our tradition? The Moslem who comes here may worship as he pleases, and may hold public office without discrimination. That is as it should be. But why should it follow that he can require others to give up their Christian tradition merely because he is a tolerated and welcomed member of the community?

Cultural Heritage

Though we have a considerable common cultural heritage, there have always been minority groups in our country. This, I am sure, has been healthy and educational for all concerned. We have surely gained from having a less homogeneous population. Of course, the rights of all, especially those of minorities, must be protected and preserved. But does that require that the majority, where there is such a majority, must give up its cultural heritage and tradition? Why?

Let us consider the Jewish child, or the Catholic child, or the nonbeliever, or the Congregationalist, or the Quaker. He, either alone, or with a few or many others of his views, attends a public school, whose school district, by local action, has prescribed the regents' prayer. When the prayer is recited, if this child or his parents feel that he cannot participate, he may stand or sit, in respectful attention, while the other children take part in the ceremony. Or he may leave the room. It is said that this is bad, because it sets him apart from other children. It is even said that there is an element of compulsion in this—what the Supreme Court has called an "indirect coercive pressure upon religious minorities to conform."

But is this the way it should be looked at? The child of a nonconforming or a minority group is, to be sure, different in his beliefs. That is what it means to be a member of a minority. Is it not desirable, and educational, for him to learn and observe this, in the atmosphere of the school—not so much that he is different, as that other children are different from him? And is it not desirable that, at the same time, he experiences and learns the fact that his difference is tolerated and accepted? No compulsion is put upon him. He need not participate. But he, too, has the opportunity to be tolerant. He allows the majority of the group to follow their own tradition, perhaps coming to understand and to respect what they feel is significant to them.

Spiritual Experience

Is this not a useful and valuable and educational and, indeed, a spiritual experience for the children of what I have called the majority group? They experience the values of their own culture; but they also see that there are others who do not accept those values, and that they are wholly tolerated in their non-acceptance. Learning tolerance for other persons, no matter how different, and respect for their beliefs, may be an important part of American education, and wholly consistent with the First Amendment. No one would think otherwise were it not for parents who take an absolutist approach to the problem, perhaps encouraged by the absolutist expressions of justices of the Supreme Court, on and off the bench.

Chapter 6

Thomas Jefferson as
Authority and Witness

By general consent Thomas Jefferson is our third greatest President, though he deliberately omitted the Presidency in his list of the achievements he wished to have commemorated on his tombstone.

In versatility and in range and variety of interests Jefferson is perhaps the first American. He has been called the last great figure of the Renaissance. One might more accurately describe him as a man of the Renaissance born out of due time and on the wrong Continent. He deserves, if any of our countrymen does, to be called the American Leonardo.

It has become conventional in academic and intellectual circles to disparage the religious faith of the Founding Fathers in general and of Jefferson in particular. Norman Cousins has spoken of "the fallacy that holds that most of the Founding Fathers were essentially agnostics or atheists."[1] Once while lecturing at the National War College to a diversified group of Reserve Officers from all over the nation, I had occasion to speak of the extraordinary debt Americans owe Jefferson for having stamped our state tradition and ideology so strongly with a religious seal. Afterward in an informal general discussion a young professor of history remarked: "I was much interested in what you said about religion in the American tradition. But Jefferson of course was personally not a believer."

I attempted to set the record straight for that young man, and through him for his pupils, pointing out that Jefferson was indeed a Deist but that this actually meant Theist, the difference being merely a matter of Latin versus Greek derivation, and

---

[1] "In God We Trust," pp. 13-14.

131

that in any case his rational faith in God and in the moral law most purely embodied in Jesus was in no way perfunctory but was in his view the very foundation of human existence.

This is a fact and a deeply significant one. It is no accident that Jefferson's contributions to the living American tradition are without exception charged in the highest degree with religious conviction. His own life and thought were. Reason and experience combined to persuade him beyond peradventure of a doubt that there was a benevolent Creator of the universe and in particular of its highest creature, man. Man's personal fulfillment and happiness consisted, in the first instance, in living in accordance with conscience. "The moral sense, or conscience, is as much a part of man as his leg or arm. It is given to all human beings in a stronger or weaker degree, as force of members is given them in greater or less degree. It may be strengthened by exercise as may any particular limb of the body."[2]

Jefferson was inclined to stress what he called the moral branch of religion or theology. He disliked dogmas and dogmatic systems. In fact it must be admitted that he was himself somewhat dogmatic in his anti-dogmatism and in his thorough and uncompromising dislike of the sectarian temper. Like John Milton more than a century earlier, he too found that presbyter was priest writ large. He had a special dislike for the Presbyterian clergy: the "loudest; the most intolerant of all sects, the most tyrannical and ambitious"; and the clergy of New England were a continual pain to him, as he was to them.

It would however be a complete mistake to infer that for Jefferson morality was the same thing as religion or that he was what has come to be known in our century as a religious humanist. Rather he sees true religion as the perfect union of communion with God and morality. The key here is the spirit and doctrine of the loftiest portions of the Old Testament and the life and teachings of Jesus.

Jefferson has made his concept clear in many passages and it will be helpful to the student of this pivotal Founding Father to have a few of them for ready reference.

I believe, with the Quaker preacher, that he who

[2] Letter to Peter Carr, August 10, 1787.

steadily observes those moral precepts in which all religions concur, will never be questioned at the gates, as to the dogmas in which they all differ. That on entering there, all these are left behind us, and the Aristides and Catos, the Penns and Tillotsons, Presbyterians and Baptists, will find themselves united in all principles which are in concert with the reason of the supreme mind.

Of all the systems of morality, ancient or modern, which have come under my observation, none appears to me so pure as that of Jesus.[3]

I, too, have made a wee-little book from the same materials (i.e., the four Evangelists), which I call the Philosophy of Jesus; it is a paradigma of his doctrines, made by cutting the texts out of the book, and arranging them on the pages of a blank book, in a certain order of time or subject. A more beautiful or precious morsel of ethics I have never seen; it is a document in proof that I am a *real Christian,* that is to say, a disciple of the doctrines of Jesus, very different from the Platonists, who call *me* infidel and *themselves* Christians and preachers of the gospel, while they draw all their characteristic dogmas from what its author never said nor saw.[4]

The two passages quoted above were written after Jefferson left the White House. While he was President, in fact during his first term, he corresponded extensively with the eminent Dr. Joseph Priestley and with Dr. Benjamin Rush on the nature of true Christianity and the desirability of an amended version of the Gospel or life and teachings of Jesus which would do full justice to his originality and sublimity. The following passage represents perhaps the most complete summary of his religious views ever drawn up by the Sage of Monticello.

To the corruptions of Christianity I am indeed opposed; but not to the genuine precepts of Jesus himself. I am a Christian, in the only sense in which he wished any one to be; sincerely attached to his doctrines, in preference to all others; ascribing to him

[3] Letter to William Canby, September 18, 1813. The preacher referred to was Richard Motte.

[4] Letter to Charles Thomson, January 9, 1816.

every human excellence; and believing he never claimed any other. . . .

1. Jesus corrected the Deism of the Jews, confirming them in their belief of one only God, and giving them juster notions of his attributes and government.

2. His moral doctrines, relating to kindred and friends, were more pure and perfect than those of the most correct of the philosophers, and greatly more so than those of the Jews; and they went far beyond both in inculcating universal philanthropy. . . .

3. The precepts of philosophy, and of the Hebrew code, laid hold of actions only. He pushed his scrutinies into the heart of man; erected his tribunal in the region of his thoughts, and purified the waters at the fountain head.

4. He taught, emphatically, the doctrines of a future state, which was either doubted or disbelieved by the Jews; and wielded it with efficacy, as an important incentive, supplementary to the other motives to moral conduct.[5]

We have looked at the religion of Thomas Jefferson. Now we must glance at his political views, especially in relation to the new Constitutional Republic, the United States of America.

There are, in spite of Gilbert and Sullivan and American twentieth-century party stereotypes, three main attitudes or tendencies in politics. These are conservative, radical, and liberal. More frequently than not, a given individual is a blend of two of these stances or outlooks. Sometimes a political leader has traces of all three. This is perhaps especially true in the United States where we tend to ride lightly to theory and to follow the practical or the pragmatic path to political power.

The conservative is a man who is distrustful of change because he is not very optimistic about human nature, particularly in its unregenerate form. He sees civilization as a plant of slow growth, essentially delicate and liable to receive injury from careless or too frequent tinkering. He wants to conserve the great values man has inherited from the past and is very much afraid of the bulldozer approach to the temple of civilization.

The opposite of the conservative is not the liberal, but the radical. The radical is the true lover of change, because he dis-

[5] Letter to Benjamin Rush, April 21, 1803.

likes or hates the old order and is desirous of realizing something worthy and good in a short time. He is by nature a reformer, often a Puritan; and he is likely to be a statist, putting his trust in the human ultimate of political power as embodied in Leviathan—the mortal god under the Infinite Deity. The radical is not afraid of the social bulldozer. He believes that it is often necessary to have a destructive and thorough revolution in order to sweep away past abuses and institute an order truly rational and human.

The third political temperament is that of the liberal. His creed is "I believe in man." He is the man who values above all else liberty for the individual, distrusting every concentration of power and fearing as the worst of evils, unless it be utter chaos, the formidable tyranny of the centralized omnicompetent state.

It was a great liberal, Lord Acton, who wrote: "Power always tends to corrupt, and absolute power corrupts absolutely." The heyday of liberalism was the 19th century and perhaps the purest example of a liberal who ever lived was John Stuart Mill. "The spirit of improvement is not always a spirit of liberty, for it may aim at forcing improvements on an unwilling people; and the spirit of liberty, in so far as it resists such attempts, may ally itself locally and temporarily with the opponents of improvement; but the only unfailing and permanent source of improvement is liberty, since by it there are as many possible independent centres of improvement as there are individuals." William E. Gladstone was a Conservative Liberal—how conservative his views on the Church of England perhaps show. In our time Woodrow Wilson has seemed to many the incarnation of the liberal spirit, but there was in him also a good deal of the reformer and the Calvinist. Perhaps he must be called a Radical Liberal. At least he made a substantial contribution to the rising synthesis of liberal idealism and state activism which was to characterize particularly the Democratic Party in the 20th century and to result in an American redefinition of liberalism.

The characteristic radical of modern history is Karl Marx— an alienated and bitter man of great ability but with a messiah-complex so illimitable that he prophesied a wholly new advent or beginning for history and a millennium not of spiritual dreams but in the here and now as a result of human cooperation with dialectically directed historic necessity. Marx is close to a pure type. He was all radical. There was nothing at all of the conservative in him and very little of the liberal.

Many people today want to begin Communism with Plato. This sort of statement is more false than true as a rule, but it does contain a grain of truth. Plato was a radical up to a point and he succumbed as a young philosopher to the temptation of statism. To some extent this was inherent in Greek and ancient experience, for it is the Hebraic-Christian tradition that has separated state and church and magnified the sacredness and dignity of the individual. But Plato was also very impatient and a good deal of a Puritan. He was in a hurry to see and feel perfection, not merely in the eternal coldness of a world invisible and unseen, but in the warm present order of time, flesh, and materiality.

Radicalism was however only one aspect of the Platonic temperament and mentality. Plato was essentially a conservative in his view of man, always a telltale test. The Republic is a work of radicalism, though it embodies many conservative views. Archbishop William Temple once reminded me that for all the statism and extremism of this work, the subject on which it concludes and hinges is the immortality of the soul. The Laws, a political treatise of Plato's old age, is conservative, though mildly reformatory and Puritanical. In this work the philosopher gives a description of human nature that is amazing in its realism. If it were once again taken to heart in the United States, we would have fewer problems. He says, through the Athenian stranger:

> And of all animals the boy is the most unmanageable, inasmuch as he has the fountain of reason in him not yet regulated; he is the most insidious, sharp-witted, and insubordinate of animals. Wherefore he must be bound with many bridles.

Returning to the 18th century and the views of Thomas Jefferson, it must be borne in mind that theoretical liberalism was very much in the air. John Locke was perhaps its major prophet.

Adam Smith published his *Wealth of Nations* in the year 1776. The two great revolutions which marked off a new historical period, the American and the French, were pretty much alike in their ideology. Yet the first, the American, was a conservative revolution. The French in its upshot was extremely radical.

Of all our Founding Fathers, the Sage of Monticello came the closest to being a pure type in his instinctive political and social outlook. He was a liberal from the crown of his noble head down to his toes and out to his very finger tips. He would have agreed with John Stuart Mill on liberty being the only unfailing and permanent source of improvement. Furthermore, thrown as he was into the hurly-burly of responsible politics in the life of a young republic regulated by a mixed constitution, with governmental powers clearly divided, his faith was attested by his works with a rare consistency and steadfastness. It can be said of him that from 1776, when as a young man of 33 he wrote out the Declaration of Independence, until the end of his long pilgrimage on July 4, 1826, his life and thought were of a single piece. They constituted a seamless robe.

Jefferson believed in man, in self-government, in democracy, in the people, in individual rights and liberties as an absolute political principle. He hated and feared tyranny in every form. His greatest passion was to keep it out of America and the new world.

He wrote in 1787, to David Hartley: "I have no fear, but that the result of our experiment will be that men may be trusted to govern themselves without a master. Could the contrary of this be proved, I should conclude, either that there is no God, or that he is a malevolent being." In 1800, the year he was elected the third President of the United States, he wrote to Dr. Rush: "I have sworn upon the altar of God, eternal hostility to every form of tyranny over the mind of man." In 1813 he wrote to J. Melish: "General Washington did not harbor one principle of federalism. He was neither an Angloman, a monarchist, nor a separatist. He sincerely wished the people to have as much self-government as they were competent to exercise themselves. The only point on which he and I ever differed in opinion, was, that I had more confidence than he had in the natural integrity and discretion of the people, and in the safety and extent to which they might trust themselves with a control over their own government."

These are the general views of Jefferson. It was given to him to be our most influential political philosopher. He is, as someone has well said, the St. Paul of American democracy. No less an American than Abraham Lincoln said of him: "The principles of Jefferson are the definitions and axioms of free society."

This being the stature of the proprietor of Monticello, it is not wonderful that the Justices of the Supreme Court have in our time been consistent and persistent in appealing to Jefferson. This is not without irony, for of all the Founding Fathers he looked on the highest Court with the most suspicion and would, as far as positive evidence goes, have been the most shocked and amazed to see the power wielded today by the Court and the degree of its interference with customs and liberties long taken for granted and believed to lie in any case within the jurisdiction of state and local governments.

Thus in 1799 Jefferson in writing Elbridge Gerry nailed his colors to the mast: "I am for preserving to the States the powers not yielded by them to the Union, and to the legislature of the Union its constitutional share in the division of powers; and I am not for transferring all the powers of the States to the General Government, and all those of that government to the executive branch." In 1820 he wrote, to T. Richie: "The judiciary of the United States is the subtle corps of sappers and miners constantly working under ground to undermine the foundations of our confederated fabric. They are construing our constitution from a coordination of a general and special government to a general and supreme one alone. This will lay all things at their feet." The same year, in a letter to W. C. Jarvis, he declared: "To consider the judges as the ultimate arbiters of all constitutional questions (is) a very dangerous doctrine indeed, and one which would place us under the despotism of an oligarchy." And the following year, writing to Pleasants: "It is a misnomer to call a government republican, in which a branch of the supreme power is independent of the nation."

We are not attempting to prove anything by these citations, but it is both interesting and useful to know the views of Jefferson on problems that are still very much with us. What now of his opinions on Church and State, the First Amendment, and religion in public education?

Jefferson was in Europe when the Constitution was planned and had no part at all in drawing it up. What he did do when he finally saw it was to urge on Madison the need of a Bill of Rights. One of the great passions of his life was religious liberty. The Virginia Statute of Religious Liberty, which he wrote, is concerned to rule out all compulsion "to frequent or support any religious worship, place or ministry whatsoever" and to guarantee to individuals the utmost freedom in professing and maintaining religious opinions, without detriment to their civil capacities.

In order to have such liberty, it was necessary to do away with the institution of an established church. Jefferson believed that this institution was pernicious because it got priests into government and government into churches. The two should be separated completely so far as management and authority were concerned; and all churches and sects should be on an equality so far as government consideration was concerned.

This is the point of view which was put succinctly in the celebrated Address of President Jefferson to a Committee of Danbury Baptists on January 1, 1802:

> Believing with you that religion is a matter which lies solely between man and his God, that he owes account to none other for his faith or his worship, that the legislative powers of government reach actions only, and not opinions, I contemplate with solemn reverence that act of the whole American people which declared that their legislature should "make no law respecting an establishment of religion, or prohibiting the free exercise thereof," thus building a wall of separation between Church and State. Adhering to this expression of the supreme will of the nation in behalf of the rights of conscience, I shall see with sincere satisfaction the progress of those sentiments which tend to restore to man all his natural rights, convinced he has no natural right in opposition to his social duties.

This is a weighty statement, and for that reason has been set down in full. It is not remarkable that it has been influential. If it stood alone, or it we had no testimony from its author pointing in other directions, we might acquiesce with the modern Supreme Court in claiming the authority of Jefferson, despite his clear rejection of the authority of the Court as against the will of the nation. But counter testimony does exist.

Here is another address, to a clergyman, Rev. Samuel Miller, in a letter of January 23, 1808:

> I consider the government of the United States as interdicted by the Constitution from intermeddling with religious institutions, their doctrines, discipline, or exercises. This results not only from the provision that no law shall be made respecting an establishment or free exercise of religion, but *from that also which reserves to the States the powers not delegated to the United States. Certainly, no power to prescribe any religious exercise, or to assume authority in religious discipline, has been delegated to the General Government. It must then rest with the States, as far as it can be in any human authority. . . .*
>
> I am aware that the practice of my predecessors may be quoted (in the matter of proclaiming religious days). But I have ever believed, that the example of State executives led to the assumption of that authority by the General Government, without due examination, *which would have discovered that what might be a right in a State government, was a violation of that right when assumed by another.* (Emphasis supplied)

This passage proves beyond any doubt that Jefferson regarded civil authority in relation to religion as an area of power reserved to the States. It was something that had not been delegated to "the General Government." He considered that not only the Congress, in accordance specifically with the First Amendment, but also the President should stay clear of action in the religious sphere. It is clear that he would have applied the same rule to the United States Judiciary.

This pushes us back to actions taken or withheld, allowed or prohibited by the State authorities with respect to religion, as for example in relation to public education. A great deal of attention has been given to Jefferson's views in this area in the last decade or so. It is, we believe, possible to be sure today what Jefferson thought and advocated in his day. This may or may not prove a great deal regarding the present with its different circumstances and complications. Nevertheless, the authority of the

Sage of Monticello is so great that people from our eminent Justices down persist in seeking to wrap round them the mantle of this unique father of our liberties. We therefore present as not the least of the services which this work may render the American public the following correspondence occasioned by the decision of the Supreme Court in *School District v. Schempp* and *Murray v. Curlett.*

The reader, if he has happened to follow carefully the preceding chapters, will be aware that to a limited extent the subject is covered in them. The following summations taken together with the earlier material should leave no doubt as to what Jefferson believed, desired, and advocated with respect to religion in public education. In fairness to him and in loyalty to truth, let all Americans abandon the myths of his religious indifferentism and secularism and listen to his own testimony.

June 20, 1963
(Letter not published)

To the Editor of The New York Times:

I always read Arthur Krock's column with interest and benefit. Frequently I am in agreement with him.

I am compelled to dissent from his view, as set forth in your issue of June 18, that the Supreme Court's decision in banning Bible reading and prayer in the public schools is in the spirit of the 18th century.

I would say that the current decision, which is in every way a climactic one, denoting a turning point in our national life, is notably of the 20th century. The accent of this decision is on *neutrality* with respect to religion in every phase. Religion and irreligion or nonreligion are put on a par. The state is to be unconcerned either way.

This doctrine of neutrality is a novel one. The characteristic view of our jurists in the 19th century was that of Mr. Justice Brewer, speaking for the Court in 1892 and noting many matters which "add a volume of unofficial declarations to the mass of organic utterances that this is a Christian nation." This reflected a dictum of Mr. Justice Story in 1844: "It is also said, and truly, that the Christian religion is a part of the common law of Pennsylvania."

But what of the 18th century and Thomas Jefferson? First of all, Jefferson libertarian though he was, never contemplated that the right of any state to a church establishment or any other kind should be interfered with by the Federal government. The same went for whatever school arrangements a state chose to work out. Whatever we may think today, the Sage of Monticello believed in territorial democracy. He feared central government and he both foresaw and dreaded the possibility that the Supreme Court would achieve supreme power under the Federal Constitution.

Second, Jefferson differed from both the 19th century and our period in his outlook on religion and morality and their relation to education and the state. God was a tremendous reality to him and He was the author of morality. The prime aims of education, in which Jefferson had a particular, lifelong interest, were morality, health, and knowledge.

For Jefferson as for Washington and Hamilton, the detachment of morality from religion was inconceivable. But religion was not churches, sects, or, primarily, worship. It was life lived according to the will of a rational and benevolent God, revealing Himself in the conscience and mind of man. Religion thus understood was truth and was vital and binding on every rational mind. Jefferson's apprehension respecting tender minds and the first stage of education was of sectarian strife and the dogmatic temper, not religion in its pure essence.

Finally, Jefferson was deeply concerned with the duty of civilizing the Indians and this led to his most obvious breaching of a wall of strict separation between church and state. In 1779 he had advocated that the state-supported College of William and Mary maintain "a perpetual mission among the Indian tribes" the object of which should be research into all phases of Indian culture as well as instruction in the principles of Christianity. In 1803 as President he sent to the Senate a treaty with the Kaskaskia Indians which provided for support of a Catholic priest over a 7-year period and the sum of $300.00 toward the erection of a church.

Charles Wesley Lowry

THE NEW YORK TIMES
Washington Bureau

June 22, 1963

Charles Wesley Lowry, Esq.
Foundation for Religious Action
In The Social and Civil Order
Washington 6, D. C.

Dear Mr. Lowry,

Thank you for your courtesy in sending me a copy of your letter to The Times about my "18th Century" piece. While it is true that Jefferson was an all-out State's Righter, his social philosophy was as I pointed out—that religious reading should not be part of the public school education.

I don't know whether you agree that Dr. Julian Boyd of Princeton is the leading authority on Jefferson's writings and beliefs. But I read him that article over the telephone and he agreed with me.

Yours faithfully,
Arthur Krock

. June 26, 1963

Mr. Arthur Krock
Washington, D. C.

Dear Mr. Krock:

Your courteous letter is appreciated.

Far be it from me to set myself up against Professor Boyd, though I can perhaps be allowed to say that Jefferson is a little like Plato and the Bible. Pinning him down is sometimes difficult.

There is a new book *Jefferson on Religion in Public Education*, by Robert M. Healey (Yale University Press, 1962). It is an expanded Yale Ph.D. thesis by Dr. Healey and seems to me as definitive a work as we are likely to get on this facet of Jefferson. I have been heavily fortified by this book in my reactions to the Bible-prayer opinions of the Supreme Court.

Perhaps you will find two quotes of interest. One is general, the other specific in reference to your recent column.

I

"The question of whether Jefferson felt that religion had any place in a system of education . . . will depend upon his concept of morality, what connection he saw between morality and religion, and how he proposed to have education produce the moral individual.

"Jefferson perceived an intimate connection between religion and morality. His concept of morality was grounded in his religious belief. He believed that the benevolent Creator had made man a moral agent in order to promote the happiness of man in society. . . .

". . . If an aim of education was to produce moral adults, 'true religion' had to be included. The exposition and inculcation of the benevolence of God was essential.

". . . The advice given to his namesakes was invariably religious, a brief summation of his views on the Christian religion resulting from a life of inquiry and reflection. Religion was how man acted, and education was really a perversion if it did not provide for the development of morality through religion." (Pages 159-161)

(Note. This is what I understand in general by the 18th century outlook.)

II

"Those doctrines which could ruin the mind were not the beliefs all men held in common but the conflicting dogmas and assertions of particular sects. . . .

"On this basis Jefferson felt that those aspects of religion whose effects could only be pernicious might properly be excluded from democratic public education. In no way did he see this as an attack upon religion. Instead, it was a way of guaranteeing religious freedom. It provided simply that no sect or group of sects could get any advantage over others through control of, or establishment within, public education. . . .

"To Jefferson the elimination of whatever was inconsistent with the tenets of any particular sect did not mean that religion itself was to be outlawed in public education, any more than the interdiction of the government from meddling with religious institutions, doctrines, disciplines, or exercises meant to Jefferson that the government was without religion. This he denied. Rather, the purpose of this provision was to guarantee and encourage religious freedom. This meant that those areas of religion upon which all sects agreed were certainly to be included within the framework of public education.

". . . All religions agreed on the precepts of morality, which could be summed up in a few words: 'Be just and good—Fear God and love thy neighbor.' This was common ground for use at all levels of education." (Pages 206-208)

Does this not indicate that our people—the Justices and many others — reverse the 18th century. They say, Leave it to the Churches and the homes. They have no worry about but would encourage sectarian teaching of religion. Jefferson was more of a reformer and saw a mission for public schools in the field of morality and religion. He is a fascinating man!

Most cordially,
Charles Wesley Lowry

LETTER BY CHARLES WESLEY LOWRY

(Published July 21, 1963)
To the Editor of The New York Times:

Professor Norman Redlich in his letter published July 14 criticises President Henry P. Van Dusen for offering the public nothing "more than sweeping and undocumented statements concerning the intent of the Founding Fathers." May I be permitted to supply some pertinent documentation which tells heavily in favor of Dr. Van Dusen's view.[6]

The crux of the discussion on the American position respecting religion, prayer, and the Bible is not an establishment of some form of organized religion or direct support through taxation of one or some or all churches or sects. Such activities are not at issue today. It was direct tax support of salaries of teachers of the Christian religion which Patrick Henry favored and James Madison opposed successfully in his famous *Remonstrance*.

The real issue is the public status and national role of religion understood not denominationally but in terms of essential con-

[6] For Dr. Van Dusen's letter, see supra, p. 113.

sensus respecting God, man, and the moral law. It is in this sense that the Declaration of Independence is profoundly and centrally a religious document.

Thomas Jefferson had a lifelong interest in education and has a good claim to be called the founder of public education in the United States. He is on record as to what should and should not be done religiously in such education. This was his proposal in a Bill for Establishing Elementary Schools:

> The said teachers shall, in all things relating to the education and government of their pupils, be under the direction and control of the Visitors; but no religious reading, instruction, or exercise, shall be prescribed or practiced inconsistent with the tenets of any religious sect or denomination. (Quoted, Healey, *Jefferson on Religion in Public Education*, Yale Un. Press, pp. 207-208)

The University of Virginia was in his own view the crown of Jefferson's life and work. In 1822 as Rector of the University he wrote: "It was not, however, to be understood that instruction in religious opinion and duties was meant to be precluded by the public authorities, as indifferent to the interests of society. On the contrary, the relations which exist between man and his Maker, and the duties resulting from these relations are the most interesting and important to every human being, and the most incumbent on his study and investigation." (Healey, p. 219)

These are but samples of a tremendous body of evidence which shows that the Sage of Monticello had a clear position and took for granted the intimate union of "religion, morality and knowledge" (Northwest Ordinance) in the educational process.

As for James Madison, five years after the *Remonstrance*, in 1789, he introduced in Congress the first version of the Bill of Rights. He was a member of the Joint Committee for appointing Chaplains for the two bodies of the same Congress. Later as President he approved bills appropriating funds for payment of Chaplains for the Congress and the Armed Forces and—as Jefferson had done—for promotion of religion and religious education among the Indians.

Finally, it is surely of critical significance historically that on September 25, 1789, the Congress not only submitted the First Amendment to the States. It also passed, after debate, a Resolution recommending to all the people "A day of public thanksgiving and prayer" so that they could acknowledge with grateful hearts the favor of God in "affording them an opportunity peaceably to establish a Constitution of government for their safety and happiness."[7]

[7] See Appendix B.

Appendix B

First Thanksgiving Day
Proclamation Under
the New Constitution

Issued by the President, George Washington
New York City, October 3, 1789

Whereas it is the duty of all Nations to acknowledge the providence of Almighty God, to obey his will, to be grateful for his benefits, and humbly to implore his protection and favor, and Whereas both Houses of Congress have by their joint Committee requested me to "recommend to the People of the United States a day of public thanksgiving and prayer to be observed by acknowledging with grateful hearts the many signal favors of Almighty God, especially by affording them an opportunity peaceably to establish a form of government for their safety and happiness."

Now therefore I do recommend and assign Thursday the 26th day of November next to be devoted by the People of these States to the Service of that great and glorious Being, who is the beneficent Author of all the good that was, that is, or that will be. That we may then all unite in rendering unto him our sincere and humble thanks, for his kind care and protection of the People of this country previous to their becoming a Nation, for the signal and manifold mercies, and the favorable interpositions of his providence, which we experienced in the course and conclusion of the late war, for the great degree of tranquility, union, and plenty, which we have since enjoyed, for the peaceable and rational manner in which we have been enabled to establish constitutions of government for our safety and happiness, and particularly the national One now lately instituted, for the civil and religious liberty with which we are blessed, and the means we have of acquiring and diffusing useful knowledge and in general for all the great and various favors which he hath been pleased to confer upon us.

And also that we may then unite in most humbly offering our prayers and supplications to the great Lord and Ruler of Nations and beseech him to pardon our national and other transgressions, to enable us all, whether in public or private stations, to perform our several and relative duties properly and punctually, to render our national government a blessing to all the people, by constantly being a government of wise, just and constitutional laws, discreetly and faithfully executed and obeyed, to protect and guide all Sovereigns and Nations (especially such as have shown kindness unto us) and to bless them with good government, peace and concord. To promote the knowledge and practice of true religion and virtue, and the increase of science among them and us, and generally to grant unto all Mankind such a degree of temporal prosperity as he alone knows to be best.

Chapter 7

The Heart of Earlier
Church-State Decisions

It cannot escape the thoughtful historian or student of American history that the first century and a third of our existence as a nation witnessed almost no serious problems of a constitutional character in the sphere of Church-State relationships. This fact must surely possess deep significance sociologically or juristically: from the standpoint of Constitutional law. Most probably influential factors can be discerned from both angles. In any case we note here a fact of American history that is massive in proportion and impressive in implication.

Beginning with the case of *United States v. Macintosh* in 1931, we get a rash of litigation carried to the highest Court in the area of the liberty of conscience as between the individual and the state. Professor Macintosh of the Yale Divinity School was a Canadian who was unwilling to promise to bear arms unless he believed a given war to be morally justified and was for this reason denied naturalization. Then there is a series of cases involving Jehovah's Witnesses. Two types of issue are involved: the attempts of communities to regulate aggressive proselytizing and refusal of children to salute the national flag as part of a school exercise.

The period covering these classifications of cases is fifteen years—from 1931 to 1946. What is most striking is the inability of the Court during this period and on these issues to make up its mind. There were many sharply split decisions and on almost every issue the Court finally reversed itself. One has a strong sense in reading the numerous and lengthy opinions, especially of concurrence and dissent, that the learned Justices were indeed adepts at hair-splitting.

Beginning with *Everson v. Board of Education* in 1947, we reach the current phase of preoccupation with religion and public education on the part of the highest Court. The issues are now more momentous and emotionally charged from a public standpoint. The Court seems to have felt this for some time and to have moved at first with genuine circumspection. To a certain extent it tacked back and forth, giving in one case and taking away in the next. Thus in *Everson* bus transportation for parochial school pupils was adjudged a service to individual children and not an act involving an establishment of religion. At the same time Mr. Justice Black, who was to write three out of five of the crucial opinions in this series of cases, was at pains to lay down a sweeping and, we think, a novel definition of the establishment clause of the First Amendment.

This broad construction of establishment was made to order for the next case, *McCollum v. Board of Education,* involving "released-time" for religious education. This was in 1948 and the opinion of the Court was delivered by Mr. Justice Black.

Four years later in *Zorach v. Clauson* the Court did not exactly reverse itself. It did however do a neat job of tacking to the right on a new version of released time, and the layman certainly gets the feeling that the Court was anxious not to go too far in the radical direction and tone of *McCollum.* This is borne out by Mr. Justice Black's injured and indignant, dissenting opinion. This opinion of the Court delivered by Mr. Justice Douglas is one of the great conservative legal verdicts in our history.

This brings us up to contemporary events and concerns, specifically to *Engel v. Vitale* and the double-barreled *School District v. Schempp: Murray v. Curlett.* The opinions of the Court in these landmark cases have already been presented in full with the lonely dissents of Mr. Justice Stewart. The material which follows will enable the inquiring student to acquire a broad historical perspective in constitutional decisions in this general field and some familiarity with conclusions that have tended in the past generation to become axioms and assumptions in the tradition of the highest Court. An outstanding example of this is the role assigned the 14th Amendment in Church-State matters, beginning with *Cantwell v. Connecticut (1940),* despite a good deal of highly concrete evidence that what has now become a dogma and an axiom for the Court never entered the minds of the generation that produced the 14th Amendment.

Thus in 1875 James G. Blaine, a close friend of the famous and eloquent rationalist Bob Ingersoll and later the Republican presidential candidate against Grover Cleveland, introduced into the House of Representatives a constitutional amendment extending to the States existing restrictions upon the Federal Government with regard to an establishment of religion or interfering with its free exercise. The following year, on August 4, 1876, the House passed the Blaine amendment by a vote of 180 to 7.

The Senate was more conservative. First, it tacked on a sentence which read: "This article shall not be construed to prohibit the reading of the Bible in any school or institution." Then it approved the amendment but only by a vote of 28 to 16, thus failing to secure the necessary two-thirds vote.

This is evidence of deep and telling import. It does not depend on the tangled issues of the voting by states on the 14th Amendment and the potential challenge to its legality inherent in the fact that the Southern States were denied an opportunity to vote on this decisive alteration in the Federal Constitution, in contrast to the procedure followed in the case of the 13th Amendment. The Blaine Amendment proves beyond any doubt that the Members of the 44th Congress—many of whom like Blaine had been in Congress less than ten years earlier when the 14th Amendment was adopted—did not regard the religion clauses of the First Amendment as automatically applied to the States by the 14th Amendment.

TERRETT v. TAYLOR (1815)

This is the first "Church-State" decision of the Supreme Court. It reaches back to an act of the Legislature of the Commonwealth of Virginia of 1801 and thus really confronts the complex legacy of problems bequeathed by the breakup of an established Church in our oldest Colony. This disestablishment of the Episcopal (formerly Anglican) Church in Virginia was voluntary on the part of the State. In the Commonwealth of Massachusetts, our second oldest Colony, the Congregational Church remained an establishment until 1833.

Mr. Justice Story delivered the opinion of the Court.

. . . This summary view of so much of the Virginia statutes as bears directly on the subject in controversy, presents not only a most extraordinary diversity of opinion in the legislature as to the nature and propriety of aid in the temporal concerns of religion, but the more embarrassing considerations of the constitutional character and efficacy of those laws touching the right and property of the Episcopal Church.

It is conceded on all sides that, at the revolution, the Episcopal Church no longer retained its character as an exclusive religious establishment. And there can be no doubt that it was competent to the people and to the legislative to deprive it of its superiority over other religious sects, and to withhold from it any support by public taxation. But, although it may be true that "religion can be directed only by reason and conviction, not by force or violence," and that "all men are equally entitled to the free exercise of religion according to the dictates of conscience," as the bill of rights of Virginia declares, yet it is difficult to perceive how it follows as a consequence that the legislature may not enact laws more effectually to enable all sects to accomplish the great objects of religion by giving them corporate rights for the management of their property, and the regulation of their temporal as well as spiritual concerns. Consistent with the constitution of Virginia the legislature could not create or continue a religious establishment which should have exclusive rights and prerogatives, or compel the citizens to worship under a stipulated form or discipline, or to pay taxes to those whose creed they could not conscientiously believe. But the free exercise of religion cannot be justly deemed to be restrained by aiding with equal attention the votaries of every sect to perform their own religious duties, or by establishing funds for the support of ministers, for public charities, for the endowment of churches, or for the sepulture of the dead. And that these purposes could be better secured and cherished by corporate powers, cannot be doubted by any person who has attended to the difficulties which surround all voluntary associations. While, therefore, the legislature might exempt the citizens from a compulsive attendance and payment of taxes in support of any particular sect, it is not perceived that either public or constitutional principles required the abolition of all religious corporations.

Be, however, the general authority of the legislature as to the subject of religion as it may, it will require other arguments to establish the position that, at the revolution, all the public property acquired by the Episcopal churches, under the sanction of the laws, became the property of the state. . . .

VIDAL v. GIRARD'S EXECUTORS (1844)

This case is possibly of more interest than significance. The venerable Justice Story was still going strong. The chief lawyer for the plaintiff, attempting to upset the will of the wealthy rationalist Stephen Girard, was Daniel Webster. Said the illustrious orator before the Court: "A cruel experiment is to be made upon these orphans, to ascertain whether they can be brought up without religion." And again: "No fault can be found with Girard for wishing a marble college to bear his name forever, but it is not valuable unless it has a fragrance of Christianity about it." The Court pays its respect to the characteristic 19th century axiom that we are in some real sense a Christian nation but finds sufficient reasons for not pressing this point to interfering with the substantial liberty of an individual to do what he wills with his own.

Mr. Justice Story delivered the opinion of the Court.

. . . The case . . . is that of a valid charity in Pennsylvania, unless it is rendered void by the remaining objection which has been taken to it.

This objection is that the foundation of the college upon the principles and exclusions prescribed by the testator, is derogatory and hostile to the Christian religion, and so is void, as being against the common law and public policy of Pennsylvania. . . .

It is also said, and truly, that the Christian religion is a part of the common law of Pennsylvania. But this proposition is to be received with its appropriate qualifications, and in connection with the bill of rights of that State, as found in its constitution of government. . . .

It is unnecessary for us, however, to consider what would be the legal effect of a devise in Pennsylvania for the establishment of a school or college, for the propagation of Judaism, or Deism, or any other form of infidelity. Such a case is not to be presumed to exist in a Christian country; and therefore it must be made out by clear and indisputable proof. . . .

Looking to the objection, therefore, in a mere juridical view, which is the only one in which we are at liberty to consider it, we are satisfied that there is nothing in the devise establishing the college, or in the regulations and restrictions contained therein, which are inconsistent with the Christian religion, or are opposed to any known policy of the State of Pennsylvania. . . .

REYNOLDS v. UNITED STATES (1879)

The problem which brought into prominence in the 19th century the religion clauses of the First Amendment was the Mormon insistence on practicing polygamy as a religious duty in the Territories of Utah and Idaho. This is the first of a series of cases. In this one we have the Court's first discussion of "free exercise of religion," the first reference to Madison's *Remonstrance,* and the first citation of Jefferson's celebrated gloss on the First Amendment as erecting a wall of separation between Church and State.

Mr. Chief Justice Waite delivered the opinion of the Court.

. . . Congress cannot pass a law for the government of the Territories which shall prohibit the free exercise of religion. . . . Religious freedom is guaranteed everywhere throughout the United States, so far as Congressional interference is concerned. The question to be determined is, whether the law now under consideration comes within the prohibition.

The word "religion" is not defined in the Constitution. We must go elsewhere, therefore, to ascertain its meaning, and nowhere more appropriately, we think, than to the history of those times in the midst of which the provision was adopted. The precise point of the inquiry is, what is the religious freedom which has been guaranteed?

Before the adoption of the Constitution, attempts were made in some of the Colonies and States to legislate not only in respect to the establishment of religion, but in respect to its doctrines and precepts as well. The people were taxed, against their will, for the support of religion, and sometimes for the support of particular sects to whose tenets they could not and did not subscribe. Punishments were prescribed for a failure to attend public worship, and sometimes for entertaining heretical opinions. The controversy upon this general subject was animated in many of the States, but seemed at last to culminate in Virginia. . . .

At the next session the proposed bill ("establishing provision for teachers of the Christian religion") was not only defeated, but another, "for establishing religious freedom," drafted by Mr. Jefferson was passed. In the preamble of this Act, religious freedom is defined; and after a recital "That to suffer the civil magistrate to intrude his powers into the field of opinion, and to restrain the profession or propagation of principles on supposition of their ill tendency, is a dangerous fallacy which at once destroys all religious liberty," it is declared "that it is time enough for the rightful purposes of civil government for its officers to interfere when principles break out into overt acts against peace and good order." In these two sentences is found the true distinction between what properly belongs to the Church and what to the State. . . .

Coming as this (Mr. Jefferson's gloss about a wall of separation to the Danbury Baptists) does from an acknowledged leader of the advocates of the measure, it may be accepted almost as an authoritative declaration of the scope and effect of the amendment thus secured. Congress was deprived of all legislative power over mere opinion, but was left free to reach actions which were in violation of social duties or subversive of good order. . . .

DAVIS v. BEASON (1890)

Mr. Justice Field delivered the opinion of the Court.

. . . The term "religion" has reference to one's views of his relations to his Creator, and to the obligations they impose of reverence for his being and character, and of obedience to his will. It is often confounded with the cultus or form of worship of a particular sect, but is distinguishable from the latter. The First Amendment to the Constitution, in declaring that Congress shall make no law respecting the establishment of religion, or forbidding the free exercise thereof, was intended to allow everyone under the jurisdiction of the United States to entertain such notions respecting his relations to his Maker and the duties they impose as may be approved by his judgment and conscience, and to exhibit his sentiments in such form of worship as he may think proper, not injurious to the equal rights of others, and to prohibit legislation for the support of any religious tenets, or the modes of worship of any sect. . . .

THE LATE CORPORATION OF THE CHURCH OF JESUS CHRIST OF LATTER-DAY SAINTS v. UNITED STATES (1890)

Mr. Justice Bradley delivered the opinion of the Court.

. . . Notwithstanding the stringent laws which have been passed by Congress—notwithstanding all the efforts made to suppress this barbarous practice—the sect or community composing the Church of Jesus Christ of Latter-Day Saints perseveres, in defiance of law, in preaching, upholding, promoting and defending it. It is a matter of public notoriety that its emissaries are engaged in many countries in propagating this nefarious doctrine, and urging its converts to join the community in Utah. The existence of such a propaganda is a blot on our civilization. The organization of a community for the spread and practice of polygamy is, in a measure, a return to barbarism. It is contrary to the spirit of Christianity and of the civilization which Christianity has produced in the Western world. . . .

CHURCH OF THE HOLY TRINITY v. UNITED STATES (1892)

This is a famous and oft cited case. The issue was the hiring by the Vestry of an English minister as Rector of ancient and wealthy Trinity Parish, New York City, in technical violation of an Act of Congress prohibiting the importation under contract of aliens "to perform labor or service of any kind in the United States." The opinion of the Court

concedes a literal and technical violation but sets aside a decision of
the Circuit Court to that effect by recourse in eloquent language and
with innumerable illustrations to the religious and Christian character
of American traditions from the beginning. The argument is really not
from the Constitution at all, but is in effect for special privilege in the
religious field because of the special status and regard unanimously accorded religion by the American people and nation. The importance of
the opinion lies in its summation of the 19th century outlook on religion
and the American state.

Mr. Justice Brewer delivered the opinion of the Court.

. . . But beyond all these matters no purpose of action against
religion can be imputed to any legislation, State or Nation, because this is a religious people. This is historically true. From the
discovery of this continent to the present hour there is a single
voice making this affirmation. . . .

If we examine the constitutions of the various states we find
in them a constant recognition of religious obligations. Every constitution of every one of the forty-four states contains language
which either directly or by clear implication recognizes a profound reverence for religion and an assumption that its influence
in all human affairs is essential to the well being of the community. This recognition may be in the preamble, such as is
found in the constitution of Illinois, 1870: "We, the people of the
State of Illinois, grateful to Almighty God for the civil, political,
and religious liberty which He hath so long permitted us to
enjoy, and looking to Him for a blessing upon our endeavors
to secure and transmit the same unimpaired to succeeding generations," etc. . . .

There is no dissonance in these declarations. There is a universal language pervading them all, having one meaning; they
affirm and reaffirm that this is a religious nation. These are not
individual sayings, declarations of private persons; they are
organic utterances; they speak the voice of the entire people.
While because of a general recognition of this truth the question has seldom been presented to the courts, yet we find that
in Updegraph v. Com., it was decided that, "Christianity, general Christianity, is, and always has been, a part of the common
law of Pennsylvania; . . . not Christianity with an established
church, and tithes, and spiritual courts; but Christianity with

liberty of conscience to all men." And in People v. Ruggles, Chancellor Kent, the great commentator on American law, speaking as Chief Justice of the Supreme Court of New York, said: "The people of this State, in common with the people of this country, profess the general doctrines of Christianity, as the rule of their faith and practice. . . ."

These, and many other matters which might be noticed, add a volume of unofficial declarations to the mass of organic utterances that this is a Christian nation. . . .

PIERCE v. SOCIETY OF SISTERS (1925)

An Oregon law would have required, effective September 1, 1926, every child between 8 and 16 years to be sent to a public school, with failure to do so accounted a misdemeanor. This case, which had the effect of striking down the Oregon Act, is often called the parochial school Magna Carta. The same, of course, applies to all private schools.

Mr. Justice McReynolds delivered the opinion of the Court.

. . . As often heretofore pointed out, rights guaranteed by the Constitution may not be abridged by legislation which has no reasonable relation to some purpose within the competency of the state. The fundamental theory of liberty upon which all governments in this Union repose excludes any general power of the state to standardize its children by forcing them to accept instruction from public teachers only. The child is not the mere creature of the state; those who nurture him and direct his destiny have the right, coupled with the high duty, to recognize and prepare him for additional obligations. . . .

COCHRAN v. BOARD OF EDUCATION (1930)

In this case the Court upholds a Louisiana law providing free textbooks for school children whether in public or parochial schools. It is the precursor of the Everson case 17 years later. But the appellant had invoked not the First but the 14th Amendment, charging a taking of private property for a private purpose in taxation to buy the school books.

Mr. Chief Justice Hughes delivered the opinion of the Court.

. . . The operation and effect of the legislation in question were described by the Supreme Court of the State as follows:

". . . The schools, however, are not the beneficiaries of these appropriations. . . . The school children and the state alone are the beneficiaries. . . ."

Viewing the statute as having the effect thus attributed to it, we can not doubt that the taxing power of the State is exerted for a public purpose. . . . Individual interests are aided only as the common interest is safeguarded.

Judgment affirmed.

UNITED STATES v. MACINTOSH (1931)

Mr. Justice Sutherland delivered the opinion of the Court.

. . . When he speaks of putting his allegiance to the will of God above his allegiance to the government, it is evident, in the light of his entire statement, that he means to make *his own interpretation* of the will of God the decisive test which shall conclude the government and stay its hand. We are a Christian people, according to one another the equal right of religious freedom, and acknowledging with reverence the duty of obedience to the will of God. But, also, we are a nation with the duty to survive; a nation whose Constitution contemplates war as well as peace; whose government must go forward upon the assumption, and safely can proceed upon no other, that unqualified allegiance to the nation and submission and obedience to the laws of the land, as well those made for war as those made for peace, are not inconsistent with the will of God. . . .

Mr. Chief Justice Hughes, dissenting.

. . . I think that the requirement of the oath of office should be read in the light of our regard from the beginning for freedom of conscience. While it has always been recognized that the supreme power of government may be exerted and disobedience to its commands may be punished, we know that with many of our worthy citizens it would be a most heart-searching question if they were asked whether they would promise to obey a law believed to be in conflict with religious duty. Many of their most honored exemplars in the past have been willing to suffer imprisonment or even death rather than to make such a promise. . . .

One cannot speak of religious liberty, with proper appreciation of its essential and historic significance, without assuming
the existence of a belief in supreme allegiance to the will of
God. Professor Macintosh, when pressed by the inquiries put to
him, stated what is axiomatic in religious doctrine. And, putting
aside dogmas with their particular conceptions of deity, freedom
of conscience itself implies respect for an innate conviction of
paramount duty. The battle for religious liberty has been fought
and won with respect to religious beliefs and practices, which
are not in conflict with good order, upon the very ground of
the supremacy of conscience within its proper field. . . .

CANTWELL v. CONNECTICUT (1940)

This is the first of the Jehovah's Witnesses cases. The highest Court
has perhaps never gotten more intricately and tortuously involved than in
these cases. This one concerns proselytizing without the approval of the
public welfare council in accordance with Connecticut law. A momentous
step also is taken with respect to the 14th Amendment.

Mr. Justice Roberts delivered the opinion of the Court.

. . . We hold that the statute, as construed and applied to the
appellants, deprives them of their liberty without due process
of law in contravention of the Fourteenth Amendment. The
fundamental concept of liberty embodied in that Amendment
embraces the liberties guaranteed by the First Amendment. The
First Amendment declares that Congress shall make no law
respecting an establishment of religion or prohibiting the free
exercise thereof. The Fourteenth Amendment has rendered the
legislatures of the states as incompetent as Congress to enact
such laws. The constitutional inhibition of legislation on the subject of religion has a double aspect. On the one hand, it forestalls compulsion by law of the acceptance of any creed or the
practice of any form of worship. Freedom of conscience and
freedom to adhere to such religious organization or form of
worship as the individual may choose cannot be restricted by
law. On the other hand, it safeguards the free exercise of the
chosen form of religion. Thus the Amendment embraces two
concepts,—freedom to believe and freedom to act. The first is
absolute but, in the nature of things, the second cannot be. Con-

duct remains subject to regulation for the protection of society.
. . .

We find in the instant case no assault or threatening of bodily harm, no truculent bearing, no intentional discourtesy, no personal abuse. . . .

Although the contents of the record not unnaturally aroused animosity, we think that, in the absence of a statute narrowly drawn to define and punish specific conduct as constituting a clear and present danger to a substantial interest of the State, the petitioner's communication, considered in the light of the constitutional guarantees, raised no such clear and present menace to public peace and order as to render him liable to conviction of the common law offense in question. . . .

MINERSVILLE SCHOOL DISTRICT v. GOBITIS (1940)

This decision, involving the flag salute in school, shows the highest court in a conservative frame of mind.

Mr. Justice Frankfurter delivered the opinion of the Court.

. . . Centuries of strife over the erection of particular dogmas as exclusive or all-comprehending faiths led to the inclusion of a guarantee for religious freedom in the Bill of Rights. The First Amendment, and the Fourteenth through its absorption of the First, sought to guard against repetition of those bitter struggles by prohibiting the establishment of a state religion and by securing to every sect the free exercise of its faith. So pervasive is the acceptance of this precious right that its scope is brought into question, as here, only when the conscience of individuals collides with the felt necessities of society. . . .

The preciousness of the family relation, the authority and independence which give dignity to parenthood, indeed the enjoyment of all freedom, presuppose the kind of ordered society which is summarized by our flag. A society which is dedicated to the preservation of these ultimate values of civilization may in self-protection utilize the educational process for inculcating those almost unconscious feelings which bind men together in a comprehending loyalty, whatever may be their lesser differences and difficulties. That is to say, the process may be utilized so long as men's right to believe as they please, to win others to their way of belief, and their right to assemble in their chosen places of worship for the devotional ceremonies of their faith, are fully respected.

Judicial review, itself a limitation on popular government, is a fundamental part of our constitutional scheme. But to the legislature no less than to courts is committed the guardianship of deeply-cherished liberties. Where all the effective means of inducing political changes are left free from interference, education in the abandonment of foolish legislation is itself a training in liberty. To fight out the wise use of legislative authority in the forum of public opinion and before legislative assemblies rather than to transfer such a contest to the judicial arena, serves to vindicate the self-confidence of a free people.

JONES v. CITY OF OPELIKA (1942)

This is another Jehovah's Witnesses case. City ordinances imposing license taxes upon the sale of printed matter are upheld. But the court divides 5 to 4 and there are three different dissenting opinions. The third of these, prophetic of things to come, is reproduced here.

Mr. Justice Black, Mr. Justice Douglas, Mr. Justice Murphy.

The opinion of the Court sanctions a device which in our opinion suppresses or tends to suppress the free exercise of a religion practiced by a minority group. This is but another step in the direction which Minersville School District v. Gobitis, took against the same religious minority and is a logical extension of the principles upon which that decision rested. Since we joined in the opinion in the Gobitis case, we think this is an appropriate occasion to state that we now believe that it was also wrongly decided. Certainly our democratic form of government functioning under the historic Bill of Rights has a high responsibility to accommodate itself to the religious views of minorities however unpopular and unorthodox those views may be. The First Amendment does not put the right freely to exercise religion in a subordinate position. We fear, however, that the opinions in these and in the Gobitis case do exactly that.

MURDOCK v. COMMONWEALTH
OF PENNSYLVANIA (1943)

In a 5 to 4 decision the Court now reverses *Jones v. City of Opelika*. Note the tendency in this opinion to give religion a privileged position.

Mr. Justice Douglas delivered the opinion of the Court.

. . . But the mere fact that the religious literature is "sold" by the itinerant preachers rather than "donated" does not transform evangelism into a commercial enterprise. If it did, then the passing of a collection plate in Church would make the Church service a commercial project. The constitutional rights of those spreading their religious beliefs through the spoken and printed word are not to be gauged by standards governing retailers or wholesalers of books. The right to use the press for expressing one's views is not to be measured by the protection afforded commercial handbills. It should be remembered that the pamphlets of Thomas Paine were not distributed free of charge. It is plain that a religious organization needs funds to remain a going concern. But an itinerant evangelist, however misguided or intolerant he may be, does not become a mere book agent by selling the Bible or religious tracts to help defray his expenses or to sustain him. . . .

JONES v. CITY OF OPELIKA (1943)

In his dissent to the reversal, a year later, of the earlier *Jones v. City of Opelika*, Mr. Justice Reed goes into the immediate historical background of the Bill of Rights.

Mr. Justice Reed, dissenting.

. . . The available evidence of Congressional action shows clearly that the draftsmen of the amendments had in mind the practice of religion and the right to be heard, rather than any abridgment or interference with either by taxation in any form. The amendments were proposed by Mr. Madison. He was careful to explain to the Congress the meaning of the amendment on religion. The draft was commented upon by Mr. Madison when it read: "No religion shall be established by law, nor shall the equal rights of conscience be infringed."

He said that he apprehended the meaning of the words on religion to be that Congress should not establish a religion and enforce the legal observation of it by law, nor compel men to worship God in any manner contrary to their conscience. No such specific interpretation of the amendment on freedom of expression has been found in the debates. The clearest is probably from Mr. Benson who said that "The committee who framed this report proceeded on the principle that these rights belonged to the people; they conceived them to be inherent; and all that they meant to provide against was their being infringed by the Government." . . .

DOUGLAS v. CITY OF JEANNETTE (1943)

This case is taken as a text in a celebrated opinion which is technically a concurrence in the opinion of the Court in *Douglas,* but is a dissent in *Murdock* and a similar case *Martin v. Struthers.* Mr. Justice Frankfurter joined in this dissent.

Mr. Justice Jackson.

. . . If we should strip these cases to the underlying questions, I find them too difficult as constitutional problems to be disposed of by a vague but fervent transcendentalism.

In my view the First Amendment assures the broadest tolerable exercise of free speech, free press, and free assembly, not merely for religious purposes, but for political, economic, scientific, news or informational ends as well. When limits are reached which such communications must observe, can one go farther under the cloak of religious evangelism? Does what is obscene, or commercial, or abusive or inciting become less so if employed to promote a religious ideology? I had not supposed that the rights of secular and non-religious communications were more narrow or in any way inferior to those of avowed religious groups.

It may be asked why then does the First Amendment separately mention free exercise of religion? The history of religious persecution gives the answer. Religion needed specific protection because it was subject to attack from a separate quarter. It was often claimed that one was an heretic and guilty of blasphemy, because he failed to conform in mere belief, or in support of prevailing institutions and theology. It was to assure religious teaching as much freedom as secular discussion, rather than to assure it greater license, that led to its separate statement.

The First Amendment grew out of an experience which taught that society cannot trust the conscience of a majority to keep its religious zeal within the limits that a free society can tolerate. I do not think it any more intended to leave the conscience of a minority to fix its limits. Civil government can not let any group ride roughshod over others simply because their "consciences" tell them to do so. . . .

This Court is forever adding new stories to the temples of constitutional law, and the temples have a way of collapsing when one story too many is added. . . . The Court is adding a new privilege to override the rights of others to what has before been regarded as religious liberty. . . .

Civil liberties had their origin and must find their ultimate guaranty in the faith of the people. If that faith should be lost, five or nine men in Washington could not long supply its want. . . .

WEST VIRGINIA STATE BOARD OF EDUCATION v. BARNETTE (1943)

The Court in this case reverses its stand on the flag salute in *Gobitis*. It says "No" to West Virginia on the policy of enforcing this symbolism and ritual. Many readers will be fascinated by what Justice Frankfurter in his dissent says about Bible-reading.

Mr. Justice Jackson delivered the opinion of the Court.

. . . There is no doubt that . . . the flag salute is a form of utterance. Symbolism is a primitive but effective way of communicating ideas. The use of an emblem or flag to symbolize some system, idea, institution, or personality, is a short cut from mind to mind. . . .

To sustain the compulsory flag salute we are required to say that a Bill of Rights which guard the individual's right to speak his own mind, left it open to public authorities to compel him to utter what is not in his mind. . . .

Nor does the issue as we see it turn on one's possession of

particular religious views or the sincerity with which they are held. . . .

The Fourteenth Amendment, as now applied to the States, protects the citizen against the State itself and all of its creatures —Boards of Education not excepted. . . .

If there is any fixed star in our constitutional constellation, it is that no official, high or petty, can prescribe what shall be orthodox in politics, nationalism, religion, or other matters of opinion or force citizens to confess by word or act their faith therein. If there are any circumstances which permit an exception, they do not now occur to us. . . .

Mr. Justice Frankfurter, dissenting.

. . . When Mr. Justice Holmes, speaking for this Court, wrote that "It must be remembered that legislatures are ultimate guardians of the liberties and welfare of the people in quite as great a degree as the courts," he went to the very essence of our constitutional system and the democratic conception of our society. He did not mean that for only some phases of civil government this Court was not to supplant legislatures and sit in judgment upon the right or wrong of a challenged measure. He was stating the comprehensive judicial duty and role of this Court in our constitutional scheme whenever legislation is sought to be nullified on any ground, namely, that responsibility for legislation lies with the legislatures, answerable as they are, directly to the people, and this Court's only and very narrow function is to determine whether within this broad grant of authority vested in legislatures they have exercised a judgment for which reasonable justification can be offered. . . .

The reason why from the beginning even the narrow judicial authority to nullify legislation has been viewed with a jealous eye is that it serves to prevent the full play of the democratic process. The fact that it may be an undemocratic aspect of our scheme of government does not call for its rejection or its disuse. But it is the best of reasons . . . for the greatest caution in its use. . . .

We are not reviewing merely the action of a local school board. The flag salute requirement in this case comes before us with full authority of the State of West Virginia. We are in fact passing judgment on the power of the State as a whole. . . .

What one can say with assurance is that the history out of which grew constitutional provisions for religious equality, and the writings of the great exponents of religious freedom—Jefferson, Madison, John Adams, Benjamin Franklin—are totally wanting in justification for a claim by dissidents of exceptional immunity from civic measures of general applicability, measures not in fact disguised assaults upon such dissident views. . . . And so Jefferson and those who followed him wrote guarantees of religious freedom into our constitutions. Religious minorities as well as religious majorities were to be equal in the eyes of the political state. But Jefferson and the others also knew that minorities may disrupt society. It never would have occurred to them to write into the Constitution the subordination of the general civil authority of the state to sectarian scruples. . . .

Consider the controversial issue of compulsory Bible-reading in public schools. The educational policies of the states are in great conflict over this, and the state courts are divided in their decisions on the issue whether the requirement of Bible-reading offends constitutional provisions dealing with religious freedom. The requirement of Bible-reading has been justified by various state courts as an appropriate means of inculcating ethical precepts and familiarizing pupils with the most lasting expressions of great English literature. Is this Court to overthrow such variant state educational policies by denying states the right to entertain such convictions in regard to their school systems because of a belief that the King James version is in fact a sectarian text to which parents of the Catholic and Jewish faiths and of some Protestant persuasions may rightly object to having their children exposed? On the other hand the religious consciences of some parents may rebel at the absence of any Bible-reading in the schools. Or is this Court to enter the old controversy between science and religion by unduly defining the limits within which a state may experiment with its school curricula? . . .

EVERSON v. BOARD OF EDUCATION (1947)

We come now to three landmark cases. This one deals with free bus transportation for parochial school pupils. Mr. Justice Black takes the occasion, however, speaking for the Court, to go into questions of establishment and the meaning of separation of church and state. He lays out clearly the so-called broad interpretation of the establishment clause of the First Amendment in an opinion that is remarkably prophetic of things to come. However in all fairness, the precise import of this decision was conservative. The opinion of the Court incidentally appears to be in error in asserting that James Madison's "great Memorial and Remonstrance" was written against "Virginia's tax levy for the support of the established church." The law which Madison opposed successfully, and which Patrick Henry was as strongly for, proposed a tax levy for the support of Christian teachers of the various denominations according to the designation of the taxpayer in each case.

Mr. Justice Black delivered the opinion of the Court.

. . . The "establishment of religion" clause of the First Amendment means at least this: Neither a state nor the Federal Government can set up a church. Neither can pass laws which aid one religion, aid all religions, or prefer one religion over another. Neither can force nor influence a person to go to or to remain away from church against his will or force him to profess a belief or disbelief in any religion. No person can be punished for entertaining or professing religious beliefs or disbeliefs, for church attendance or non-attendance. No tax in any amount, large or small, can be levied to support any religious activities or institutions, whatever they may be called, or whatever form they may adopt to teach or practice religion. Neither a state nor the Federal Government can, openly or secretly, participate in the affairs of any religious organizations or groups and vice versa. In the words of Jefferson, the clause against establishment of religion by law was intended to erect "a wall of separation between Church and State."

We must consider the New Jersey statute in accordance with the foregoing limitations imposed by the First Amendment. But we must not strike that state statute down if it is within the state's constitutional power even though it approaches the verge of that power. New Jersey cannot consistently with the "establishment of religion" clause of the First Amendment contribute tax-raised funds to the support of an institution which teaches the tenets and faith of any church. On the other hand, other language of the amendment commands that New Jersey cannot exclude individual Catholics, Lutherans, Mohammedans, Baptists,

Jews, Methodists, Nonbelievers, Presbyterians, or the members of any other faith, because of their faith, or lack of it, from receiving the benefits of public welfare legislation. . . .

ILLINOIS ex rel. McCOLLUM v.
BOARD OF EDUCATION (1948)

The issue in this case is "released-time" from public school for religious education. Mr. Justice Black again delivers the opinion of the Court and is able now to apply "line upon line, precept upon precept" the view of the establishment clause set forth somewhat gratuitously in *Everson*.

Mr. Justice Black delivered the opinion of the Court.

. . . Recognizing that the Illinois program is barred by the First and Fourteenth Amendments if we adhere to the views expressed both by the majority and the minority in the Everson case, counsel for the respondents challenge those views as dicta and urge that we reconsider and repudiate them. They argue that historically the First Amendment was intended to forbid only government preference of one religion over another, not an impartial governmental assistance of all religions. In addition they ask that we distinguish or overrule our holding in the Everson case that the Fourteenth Amendment made the "establishment of religion" clause of the First Amendment applicable as a prohibition against the states. After giving full consideration to the arguments presented we are unable to accept either of these contentions.

To hold that a state cannot consistently with the First and Fourteenth Amendments utilize its public school system to aid any or all religious faiths or sects in the dissemination of their doctrines and ideals does not, as counsel urge, manifest a governmental hostility to religion or religious teachings. A manifestation of such hostility would be at war with our national tradition as embodied in the First Amendment's guaranty of the free exercise of religion. For the First Amendment rests upon the premise that both religion and government can best work to achieve their lofty aims if each is left free from the other within its respective sphere. Or, as we said in the Everson case, the First Amendment has erected a wall between Church and State which must be kept high and impregnable.

Here not only are the state's tax-supported public school buildings used for the dissemination of religious doctrines. The State also affords sectarian groups an invaluable aid in that it helps to provide pupils for their religious classes through use of the state's compulsory public school machinery. This is not separation of Church and State.

The cause is reversed and remanded to the State Supreme Court for proceedings not inconsistent with this opinion.

Mr. Justice Frankfurter delivered the following opinion, in which Mr. Justice Jackson, Mr. Justice Rutledge and Mr. Justice Burton join.

. . . We are all agreed that the First and the Fourteenth Amendments have a secular reach far more penetrating in the conduct of Government than merely to forbid an "established church." But agreement, in the abstract, that the First Amendment was designed to erect "a wall of separation between Church and State," does not preclude a clash of views as to what the wall separates. . . . We cannot illuminatingly apply the "wall-of-separation" metaphor until we have considered the relevant history of religious education in America, the place of the "released time" movement in that history, and its precise manifestation in the case before us. . . .

We do not consider, as indeed we could not, school programs not before us which, though colloquially characterized as "released time," present situations differing in aspects that may well be constitutionally crucial. . . . We find that the basic Constitutional principle of absolute separation was violated when the State of Illinois, speaking through its Supreme Court, sustained the school authorities of Champaign in sponsoring and effectively furthering religious beliefs by its educational arrangement.

Separation means separation not something less. Jefferson's metaphor in describing the relation between Church and State speaks of a "wall of separation," not of a fine line easily overstepped. The public school is at once the symbol of our democracy and the most pervasive means for promoting our common destiny. In no activity of the State is it more vital to keep out divisive forces than in its schools, to avoid confusing, not to say fusing, what the Constitution sought to keep strictly apart. . . .

Mr. Justice Jackson, concurring.

. . . The plaintiff, as she has every right to be, is an avowed atheist. What she has asked of the courts is that they not only end the "released time" plan but also ban every form of teaching which suggests or recognizes that there is a God. She would ban all teaching of the Scriptures. She especially mentions as an example of invasion of her rights "having pupils learn and recite such statements as, 'The Lord is my Shepherd, I shall not want.'" And she objects to teaching that the King James version of the Bible "is called the Christian's Guide Book, the Holy Writ and the Word of God," and many other similar matters. This Court is directing the Illinois courts generally to sustain plaintiff's complaint without exception of any of these grounds of complaint, without discriminating between them and without laying down any standards to define the limits of the effect of our decision.

To me, the sweep and detail of these complaints is a danger signal which warns of the kind of local controversy we will be required to arbitrate if we do not place appropriate limitations on our decision and exact strict compliance with jurisdictional requirements. . . . If we are to eliminate everything that is objectionable to any of these warring sects or inconsistent with any of their doctrines, we will leave public education in shreds. Nothing but educational confusion and a discrediting of the public school system can result from subjecting it to constant lawsuits. . . .

The task of separating the secular from the religious in education is one of magnitude, intricacy and delicacy. To lay down a sweeping constitutional doctrine as demanded by complainant and apparently approved by the Court . . . is to decree a uniform, rigid and, if we are consistent, an unchanging standard for countless school boards representing and serving highly localized groups. . . .

It is idle to pretend that this task is one for which we can find in the Constitution one word to help us. . . . It is a matter on which we can find no law but our own prepossessions. If with no surer legal guidance we are to take up and decide every variation of this controversy . . . we are likely to make the legal "wall of separation between church and state" as winding as the famous serpentine wall designed by Mr. Jefferson for the University he founded.

Mr. Justice Reed, dissenting.

. . . As no issue of prohibition upon the free exercise of religion is before us, we need only examine the School Board's action to see if it constitutes an establishment of religion. . . .

The phrase "an establishment of religion" may have been intended by Congress to be aimed only at a state church. When the First Amendment was pending in Congress in substantially its present form, "Mr. Madison said, he apprehended the meaning of the words to be, that Congress should not establish a religion, and enforce the legal observation of it by law, nor compel men to worship God in any manner contrary to their conscience." Passing years, however, have brought about acceptance of a broader meaning, although never until today, I believe, has this Court widened its interpretation to any such degree as holding that recognition of the interest of our nation in religion, through the granting, to qualified representatives of the principal faiths, of opportunity to present religion as an optional, extracurricular subject during released school time in public school buildings, was equivalent to an establishment of religion. . . .

Mr. Jefferson, as one of the founders of the University of Virginia, a school which from its establishment in 1819 has been wholly governed, managed and controlled by the State of Virginia, was faced with the same problem that is before this Court today: The question of the constitutional limitation upon religious education in public schools. In his annual report as Rector, to the President and Directors of the Literary Fund, dated October 7, 1822, approved by the Visitors of the University of whom Mr. Madison was one, Mr. Jefferson set forth his views at some length. These suggestions of Mr. Jefferson were adopted and Ch. II, 1, of the Regulations of the University of October 4, 1824, provided that:

"Should the religious sects of this State, or any of them, according to the invitation held out to them, establish within, or adjacent to, the precincts of the University, schools for instruction in the religion of their sect, the students of the University will be free, and expected to attend religious worship at the establishment of their respective sects, in the morning, and in time to meet their school in the University at its stated hour."

Thus, the "wall of separation between Church and State" that Mr. Jefferson built at the University which he founded did not exclude religious education from that school. The difference between the generality of his statements on the separation of church and state and the specificity of his conclusions on education are considerable. A rule of law should not be drawn from a figure of speech. . . .

It is clear from its historical setting and its language that the Remonstrance was a protest against an effort by Virginia to support Christian sects by taxation. Issues similar to those raised by the instant case were not discussed. Thus, Mr. Madison's approval of Mr. Jefferson's report as Rector gives, in my opinion, a clearer indication of his views on the constitutionality of religious education in public schools than his general statements on a different subject. . . .

The prohibition of enactments respecting the establishment of religion do not bar every friendly gesture between church and state. It is not an absolute prohibition against every conceivable situation where the two may work together any more than the other provisions of the First Amendment—free speech, free press —are absolutes. . . . This Court cannot be too cautious in upsetting practices embedded in our society by many years of experience. . . . Devotion to the great principle of religious liberty should not lead us into a rigid interpretation of the constitutional guarantee that conflicts with accepted habits of our people. This is an instance where, for me, the history of past practices is determinative of the meaning of a constitutional clause not a decorous introduction to the study of its text. The judgment should be affirmed.

ZORACH v. CLAUSON (1952)

This notable decision, in a New York released-time case involving release of children from school to church, not as in *McCollum* to classrooms on school premises with instruction there by pastors, priests, or rabbis, is in the long tradition of a constructive and conservative as opposed to a radical outlook on established, traditional society and its relation to Constitutional norms and protections. It gives the impression of a strong feeling for the religious imperatives in the American experiment, without minimizing or jeopardizing the rights of individuals. The reverse of this, emotionally, can be sensed in the excerpt given after the opinion of the Court in the dissent of Mr. Justice Black. *Zorach*, coming after *McCollum*, as the latter came after *Everson*, encouraged many to believe that the Supreme Court continued in our time to be characterized by caution, moderation, and restraint. It even encouraged the hope, vain as it now seems, that the Court would take advantage of the narrow base of the decision in *Engel* (New York School Prayer case) and move conservatively in the matter of Bible-reading and the Lord's Prayer. The question now is whether the Court has left itself room for turning or feels, as some of us fear, that it has burned its bridges on religion in public education. Only time and tides of public opinion can answer this query.

Mr. Justice Douglas delivered the opinion of the Court.

. . . The First Amendment within the scope of its coverage permits no exception; the prohibition is absolute. The First Amendment, however, does not say that in every and all respects there shall be a separation of Church and State. Rather, it studiously defines the manner, the specific ways, in which there shall be no concert or union or dependency one on the other. This is the common sense of the matter. Otherwise the state and religion would be aliens to each other—hostile, suspicious, and even unfriendly. . . . A fastidious atheist or agnostic could even object to the supplication with which the Court opens each session: "God save the United States and this Honorable Court."
. . .

We are a religious people whose institutions presuppose a Supreme Being. We guarantee the freedom to worship as one chooses. We make room for as wide a variety of beliefs and creeds as the spiritual needs of man deem necessary. We sponsor an attitude on the part of government that shows no partiality to any one group and that lets each flourish according to the zeal of its adherents and the appeal of its dogma. When the state encourages religious instruction or cooperates with religious authorities by adjusting the schedule of public events to sectarian needs, it follows the best of our traditions. For it then respects the religious nature of our people and accommodates the public service to their spiritual needs. To hold that it may not would be to find in the Constitution a requirement that the government show a callous indifference to religious groups. That would be preferring those who believe in no religion over those who believe. . . .

Mr. Justice Black, dissenting.

. . . In dissenting today, I mean to do more than give routine approval to our McCollum decision. I mean also to reaffirm my faith in the fundamental philosophy expressed in McCollum and Everson v. Board of Education. . . .

Here the sole question is whether New York can use its compulsory education laws to help religious sects get attendants presumably too unenthusiastic to go unless moved to do so by the pressure of this state machinery. That this is the plan, purpose, design and consequence of the New York program cannot be denied. . . . This is not separation but combination of Church and State.

The Court's validation of the New York system rests in part on its statement that Americans "are a religious people whose institutions presuppose a Supreme Being." This was at least as true when the First Amendment was adopted; and it was just as true when eight justices of this Court invalidated the released time system in McCollum on the premise that a state can no more "aid all religions" than it can aid one. It was precisely because Eighteenth Century Americans were a religious people divided into many fighting sects that we were given the constitutional mandate to keep church and state completely separate. . . . Now as then, it is only by wholly isolating the state from the religious sphere and compelling it to be completely neutral, that the freedom of each and every denomination and of all nonbelievers can be maintained. It is this neutrality the Court abandons today when it treats New York's coercive system as a program which merely "encourages religious instruction or cooperates with religious authorities." The abandonment is all the more dangerous to liberty because of the Court's legal exaltation of the orthodox and its derogation of unbelievers.

Under our system of religious freedom. . . . The choice of all has been as free as the choice of those who answered the call to worship moved only by the music of the old Sunday morning church bells. . . . Before today, our judicial opinions have refrained from drawing invidious distinctions between those who believe in no religion and those who do believe. The First Amendment has lost much if the religious follower and the atheist are no longer to be judicially regarded as entitled to equal justice under law. . . .

Chapter 8

Religion in American
State Papers

Several years ago I made a selection of 21 documents drawn from the wealth of American state papers. The criteria employed in choosing the particular documents in question were two: a strong religious note and tested historical significance.

In a tract published in 1960, *The Meaning of American Civilization,* I listed these 21 documents as exemplifying the unique religious strain in American state papers as a whole. A distinguished author and a personal friend, Mrs. Bonaro Overstreet, who read this small tract, called me on the phone to express her interest in the documents thus singled out and asked: "Where can I get them?"

We agreed after some discussion that it would be a useful service if such a collection of selected state papers could be published as a small volume. I wish this could be done here, but considerations of space make it impossible. We must therefore be content to present here for the use of students who want to have available in handy form essential materials on Church and State, religion and government in the American tradition, appropriate excerpts from our 21 documents. In several instances where they are not long we publish the text in full or very nearly so. In addition, for the sake of a greater completeness, we are presenting very brief quotations from selected Inaugural Addresses of our Presidents other than Washington, Lincoln, and Wilson, the only Presidents whose Inaugurals are covered in the 21 documents.

It is believed that the inclusion of a representative list of American state papers in the source material made available in this volume will be of conspicuous aid to the student of recent

Supreme Court decisions and the critical issue of true Americanism raised by these opinions.

21 Landmark Documents

1. FIRST CHARTER OF JAMESTOWN

April 10, 1606

This charter gave the London and Plymouth Companies the right to
colonize in North America within specified areas. An effort by the Plymouth
Colony in Maine failed, but the London Company established at James-
town in 1607 the first permanent English colony.

I. JAMES, by the Grace of God, King of *England, Scotland,
France,* and *Ireland,* Defender of the Faith, &C. WHEREAS our
loving and well-disposed Subjects, Sir *Thomas Gates,* and Sir
George Somers, Knights, *Richard Hackluit,* Clerk, Prebendary of
Westminster, and *Edward-Maria Wingfield, Thomas Hanham,*
and *Raleigh Gilbert,* Esqrs. *William Parker* and *George Popham,*
Gentlemen, and divers others of our loving Subjects, have been
humble Suitors unto us, that We would vouchsafe unto them
our Licence, to make Habitation, Plantation, and to deduce a
Colony of sundry of our People into that Part of *America,* commonly called VIRGINIA, and other Parts and Territories in
America, either appertaining unto us, or which are not now
actually possessed by any *Christian* Prince or People, situate,
lying, and being all along the Sea Coasts, between four and
thirty Degrees of *Northerly* Latitude from the Equinoctial Line,
and five and forty Degrees of the same Latitude, and in the
main Land between the same four and thirty and five and forty
Degrees, and the Islands thereunto adjacent, or within one
hundred Miles of the Coast thereof;

And to that End, and for the more speedy Accomplishment
of their said intended Plantation and Habitation there, are desirous to divide themselves into two several Colonies and Companies; The one consisting of certain Knights, Gentlemen, Merchants, and other Adventurers, of our City of *London* and elsewhere, which are, and from time to time shall be, joined unto
them, which do desire to begin their Plantation and Habitation
in some fit and convenient Place, between four and thirty and
one and forty Degrees of the said Latitude, alongst the Coasts

of *Virginia* and Coasts of *America* aforesaid; And the other consisting of sundry Knights, Gentlemen, Merchants, and other Adventurers, of our Cities of *Bristol* and *Exeter*, and of our Town of *Plymouth*, and of other Places, which do join themselves unto that Colony, which do desire to begin their Plantation and Habitation in some fit and convenient Place, between eight and thirty Degrees and five and forty Degrees of the said Latitude, all alongst the said Coast of *Virginia* and *America*, as that Coast lyeth:

We, greatly commending, and graciously accepting of, their Desires for the Furtherance of so noble a Work, which may, by the Province of Almighty God, hereafter tend to the Glory of his Divine Majesty, in propagating of *Christian* Religion to such People, as yet live in Darkness and miserable Ignorance of the true Knowledge and Worship of God, and may in time bring the Infidels and Savages, living in those Parts, to human Civility, and to a settled and quiet Government; Do, by these our Letters Patents, graciously accept of, and agree to, their humble and well-intended Desires;

AND do therefore, for Us, our Heirs, and Successors, GRANT and agree, that the said Sir *Thomas Gates*, Sir *George Somers*, *Richard Hackluit*, and *Edward-Maria Wingfield*, Adventurers of and for our City of *London*, and all such others, as are, or shall be joined unto them of that Colony, shall be called the *first Colony. . . .*

2. THE MAYFLOWER COMPACT

November 11, 1620

The occasion of this compact was the accidents of wind and tide which had born the Mayflower far to the North and outside the jurisdiction of the London Company. The "Pilgrims" determined to settle where they had landed and made this agreement as a basis for the government of the colony they were about to found. To a degree the Mayflower Compact is a forerunner of the Declaration of Independence. The 41 signatories to the document—all the male passengers—include Mr., or Master, William Bradford, Mr. William Brewster, and plain Miles Standish and John Alden.

In the Name of God, Amen. We, whose names are underwritten, the Loyal Subjects of our dread Sovereign Lord King *James*, by the Grace of God, of *Great Britain, France,* and *Ire-*

land, King, Defender of the Faith, &c. Having undertaken for the Glory of God, and Advancement of the Christian Faith, and the Honour of our King and Country, a Voyage to plant the first colony in the northern Parts of Virginia; Do by these Presents, solemnly and mutually in the Presence of God and one another, convenant and combine ourselves together into a civil Body Politick, for our better Ordering and Preservation, and Further-ance of the Ends aforesaid; And by Virtue hereof do enact, constitute, and frame, such just and equal Laws, Ordinances, Acts, Constitutions, and Offices, from time to time, as shall be thought most meet and convenient for the general Good of the Colony; unto which we promise all due Submission and Obedi-ence. In WITNESS whereof we have hereunto subscribed our names at *Cape Cod* the eleventh of *November,* in the Reign of our Sovereign Lord King *James* of *England, France,* and *Ireland,* the eighteenth and of *Scotland,* the fifty-fourth. *Anno Domini,* 1620.

3. THE NEW ENGLAND CONFEDERATION

May 19, 1643

These articles marked the first intercolonial union in America. The purpose was defense. The parties to the union were the four colonial governments listed below. We have here an interesting anticipation of the later Articles of Confederation.

The Articles of Confederation between the Plantations under the Government of the Massachusetts, the Plantations under the Government of New Plymouth, the Plantations under the Government of Connecticut, and the Government of New Haven with the Plantations in Combination therewith:

Whereas we all came into these parts of America with one and the same end and aim, namely, to advance the Kingdom of our Lord Jesus Christ and to enjoy the liberties of the Gospel in purity with peace; and whereas in our settling (by a wise provi-dence of God) we are further dispersed upon the sea coasts and rivers than was at first intended, so that we can not according to our desire with convenience communicate in one government and jurisdiction; and whereas we live encompassed with people of several nations and strange languages which hereafter may prove injurious to us or our posterity. And forasmuch as the natives have formerly committed sundry insolence and outrages upon several Plantations of the English and have of late combined themselves against us; and seeing by reason of those sad distractions in England which they have heard of, and by which they know we are hindered from that humble way of seeking advice, or reaping those comfortable fruits of protection, which at other times we might well expect. We therefore do conceive it our bounden duty, without delay to enter into a present Cosociation amongst ourselves, for mutual help and strength in all our future concernments: That, as in nation and religion, so in other respects, we be and continue one according to the tenor and true meaning of the ensuing articles; Wherefore it is fully agreed and concluded by and between the parties or Jurisdictions above named, and they jointly and severally do by these presents agree and conclude that they all be and henceforth be called by the name of the United Colonies of New England. . . .

6. It is also agreed, that for the managing and concluding of all affairs proper, and concerning the whole Confederation two Commissioners shall be chosen by and out of each of these four Jurisdictions: namely, two for the Massachusetts, two for Plymouth, two for Connecticut, and two for New Haven, being all in Church-fellowship with us, which shall bring full power from their several General Courts respectively to hear, examine, weigh, and determine all affairs of our war, or peace, leagues, aids, charges, and numbers of men for war, division of spoils and whatsoever is gotten by conquest, receiving of more Confederates for Plantations into combination with any of the Confederates, and all things of like nature, which are the proper concomitants or consequents of such a Confederation for amity, offence, and defence: not intermeddling with the government of any of the Jurisdictions, which by the third article is preserved entirely to themselves. . . .

4. MASSACHUSETTS SCHOOL LAW OF 1647

Reading instruction had been provided for in a 1642 law, but the statute which follows in part denoted the first system of public education in America. Provisions included: townships of 50 homes had to instruct in writing and reading; towns of 100 families were required to establish grammar schools to prepare pupils for the university; teachers' salaries were to be paid by parents or the inhabitants as a whole.

It being one chiefe proiect of ye ould deluder, Satan, to keepe men from the knowledge of ye Scriptures, as in formr times by keeping ym in an unknowne tongue, . . . yt learning may not be buried in ye grave of or fathrs in ye church and commonwealth, . . .

It is therefore ordered, . . .

5. MARYLAND TOLERATION ACT

April 21, 1649

It is a feather in the cap both of the State of Maryland and of the Roman Catholic Church that the General Assembly of Maryland, at the urging of the second Lord Baltimore, a Catholic, passed the first American religious toleration act. The benefits were limited to fairly orthodox Christians and, as the language below shows, we are still far from the 18th century and the spirit of the American Constitution. Note the appearance of the phrase, "the free exercise thereof," referring to religion.

Forasmuch as in a well governed and Christian Common Wealth matters concerning Religion and the honor of God ought in the first place to bee taken, into serious consideration and endeavoured to bee settled. Be it therefore . . . enacted. . . . That whatsoever person or persons within this Province . . . shall from henceforth blaspheme God, . . . or shall deny our Saviour Jesus Christ to bee the sonne of God, or shall deny the holy Trinity the ffather sonne and holy Ghost, or the Godhead of any of the said Three persons of the Trinity or the Unity of the Godhead . . . shall be punished with death and confiscation or forfeiture of all his or her lands. . . .

And whereas the inforceing of the conscience in matters of Religion hath frequently fallen out to be of dangerous Consequence in those commonwealthes where it hath been practised, And for the more quiett and peaceable governement of this Province, and the better to preserve mutuall Love and amity amongst the Inhabitants thereof. Be it Therefore . . . enacted (except as in this present Act is before Declared and sett forth) that noe person or persons whatsoever within this Province, or

the Islands, Ports, Harbors, Creekes, or havens thereunto belonging professing to believe in Jesus Christ, shall from henceforth bee any waies troubled, Molested or discountenanced for
or in respect of his or her religion nor in the free exercise thereof
within this Province or the Islands thereunto belonging nor any
way compelled to the beleife or exercise of any other Religion
against his or her consent, or conspire against the civill Government established or to bee established in this Province under
him or his heires. And that all & every person and persons that
shall presume Contrary to this Act and the true intent and
meaning thereof directly or indirectly either in person or estate
willfully to wronge disturbe trouble or molest any person whatsoever within this Province professing to believe in Jesus Christ
for or in respect of his or her religion or the free exercise thereof
within this Province other than is provided for in this Act that
such person or persons soe offending, shalbe compelled to pay
trebble damages to the party soe wronged or molested, and for
every such offence shall also forfeit 20 s. sterling in money or
the value thereof . . . , Or if the parties soe offending as aforesaid shall refuse or bee unable to recompense the party soe
wronged, or to satisfy such ffyne or forfeiture, then such offender
shalbe severely punished by publick whipping & imprisonment
during the pleasure of the Lord proprietary, or his Leiutenant
or Chiefe Governor of this Province for the tyme being without
baile or maineprise. . . .

6. PENNSYLVANIA CHARTER OF PRIVILEGES

October 28, 1701

Pennsylvania was the freest and most advanced, from a later standpoint,
of all the colonies. Chartered in 1681 under a proprietary grant of land to
William Penn by Charles II, the colony was founded the following year.

William Penn, Proprietary and Governor of the Province of
Pensilvania and Territories thereunto belonging, To all to whom
these Presents shall come, sendeth Greeting. Whereas King
Charles *the Second,* by His Letters Patents, under the Great
Seal of *England,* bearing Date the *Fourth* Day of *March,* in the
Year *One Thousand Six Hundred and Eighty-one,* was graciously
pleased to give and grant unto me, and my Heirs and Assigns

for ever, this Province of *Pensilvania*, with divers great Powers and Jurisdictions for the well Government thereof. . . .

KNOW YE THEREFORE, That for the further Well-being and good Government of the said Province, and Territories and in Pursuance of the Rights and Powers beforementioned, I the said *William Penn* do declare, grant and confirm, unto all the Freemen, Planters and Adventurers, and other Inhabitants of this Province and Territories, these following Liberties, Franchises and Privileges, so far as in me lieth, to be held, enjoyed and kept, by the Freemen, Planters and Adventurers, and other Inhabitants of and in the said Province and Territories thereunto annexed, for ever.

FIRST. BECAUSE no People can be truly happy, though under the greatest Enjoyment of Civil Liberies, if abridged of the Freedom of their Consciences, as to their Religious Profession and Worship: And Almighty God being the only Lord of Conscience, Father of Lights and Spirits; and the Author as well as object of all divine Knowledge, Faith and Worship who only doth enlighten the Minds, and persuade and convince the Understandings of People, I do hereby grant and declare, That no Person or Persons, inhabiting in this province or Territories, who shall confess and acknowledge One Almighty God, the Creator, Upholder and Ruler of the World; and profess him or themselves obliged to live quietly under the Civil Government, shall be in any Case molested or prejudiced, in his or their Person or Estate, because of his or their conscientious Persuasion or Practice, nor be compelled to frequent or maintain any religious Worship, Place or Ministry, contrary to his or their Mind, or to do or suffer any other Act or Thing, contrary to their religious Persuasion.

AND that all Persons who also profess to believe in *Jesus Christ*, the Saviour of the World, shall be capable (notwithstanding their other Persuasions and Practices in Point of Conscience and Religion) to serve this Government in any Capacity, both legislatively and executively, he or they solemnly promising, when lawfully required, Allegiance to the King as Sovereign, and Fidelity to the Proprietary and Governor. . . .

V. THAT all Criminals shall have the same Priviliges of Witnesses and Council as their Prosecutors. . . .

VIII. BUT because the Happiness of Mankind depends so much upon the Enjoying of Liberty of their Consciences as aforesaid, I do hereby solemnly declare, promise and grant, for me, my Heirs and Assigns, That the *First* Article of this Charter relating to Liberty of Conscience, and every Part and Clause therein, according to the true Intent and Meaning thereof, shall be kept and remain, without any Alteration, inviolably for ever. . . .

7. VIRGINIA BILL OF RIGHTS

June 12, 1776

This remarkable document was drafted by George Mason except for the final paragraph on religious freedom, which was penned by Patrick Henry and is notable for its Christian ethical tone. Note the phrases, "the blessings of liberty" and "the free exercise of religion."

A declaration of rights made by the representatives of the good people of Virginia, assembled in full and free convention; which rights do pertain to them and their posterity, as the basis and foundation of government.

1. That all men are by nature equally free and independent, and have certain inherent rights, of which, when they enter into a state of society, they cannot by any compact deprive or divest their posterity; namely, the enjoyment of life and liberty, with the means of acquiring and possessing property, and pursuing and obtaining happiness and safety.

2. That all power is vested in, and consequently derived from, the people; that magistrates are their trustees and servants, and at all times amenable to them.

3. That government is, or ought to be instituted for the common benefit, protection, and security of the people, nation, or community; of all the various modes and forms of government, that is best which is capable of producing the greatest degree of happiness and safety, and is most effectually secured against the danger of maladministration; and that when any government shall be found inadequate or contrary to these purposes, a majority of the community hath an indubitable, unalienable and indefeasible right to reform, alter or abolish it, in such manner as shall be judged most conductive to the public weal.

4. That no man, or set of men, are entitled to exclusive or separate emoluments or privileges from the community, but in consideration of publick services; which, not being descendible, neither ought the offices of magistrate, legislator or judge to be hereditary.

5. That the legislative and executive powers of the state should be separate and distinct from the judiciary; and that the members of the two first may be restrained from oppression, by feeling and participating the burthens of the people, they should, at fixed periods, be reduced to a private station, return into that body from which they were originally taken, and the vacancies be supplied by frequent, certain, and regular elections, in which all, or any part of the former members to be again eligible or ineligible, as the laws shall direct.

6. That elections of members to serve as representatives of the people in assembly, ought to be free; and that all men having sufficient evidence of permanent common interest with, and attachment to the community, have the right to suffrage, and cannot be taxed or deprived of their property for publick uses, without their own consent, or that of their representatives so elected, nor bound by any law to which they have not, in like manner, assented for the public good.

7. That all power of suspending laws, or the execution of laws, by any authority without consent of the representatives of the people, is injurious to their rights, and ought not to be exercised.

8. That in all capital or criminal prosecutions a man hath a right to demand the cause and nature of his accusation, to be confronted with the accusers and witnesses, to call for evidence in his favour, and to a speedy trial by an impartial jury of his vicinage, without whose unanimous consent he cannot be found guilty; nor can he be compelled to give evidence against himself; that no man be deprived of his liberty, except by the law of the land or the judgment of his peers.

9. That excessive bail ought not to be required, nor excessive fines imposed, nor cruel and unusual punishments inflicted.

10. That general warrants, whereby an officer or messenger may be commanded to search suspected places without evidence of a fact committed, or to seize any person or persons not named,

or whose offence is not particularly described and supported by evidence, are grievous and oppressive, and ought not to be granted.

11. That in controversies respecting property, and in suits between man and man, the ancient trial by jury is preferable to any other, and ought to be held sacred.

12. That the freedom of the press is one of the great bulwarks of liberty, and can never be restrained but by despotick governments.

13. That a well-regulated militia, composed of the body of the people trained to arms, is the proper, natural and safe defence of a free state; that standing armies in time of peace should be avoided as dangerous to liberty; and that in all cases the military should be under strict subordination to, and governed by, the civil power.

14. That the people have a right to uniform government; and therefore, that no government separate from, or independent of the government of Virginia, ought to be erected or established within the limits thereof.

15. That no free government, or the blessings of liberty, can be preserved to any people, but by a firm adherence to justice, moderation, temperance, frugality and virtue, and by frequent recurrence to fundamental principles.

16. That religion, or the duty which we owe to our Creator, and the manner of discharging it, can be directed only by reason and conviction, not by force or violence; and therefore all men are equally entitled to the free exercise of religion, according to the dictates of conscience; and that it is the mutual duty of all to practise Christian forbearance, love, and charity towards each other.

8. THE DECLARATION OF INDEPENDENCE

July 4, 1776

Drawn up by Thomas Jefferson and worked over only very slightly by a committee, this inspired manifesto is with the Constitution and Bill of Rights the heart and soul of our Papers of State.

When, in the course of human events, it becomes necessary for one people to dissolve the political bands which have connected them with another, and to assume, among the powers of the earth, the separate and equal station to which the laws of nature and nature's God entitle them, a decent respect to the opinions of mankind requires that they should declare the causes which impel them to the separation.

We hold these truths to be self-evident, that all men are created equal; that they are endowed by their Creator with certain unalienable rights; that among these, are life, liberty, and the pursuit of happiness. That, to secure these rights, governments are instituted among men, deriving their just powers from the consent of the governed; that, whenever any form of government becomes destructive of these ends, it is the right of the people to alter or to abolish it, and to institute a new government, laying its foundation on such principles, and organizing its powers in such form, as to them shall seem most likely to effect their safety and happiness. Prudence, indeed, will dictate that governments long established, should not be changed for light and transient causes; and, accordingly, all experience hath shown, that mankind are more disposed to suffer, while evils are sufferable, than to right themselves by abolishing the forms to which they are accustomed. But, when a long train of abuses and usurpations, pursuing invariably the same object, evinces a design to reduce them under absolute despotism, it is their right, it is their duty, to throw off such government and to provide new guards for their future security. Such has been the patient sufferance of these colonies, and such is now the necessity which constrains them to alter their former systems of government. The history of the present King of Great Britain is a history of repeated injuries and usurpations, all having, in direct object the establishment of an absolute tyranny over these States. . . .

In every stage of these oppressions, we have petitioned for redress, in the most humble terms; our repeated petitions have been answered only by repeated injury. A prince, whose character is thus marked by every act which may define a tyrant, is unfit to be the ruler of a free people.

Nor have we been wanting in attention to our British brethren. We have warned them, from time to time, of attempts made by their legislature to extend an unwarrantable jurisdiction over us.

We have reminded them of the circumstances of our emigration and settlement here. We have appealed to their native justice and magnanimity, and we have conjured them by the ties of our common kindred, to disavow these usurpations, which would inevitably interrupt our connections and correspondence. They, too, have been deaf to the voice of justice and consanguinity. We must, therefore, acquiesce in the necessity which denounces our separation, and hold them, as we hold the rest of mankind, enemies in war, in peace, friends.

We, therefore, the representatives of the United States of America, in general Congress assembled, appealing to the Supreme Judge of the world for the rectitude of our intentions, do, in the name, and by the authority of the good people of these colonies, solemnly publish and declare, that these united colonies are, and of right ought to be, free and independent states: that they are absolved from all allegiance to the British Crown, and that all political connection between them and the state of Great Britain is, and ought to be, totally dissolved; and that, as free and independent states, they have full power to levy war, conclude peace, contract alliances, establish commerce, and to do all other acts and things which independent states may of right do. And, for the support of this declaration, with a firm reliance on the protection of Divine Providence, we mutually pledge to each other our lives, our fortunes, and our sacred honor.

9. THE ARTICLES OF CONFEDERATION

March 1, 1781

The second Continental Congress decided, before it adopted the Declaration of Independence, to create a committee to draw up articles of confederation to draw together more closely the 13 colonies. That was June 11, 1776. John Dickinson furnished the basic plan. The Congress adopted the Articles on November 15, 1777, but they did not become formally effective until their ratification by the 13th state, Maryland, on March 1, 1781. They were not adequate but they were a halfway house on the road to the Constitution.

. . . Articles of Confederation and perpetual Union between the states of Newhampshire, Massachusetts-bay, Rhodeisland and Providence Plantations, Connecticut, New-York, New Jersey,

Pennsylvania, Delaware, Maryland, Virginia, North-Carolina, South-Carolina and Georgia.

Art. I. The Stile of this confederacy shall be "The United States of America."

Art. II. Each state retains its sovereignty, freedom and independence, and every Power, Jurisdiction and right, which is not by this confederation expressly delegated to the United States, in Congress assembled.

Art. III. The said states hereby severally enter into a firm league of friendship with each other, for their common defense, the security of their Liberties, and their mutual and general welfare, binding themselves to assist each other, against all force offered to, or attacks made upon them, or any of them, on account of religion, sovereignty, trade, or any other pretence whatever. . . .

Art. XIII. Every state shall abide by the determinations of the united states in congress assembled, on all questions which by this confederation are submitted to them. And the Articles of this confederation shall be inviolably observed by every state, and the union shall be perpetual; nor shall any alteration at any time hereafter be made in any of them; unless such alteration be agreed to in a congress of the united states, and be afterwards confirmed by the legislatures of every state.

AND WHEREAS it hath pleased the Great Governor of the World to incline the hearts of the legislatures we respectively represent in congress, to approve of, and to authorize us to ratify the said articles of confederation and perpetual union. KNOW YE that we the under-signed delegates, by virtue of the power and authority to us given for that purpose, do by these presents, in the name and in behalf of our respective constituents, fully and entirely ratify and confirm each and every of the said articles of confederation and perpetual union, and all and singular the matters and things therein contained. . . .

10. VIRGINIA STATUTE OF RELIGIOUS LIBERTY

January 16, 1786

This bill was introduced by Thomas Jefferson in the Virginia House of Delegates in June, 1779. It aroused bitter opposition and was not passed until 1786. The style and fervor of this document are typical of Jefferson. He ranked its authorship alongside that of the Declaration of Independence.

SECTION 1. Well aware that the opinions and belief of men depend not on their own will, but follow involuntarily the evidence proposed to their minds; that Almighty God hath created the mind free, and manifested his supreme will that free it shall remain by making it altogether insusceptible of restraint; that all attempts to influence it by temporal punishments, or burthens, or by civil incapacitations, tend only to beget habits of hypocrisy and meanness, and are a departure from the plan of the holy author of our religion, who being lord both of body and mind, yet chose not to propagate it by coercions on either, as was in his Almighty power to do, but to extend it by its influence on reason alone; that the impious presumption of legislators and ruler, civil as well as ecclesiastical, who, being themselves but fallible and uninspired men, have assumed dominion over the faith of others, setting up their own opinions and modes of thinking as the only true and infallible, and as such endeavoring to impose them on others, hath established and maintained false religions over the greatest part of the world and through all time: That to compel a man to furnish contributions of money for the propagation of opinions which he disbelieves and abhors, is sinful and tyrannical; that even the forcing him to support this or that teacher of his own religious persuasion, is depriving him of the comfortable liberty of giving his contributions to the particular pastor whose morals he would make his pattern, and whose powers he feels most persuasive to righteousness; and is withdrawing from the ministry those temporary rewards, which proceeding from an approbation of their personal conduct, are an additional incitement to earnest and unremitting labours for the instruction of mankind; that our civil rights have no dependence on our religious opinions, any more than our opinions in physics or geometry; that therefore the proscribing any citizen as unworthy the public confidence by laying upon him an incapacity of being called to offices of trust and emolument, unless he profess or renounce this or that religious opinion, is depriving him injuriously of those privileges and advantages to which, in common with his fellow citizens, he has a natural right; that it tends also to corrupt the principles of that very religion it is meant to encourage, by bribing, with a monopoly of worldly honours and emoluments, those who will externally profess and conform to it; that though indeed these are criminal who do not withstand such temptation, yet neither are those innocent who lay the bait in their way; that the opinions of men are not the object of civil government, nor under its jurisdiction; that to suffer the civil magistrate to intrude his powers into the field of opinion and to restrain the profession or propagation of principles on supposition of their ill tendency is a dangerous fallacy, which at once destroys all religious liberty, because he being of course judge of that tendency will make his opinions the rule of judgment, and approve or condemn the sentiments of others only as they shall square with or differ from his own; that it is time enough for the rightful purposes of civil government for its officers to interfere when principles break out into overt acts against peace and good order; and finally, that truth is great and will prevail if left to herself; that she is the proper and sufficient antagonist to error, and has nothing to fear from the conflict unless by human interposition disarmed of her natural weapons, free argument and debate; errors ceasing to be dangerous when it is permitted freely to contradict them.

SECTION II. We, the General Assembly of Virginia do enact that no man shall be compelled to frequent or support any religious worship, place or ministry whatsoever, nor shall be enforced, restrained, molested or burthened in his body or goods, nor shall otherwise suffer, on account of his religious opinions or belief; but that all men shall be free to profess, and by argument to maintain, their opinions in matters of religion, and that the same shall in no wise diminish, enlarge or affect their civil capacities.

11. THE NORTHWEST ORDINANCE

July 13, 1787

This Ordinance provided for the government of the vast territory northwest of the Ohio River which was to be divided into 3 to 5 districts. These were to be made territories and then admitted as states. The Ordinance has the distinction of enactment by the last Congress functioning under the Articles of Confederation and reenactment by the first Congress assembled under the new Constitution.

An Ordinance for the government of the Territory of the United States northwest of the Ohio River.

Be it ordained by the United States in Congress assembled, That the said territory, for the purposes of temporary government, be one district, subject, however, to be divided into two districts, as future circumstances may, in the opinion of Congress, make it expedient. . . .

It is hereby ordained and declared by the authority aforesaid, That the following article shall be considered as articles of compact between the original States and the people and States in the said territory and forever remain unalterable, unless by common consent, to wit:

ART. 1. No person, demeaning himself in a peaceable and orderly manner, shall ever be molested on account of his mode of worship or religious sentiments, in the said territory.

ART. 2. The inhabitants of the said territory shall always be entitled to the benefits of the writ of *habeas corpus,* and of the trial by jury; of a proportionate representation of the people in the legislature; and of judicial proceedings according to the course of the common law. . . .

ART. 3. Religion, morality, and knowledge, being necessary to good government and the happiness of mankind, schools and the means of education shall forever be encouraged. The utmost good faith shall always be observed towards the Indians; their lands and property shall never be taken from them without their consent; and, in their property, rights, and liberty, they shall never be invaded or disturbed, unless in just and lawful wars authorized by Congress; but laws founded in justice and humanity, shall from time to time be made for preventing wrongs being done to them, and for preserving peace and friendship with them. . . .

12. THE CONSTITUTION OF THE UNITED STATES

March 4, 1789

The Constitution in its original form, minus a Bill of Rights, was adopted by the Constitutional Convention assembled in Philadelphia on September

17, 1787. It became effective with ratification by the ninth State on March 4, 1789. By May 29, 1790, all 13 States had ratified it. The Bill of Rights or First Ten Amendments were passed by the Congress on September 25, 1789, and had been ratified by three-fourths of the States on December 15, 1791. It is on first thought singular that our Constitution omits any positive reference to religion. The key to this may well be the omission of reference to the rights of man. In the Declaration it is essential to ground these in the Divine creation of man. Another factor may have been the recognition of sharp differences among the States on Church-State issues and the desire to offend none. Some have thought that the secular tone of the Constitution reflected the religious detachment of the Founding Fathers who drew up our central governmental instrument. This is forbidden by the known views of such men as the Chairman, George Washington, the acting Secretary James Madison, James Wilson, Roger Sherman, George Mason, Alexander Hamilton, John Rutledge, Edmund Pendleton, Oliver Ellsworth, William Samuel Johnson, and George Wythe among others. Also there is the moving plea of Benjamin Franklin, reproduced below as Appendix C.

THE PREAMBLE

We the people of the United States, in order to form a more perfect union, establish justice, insure domestic tranquillity, provide for the common defense, promote the general welfare, and secure the blessings of liberty to ourselves and our posterity, do ordain and establish this Constitution for the United States of America.

ARTICLE VI

3. The senators and representatives before mentioned, and the members of the several State legislatures, and all executive and judicial officers, both of the United States and of the several States, shall be bound by oath or affirmation to support this Constitution; but no religious test shall ever be required as a qualification to any office or public trust under the United States.

AMENDMENTS

ARTICLE I

Congress shall make no law respecting an establishment of religion, or prohibiting the free exercise thereof; or abridging the freedom of speech, or of the press; or the right of the people peaceably to assemble, and to petition the government for redress of grievances.

13. WASHINGTON'S FIRST INAUGURAL ADDRESS
April 30, 1789

This address is notable for the light it throws on the way in which the Father of his Country viewed as a remarkable deliverance the winning of the War of Independence. Of all American documents there is none that speaks more earnestly and personally from faith to faith. The entire Address is reproduced.

Fellow-Citizens of the Senate and of the House of Representatives:

Among the vicissitudes incident to life no event could have filled me with greater anxieties than that of which the notification was transmitted by your order, and received on the 14th day of the present month. On the one hand, I was summoned by my country, whose voice I can never hear but with veneration and love, from a retreat which I had chosen with the fondest predilection, and, in my flattering hopes, with an immutable decision, as the asylum of my declining years—a retreat which was rendered every day more necessary as well as more dear to me by the addition of habit to inclination, and of frequent interruptions in my health to the gradual waste committed on it by time. On the other hand, the magnitude and difficulty of the trust to which the voice of my country called me, being sufficient to awaken in the wisest and most experienced of her citizens a distrustful scrutiny into his qualifications, could not but overwhelm with despondence one who (inheriting inferior endowments from nature and unpracticed in the duties of civil administration) ought to be peculiarly conscious of his own deficiencies. In this conflict of emotions all I dare aver is that it has been my faithful study to collect my duty from a just appreciation of every circumstance by which it might be affected. All I dare hope is that if, in executing this task, I have been too much swayed by a grateful remembrance of former instances, or by an affectionate sensibility to this transcendent proof of the confidence of my fellow-citizens, and have thence too little consulted my incapacity as well as disinclination for the weighty and untried cares before me, my error will be palliated by the motives which mislead me, and its consequences be judged by my country with some share of the partiality in which they originated.

Such being the impressions under which I have, in obedience to the public summons, repaired to the present station, it would be peculiarly improper to omit in this first official act my fervent supplications to that Almighty Being who rules over the universe, who presides in the councils of nations, and whose providential aids can supply every human defect, that His benediction may consecrate to the liberties and happiness of the people of the United States a Government instituted by themselves for these essential purposes, and may enable every instrument employed in its administration to execute with success the functions allotted to his charge. In tendering this homage to the Great Author of every public and private good, I assure myself that it expresses your sentiments not less than my own, nor those of my fellow-citizens at large less than either. No people can be bound to acknowledge and adore the Invisible Hand which conducts the affairs of men more than those of the United States. Every step by which they have advanced to the character of an independent nation seems to have been distinguished by some token of providential agency; and in the important revolution just accomplished in the system of their united government the tranquil deliberations and voluntary consent of so many distinct communities from which the event has resulted can not be compared with the means by which most governments have been established without some return of pious gratitude, along with an humble anticipation of the future blessings which the past seem to presage. These reflections, arising out of the present crisis, have forced themselves too strongly on my mind to be suppressed. You will join with me, I trust, in thinking that there are none under the influence of which the proceedings of a new and free government can more auspiciously commence.

By the article establishing the executive department it is made the duty of the President "to recommend to your consideration such measures as he shall judge necessary and expedient." The circumstances under which I now meet you will acquit me from entering into that subject further than to refer to the great constitutional charter under which you are assembled, and which, in defining your powers, designates the objects to which your attention is to be given. It will be more consistent with those circumstances, and far more congenial with the feelings which actuate me, to substitute, in place of a recommendation of particular measures, the tribute that is due to the talents, the rectitude, and the patriotism which adorn the characters selected to devise and adopt them. In these honorable qualifications I behold the surest pledges that as on one side no local prejudices or attachments, no separate views nor party animosities, will misdirect the comprehensive and equal eye which ought to watch over this great assemblage of communities and interests, so, on another, that the foundation of our national policy will be laid in the pure and immutable principles of private morality, and the preeminence of free government be exemplified by all the attributes which can win the affections of its citizens and command the respect of the world. I dwell on this prospect with every satisfaction which an ardent love for my country can inspire, since there is no truth more thoroughly established than that there exists in the economy and course of nature an indissoluble union between virtue and happiness; between duty and advantage; between the genuine maxims of an honest and magnanimous policy and the solid rewards of public prosperity and felicity; since we ought to be no less persuaded that the propitious smiles of Heaven can never be expected on a nation that disregards the eternal rules of order and right which Heaven itself has ordained; and since the preservation of the sacred fire of liberty and the destiny of the republican model of government are justly considered, perhaps, as *deeply*, as *finally*, staked on the experiment intrusted to the hands of the American people.

Besides the ordinary objects submitted to your care, it will remain with your judgment to decide how far an exercise of the occasional power delegated by the fifth article of the Constitution is rendered expedient at the present juncture by the nature of objections which have been urged against the system, or by the degree of inquietude which has given birth to them. Instead of undertaking particular recommendations on this subject, in which I could be guided by no lights derived from official opportunities, I shall again give way to my entire confidence in your discernment and pursuit of the public good; for I assure myself that whilst you carefully avoid every alteration which might endanger the benefits of an united and effective government, or which ought to await the future lessons of experience, a reverence for the characteristic rights of freemen and a regard for the public harmony will sufficiently influence your deliberations on the question how far the former can be impregnably fortified or the latter be safely and advantageously promoted.

To the foregoing observations I have one to add, which will be most properly addressed to the House of Representatives. It concerns myself, and will therefore be as brief as possible. When I was first honored with a call into the service of my country, then on the eve of an arduous struggle for its liberties, the light in which I contemplated my duty required that I should renounce every pecuniary compensation. From this resolution I have in no instance departed; and being still under the impressions which produced it, I must decline as inapplicable to myself any share in the personal emoluments which may be indispensably included in a permanent provision for the executive department, and must accordingly pray that the pecuniary estimates for the station in which I am placed may during my continuance in it be limited to such actual expenditures as the public good may be thought to require.

Having thus imparted to you my sentiments as they have been awakened by the occasion which brings us together, I shall take my present leave; but not without resorting once more to the benign Parent of the Human Race in humble supplication that, since He has been pleased to favor the American people with opportunities for deliberating in perfect tranquillity, and dispositions for deciding with unparalleled unanimity on a form of government for the security of their union and the advancement of their happiness, so His divine blessing may be equally conspicuous in the enlarged views, the temperate consultations, and the wise measures on which the success of this Government must depend.

14. WASHINGTON'S FAREWELL ADDRESS

September 17, 1796

This address is read every year on February 22 in the Congress of the United States. It is the abiding legacy to the American people of the man whom Thomas Jefferson described in the following terms: "Perhaps the strongest feature in his character was prudence, never acting until every circumstance, every consideration was maturely weighed. . . . His integrity was most pure, his justice the most inflexible I have ever known, no motives of interest or consanguinity, of friendship or hatred, being able to bias his decision. He was, indeed, in every sense of the words, a wise, a good, and a great man."

. . . Interwoven as is the love of liberty with every ligament of your hearts, no recommendation of mine is necessary to fortify or confirm the attachment. . . .

Of all the dispositions and habits which lead to political prosperity, religion and morality are indispensable supports. In vain would that man claim the tribute of patriotism who should labor to subvert these great pillars of human happiness—these firmest props of the duties of men and citizens. The mere politician, equally with the pious man, ought to respect and to cherish them. A volume could not trace all their connections with private and public felicity. Let it simply be asked, Where is the security for property, for reputation, for life, if the sense of religious obligation desert the oaths which are the instruments of investigation in courts of justice? And let us with caution indulge the supposition that morality can be maintained without religion. Whatever may be conceded to the influence of refined education on minds of peculiar structure, reason and experience both forbid us to expect that national morality can prevail in exclusion of religious principle.

It is substantially true that virtue or morality is a necessary spring of popular government. The rule indeed extends with more or less force to every species of free government. Who that is a sincre friend to it can look with indifference upon attempts to shake the foundation of the fabric? Promote, then, as an object of primary importance, institutions for the general diffusion of knowledge. In proportion as the structure of a government gives force to public opinion, it is essential that public opinion should be enlightened. . . .

Though in reviewing the incidents of my Administration I am unconscious of intentional error, I am nevertheless too sensible of my defects not to think it probable that I may have committed many errors. Whatever they may be, I fervently beseech the Almighty to avert or mitigate the evils to which they may tend. I shall also carry with me the hope that my country will never cease to view them with indulgence, and that, after forty-five years of my life dedicated to its service with an upright zeal, the faults of incompetent abilities will be consigned to oblivion, as myself must soon be to the mansions of rest.

Relying on its kindness in this as in other things, and actuated by that fervent love toward it which is so natural to a man who views in it the native soil of himself and his progenitors for several generations, I anticipate with pleasing expectation that retreat in which I promise myself to realize without alloy the sweet enjoyment of partaking in the midst of my fellow-citizens the benign influence of good laws under a free government—the ever-favorite object of my heart, and the happy reward, as I trust, of our mutual cares, labors, and dangers.

15. LINCOLN'S HOUSE DIVIDED SPEECH

June 17, 1858

The opening sentences of this momentous speech illustrate the influence of the New Testament on the style and the thought of Abraham Lincoln.

MR. PRESIDENT AND GENTLEMEN OF THE CONVENTION: If we could first know where we are, and whither we are tending, we could better judge what to do, and how to do it. We are now far into the fifth year since a policy was initiated with the avowed object and confident promise of putting an end to slavery agitation. Under the operation of that policy, that agitation has not only not ceased, but has constantly augmented. In my opinion, it will not cease until a crisis shall have been reached and passed. "A house divided against itself cannot stand." I believe this government cannot endure permanently half slave and half free. I do not expect the Union to be dissolved; I do not expect the house to fall; but I do expect it will cease to be divided. It will become all one thing, or all the other. Either the opponents of slavery will arrest the further spread of it, and place it where the public mind shall rest in the belief that it is in the course of ultimate extinction, or its advocates will push it forward till it shall become alike lawful in all the States, old as well as new, North as well as South. . . .

16. LINCOLN'S FIRST INAUGURAL ADDRESS

March 4, 1861

This Address is of special timeliness today because of what it says about the Supreme Court and amending the Constitution. The last paragraphs reflect Lincoln's faith in God and in the right.

. . . I do not forget the position assumed by some, that constitutional questions are to be decided by the Supreme Court; nor do I deny that such decisions must be binding, in any case, upon the parties to a suit, as to the object of that suit, while they are also entitled to a very high respect and consideration in all parallel cases by all other departments of the government. And, while it is obviously possible that such decision may be erroneous in any given case, still the evil effect following it, being limited to that particular case, with the chance that it may be overruled and never become a precedent for other cases, can better be borne than could the evils of a different practice. At the same time, the candid citizen must confess that if the policy of the government, upon vital questions affecting the whole people, is to be irrevocably fixed by decisions of the Supreme Court, the instant they are made, in ordinary litigation between parties in personal actions, the people will have ceased to be their own rulers, having to that extent practically resigned the government into the hands of that eminent tribunal. Nor is there in this view any assault upon the court or the judges. It is a duty from which they may not shrink to decide cases properly brought before them, and it is no fault of theirs if others seek to turn their decisions to political purposes. . . .

This country, with its institutions, belongs to the people who inhabit it. Whenever they shall grow weary of the existing government, they can exercise their constitutional right of amending it, or their revolutionary right to dismember or overthrow it. I cannot be ignorant of the fact that many worthy and patriotic citizens are desirous of having the national Constitution amended. While I make no recommendation of amendments, I fully recognize the rightful authority of the people over the whole subject, to be exercised in either of the modes prescribed in the instrument itself and I should, under existing circumstances, favor rather than oppose a fair opportunity being afforded the people to act upon it. I will venture to add that to me the convention mode seems preferable, in that it allows amendments to originate with the people themselves, instead of only permitting them to take or reject propositions originated by others not especially chosen for the purpose, and which might not be precisely such as they would wish to either accept or refuse. I understand a proposed amendment to the Constitution—which amendment, however, I have not seen—has passed Congress, to the effect that the Federal Government shall never interfere with the domestic institutions of the States, including that of persons held to service. To avoid misconstruction of what I have said, I depart from my purpose not to speak of particular amendments so far as to say that, holding such a provision to now be implied constitutional law, I have no objection to its being made express and irrevocable. . . .

Why should there not be a patent confidence in the ultimate justice of the people? Is there any better or equal hope in the world? In our present differences is either party without faith of being in the right? If the Almighty Ruler of nations, with his eternal truth and justice, be on your side of the North, or on yours of the South, that truth and that justice will surely prevail by the judgment of this great tribunal of the American people.

By the frame of the government under which we live, this same people have wisely given their public servants but little power for mischief; and have, with equal wisdom, provided for the return of that little to their own hands at very short intervals. While the people retain their virtue and vigilance, no administration, by any extreme of wickedness or folly, can very seriously injure the government in the short space of four years.

My countrymen, one and all, think calmly and well upon this whole subject. Nothing valuable can be lost by taking time. If there be an object to hurry any of you in hot haste to a step which you would never take deliberately, that object will be frustrated by taking time; but no good object can be frustrated by it. Such of you as are now dissatisfied still have the old Constitution unimpaired, and, on the sensitive point, the laws of your own framing under it; while the new administration will have no immediate power, if it would, to change either. If it were admitted that you who are dissatisfied hold the right side in the dispute, there still is no single good reason for precipitate action. Intelligence, patriotism, Christianity, and a firm reliance on Him who has never yet forsaken this favored land, are still competent to adjust in the best way all our present difficulty.

In your hands, my dissatisfied fellow-countrymen, and not in mine, is the momentous issue of civil war. The Government will not assail you. You can have no conflict without being yourselves the aggressors. You have no oath registered in heaven to destroy the government, while I shall have the most solemn one to "preserve, protect, and defend" it.

I am loath to close. We are not enemies, but friends. We must not be enemies. Though passion may have strained, it must not break, our bonds of affection. The mystic chords of memory, stretching from every battle-field and patriot grave to every living heart and hearthstone all over this broad land, will yet swell the chorus of the Union when again touched, as surely they will be, by the better angels of our nature.

17. THE GETTYSBURG ADDRESS

March 18, 1863

As Lincoln says here, there are times when words seem powerless. This immortal elegy in prose is its own best commentary.

Four score and seven years ago our fathers brought forth on this continent, a new nation, conceived in Liberty, and dedicated to the proposition that all men are created equal.

Now we are engaged in a great civil war, testing whether that nation or any nation so conceived and so dedicated, can long endure. We are met on a great battle-field of that war. We have come to dedicate a portion of that field, as a final resting place for those who here gave their lives that that nation might live. It is altogether fitting and proper that we should do this.

But, in a larger sense, we can not dedicate—we can not consecrate—we can not hallow—this ground. The brave men, living and dead, who struggled here, have consecrated it, far above our poor power to add or detract. The world will little note, nor long remember what we say here, but it can never forget what they did here. It is for us the living, rather, to be dedicated to the great task remaining before us—that from these honored dead we take increased devotion to that cause for which they gave the last full measure of devotion—that we here highly resolve that these dead shall not have died in vain—that this nation. under God, shall have a new birth of freedom—and that government of the people, by the people, for the people, shall not perish from the earth.

18. LINCOLN'S SECOND INAUGURAL ADDRESS

March 4, 1865

This Address shows further Lincoln's gift for brevity. It also reflects the prophetic Lincoln, being one of the most Biblical of all his writings. In it he seems to have absorbed the very spirit of the prophets, Jesus the Christ, and St. Paul. In this prophetic and evangelical utterance, directed to a nation and people, the religious strain in American State Papers reaches perhaps its apex and its culmination. America is viewed as indeed "the almost chosen people."

Fellow-Countrymen:

At this second appearing to take the oath of the Presidential office there is less occasion for an extended address than there was at the first. Then a statement somewhat in detail of a course to be pursued seemed fitting and proper. Now, at the expiration of four years, during which public declarations have been constantly called forth on every point and phase of the great contest which still absorbs the attention and engrosses the energies of the nation, little that is new could be presented. The progress of our arms, upon which all else chiefly depends, is as well known to the public as to myself, and it is, I trust, reasonably satisfactory and encouraging to all. With high hope for the future, no prediction in regard to it is ventured.

On the occasion corresponding to this four years ago all thoughts were anxiously directed to an impending civil war. All dreaded it, all sought to avert it. While the inaugural address was being delivered from this place, devoted altogether to *saving* the Union without war, insurgent agents were in the city seeking to *destroy* it without war—seeking to dissolve the Union and divide effects by negotiation. Both parties deprecated war, but one of them would *make* war rather than let the nation survive, and the other would *accept* war rather than let it perish, and the war came.

One-eighth of the whole population were colored slaves, not distributed generally over the Union, but localized in the southern part of it. These slaves constituted a peculiar and powerful interest. All knew that this interest was somehow the cause of the war. To strengthen, perpetuate, and extend this interest was the object for which the insurgents would rend the Union even by war, while the Government claimed no right to do more than to restrict the territorial enlargement of it. Neither party expected for the war the magnitude or the duration which it has already attained. Neither anticipated that the cause of the conflict might cease with or even before the conflict itself should cease. Each looked for an easier triumph, and a result less fundamental and astounding. Both read the same Bible and pray to the same God, and each invokes His aid against the other. It may seem strange that any men should dare to ask a just God's assistance in wringing their bread from the sweat of other men's faces, but let us judge not, that we be not judged. The prayers of both could not be answered. That of neither has been answered fully. The Almighty has His own purposes. "Woe unto the world because of offenses; for it must needs be that offenses come, but woe to that man by whom the offense cometh." If we shall suppose that American slavery is one of those offenses which, in the providence of God, must needs come, but which, having continued through His appointed time, He now wills to remove, and that He gives to both North and South this terrible war as the woe due to those by whom the offense came, shall we discern therein any departure from those divine attributes which the believers in a living God always ascribe to Him? Fondly do we hope, fervently do we pray, that this mighty scourge of war may speedily pass away. Yet, if God wills that it continue until all the wealth piled by the bondsman's two hundred and fifty years of unrequited toil shall be sunk, and until every drop of blood drawn with the lash shall be paid by another drawn with the sword, as was said three thousand years ago, so still it must be said "the judgments of the Lord are true and righteous altogether."

With malice toward none, with charity for all, with firmness in the right as God gives us to see the right, let us strive on to finish the work we are in, to bind up the nation's wounds, to care for him who shall have borne the battle and for his widow and his orphan, to do all which may achieve and cherish a just and lasting peace among ourselves and with all nations.

19. LEE'S FAREWELL TO HIS ARMY

April 10, 1865

General Robert E. Lee and President Abraham Lincoln were very different in background but deeply alike in religious and Christian spirit. In June, 1861, a few weeks after he had been made "commander of the military and naval forces of Virgnia," a minister said to Lee: "Are you sanguine of results?" Lee answered calmly in words that anticipated the theology of Lincoln's Second Inaugural: "At present I am not concerned with results. God's will ought to be our aim, and I am quite contented that his designs should be accomplished and not mine." His Farewell Address to the Army of Northern Virginia is less profound, but breathes the serenity, unshaken self-control, restrained but deep affection for his brave men, and simple faith of Lee.

After four years of arduous service, marked by unsurpassed courage and fortitude, the Army of Northern Virginia has been compelled to yield to overwhelming numbers and resources. I need not tell the survivors of so many hard-fought battles, who have remained steadfast to the last, that I have consented to this result from no distrust of them; but, feeling that valour and devotion could accomplish nothing that could compensate for the loss that would have attended the continuation of the contest, I have determined to avoid the useless sacrifice of those whose past services have endeared them to their countrymen. By the terms of the agreement, officers and men can return to their homes and remain there until exchanged. You will take with you the satisfaction that proceeds from the consciousness of duty faithfully performed; and I earnestly pray that a merciful God will extend to you His blessing and protection. With an increasing admiration of your constancy and devotion to your country, and a grateful remembrance of your kind and generous consideration of myself, I bid you an affectionate farewell.

20. WILSON'S FIRST INAUGURAL ADDRESS

March 4, 1913

Woodrow Wilson, as is well known, employed no ghost-writers. He wrote or outlined his own speeches and spared no effort or pains in doing so. He was a self-conscious stylist and a great phrase-maker. There was nearly always something of the pulpit in the style and spirit of his utterance. This was so deep in Wilson that it was second nature. This Address is one of the most elevated and sustained in the succession of Presidential Inaugurals. It is also a work of art, finely chiseled and delicately balanced. Most of the Address is included here.

My Fellow Citizens:

There has been a change of government. It began two years ago, when the House of Representatives became Democratic by a decisive majority. It has now been completed. The Senate about to assemble will also be Democratic. The offices of President and Vice-President have been put into the hands of Democrats. What does the change mean? That is the question that is uppermost in our minds today. That is the question I am going to try to answer, in order, if I may, to interpret the occasion.

It means much more than the mere success of a party. The success of a party means little except when the Nation is using that party for a large and definite purpose. No one can mistake the purpose for which the Nation now seeks to use the Democratic Party. It seeks to use it to interpret a change of its own plans and point of view. Some old things with which we had grown familiar, and which had begun to creep into the very habit of our thought and of our lives, have altered their aspect as we have latterly looked critically upon them, with fresh, awakened eyes; have dropped their disguises and shown themselves alien and sinister. Some new things, as we look frankly upon them, willing to comprehend their real character, have come to assume the aspect of things long believed in and familiar, stuff of our own convictions. We have been refreshed by a new insight into our own life.

We see that in many things that life is very great. It is incomparably great in its material aspects, in its body of wealth, in the diversity and sweep of its energy, in the industries which have been conceived and built up by the genius of individual men and the limitless enterprise of groups of men. It is great, also, very great, in its moral force.

Nowhere else in the world have noble men and women exhibited in more striking forms the beauty and the energy of sympathy and helpfulness and counsel in their efforts to rectify wrong, alleviate suffering, and set the weak in the way of strength and hope. We have built up, moreover, a great system of government, which has stood through a long age as in many respects a model for those who seek to set liberty upon foundations that will endure against fortuitous change, against storm and accident. Our life contains every great thing, and contains it in rich abundance.

But the evil has come with the good, and much fine gold has been corroded. With riches has come inexcusable waste. We have squandered a great part of what we might have used, and have not stopped to conserve the exceeding bounty of nature, without which our genius for enterprise would have been worthless and impotent, scorning to be careful, shamefully prodigal as well as admirably efficient. We have been proud of our industrial achievements, but we have not hitherto stopped thoughtfully enough to count the human cost, the cost of lives snuffed out, of energies overtaxed and broken, the fearful physical and spiritual cost to the men and women and children upon whom the dead weight and burden of it all has fallen pitilessly the years through. The groans and agony of it all had not yet reached our ears, the solemn, moving undertone of our life, coming up out of the mines and factories and out of every home where the struggle had its intimate and familiar seat. With the great Government went many deep secret things which we too long delayed to look into and scrutinize with candid, fearless eyes. The great Government we loved has too often been made use of for private and selfish purposes, and those who used it had forgotten the people.

At last a vision has been vouchsafed us of our life as a whole. We see the bad with the good, the debased and decadent with the sound and vital. With this vision we approach new affairs. Our duty is to cleanse, to reconsider, to restore, to correct the evil without impairing the good, to purify and humanize every process of our common life without weakening or sentimentaliz-

ing it. There has been something crude and heartless and un-
feeling in our haste to succeed and be great. Our thought has
been "Let every man look out for himself, let every generation
look out for itself," while we reared giant machinery which
made it impossible that any but those who stood at the levers
of control should have a chance to look out for themselves. We
had not forgotten our morals. We remembered well enough that
we had set up a policy which was meant to serve the humblest
as well as the most powerful, with an eye single to the standards
of justice and fair play, and remembered it with pride. But we
were very heedless and in a hurry to be great.

We have come now to the sober second thought. The scales
of heedlessness have fallen from our eyes. We have made up
our minds to square every process of our national life again with
the standards we so proudly set up at the beginning and have
always carried at our hearts. Our work is a work of restoration. . . .

These are some of the things we ought to do, and not leave
the others undone, the old-fashioned, never-to-be-neglected,
fundamental safeguarding of property and of individual right.
This is the high enterprise of the new day: To lift everything
that concerns our life as a Nation to the light that shines from
the hearthfire of every man's conscience and vision of the right.
It is inconceivable that we should do this as partisans; it is inconceivable we should do it in ignorance of the facts as they are
or in blind haste. We shall restore, not destroy. We shall deal
with our economic system as it is and as it may be modified,
not as it might be if we had a clean sheet of paper to write
upon; and step by step we shall make it what it should be, in the
spirit of those who question their own wisdom and seek counsel
and knowledge, not shallow self-satisfaction or the excitement
of excursions whither they can not tell. Justice, and only justice,
shall always be our motto.

And yet it will be no cool process of mere science. The Nation
has been deeply stirred, stirred by a solemn passion, stirred by
the knowledge of wrong, of ideals lost, of government too often
debauched and made an instrument of evil. The feelings with
which we face this new age of right and opportunity sweep
across our heartstrings like some air out of God's own presence,
where justice and mercy are reconciled and the judge and the

brother are one. We know our task to be no mere task of politics
but a task which shall search us through and through, whether
we be able to understand our time and the need of our people,
whether we be indeed their spokesmen and interpreters, whether
we have the pure heart to comprehend and the rectified will to
choose our high course of action.

This is not a day of triumph; it is a day of dedication. Here
muster, not the forces of party, but the forces of humanity. Men's
hearts wait upon us; men's lives hang in the balance; men's
hopes call upon us to say what we will do. Who shall live up
to the great trust? Who dares fail to try? I summon all honest
men, all patriotic, all forward-looking men, to my side. God
helping me, I will not fail them, if they will but counsel and
sustain me!

21. F. D. ROOSEVELT'S FOUR FREEDOMS SPEECH

January 6, 1941

It is of interest to compare this speech, delivered to the Congress on
the state of the Union and not an Inaugural, with Wilson's First Inaugural.
There is a marked contrast artistically. Yet there is bite, verve, and
originality in this speech. It is a kind of declaration of American *inter-
dependence* and is a proclamation of the end of isolation. The high point
is a vision of a future world founded upon four essential freedoms. They
have altered the vocabulary of mankind.

I address you, the Members of the Seventy-Seventh Congress,
at a moment unprecedented in the history of the Union. I use
the word "unprecedented," because at no previous time has
American security been as seriously threatened from without as
it is today. . . .

It is true that prior to 1914 the United States often had been
disturbed by events in other Continents. We had even engaged
in two wars in the West Indies, in the Mediterranean and in the
Pacific for the maintenance of American rights and for the
principles of peaceful commerce. In no case, however, had a
serious threat been raised against our national safety or our
independence.

What I seek to convey is the historic truth that the United
States as a nation has at all times maintained opposition to any

attempt to lock us in behind an ancient Chinese wall while the procession of civilization went past. Today, thinking of our children and their children, we oppose enforced isolation for ourselves or for any part of the Americas.

Even when the World War broke out in 1914, it seemed to contain only small threat of danger to our own American future. But, as time went on, the American people began to visualize what the downfall of democratic nations might mean to our own democracy. . . .

Therefore, as your President, performing my constitutional duty to "give to the Congress information of the state of the Union," I find it necessary to report that the future and the safety of our country and of our democracy are overwhelmingly involved in events far beyond our borders.

Armed defense of democratic existence is now being gallantly waged in four continents. If that defense fails, all the population and all the resources of Europe, Asia, Africa and Australia will be dominated by the conquerors. The total of those populations and their resources greatly exceeds the sum total of the population and resources of the whole of the Western Hemisphere —many times over. . . .

I have called for personal sacrifice. I am assured of the willingness of almost all Americans to respond to that call. . . .

In the future days, which we seek to make secure, we look forward to a world founded upon four essential human freedoms.

The first is freedom of speech and expression—everywhere in the world.

The second is freedom of every person to worship God in his own way—everywhere in the world.

The third is freedom from want—which, translated into world terms, means economic understandings which will secure to every nation a healthy peace time life for its inhabitants— everywhere in the world.

The fourth is freedom from fear—which, translated into world terms, means a world-wide reduction of armaments to such a point and in such a thorough fashion that no nation will be in a position to commit an act of physical aggression against any neighbor—anywhere in the world.

That is no vision of a distant millennium. It is a definite

basis for a kind of world attainable in our own time and generation. That kind of world is the very antithesis of the so-called new order of tyranny which the dictators seek to create with the crash of a bomb.

To that new order we oppose the greater conception—the moral order. A good society is able to face schemes of world domination and foreign revolutions alike without fear.

Since the beginning of our American history we have been engaged in change—in a perpetual peaceful revolution—a revolution which goes on steadily, quietly adjusting itself to changing conditions—without the concentration camp or the quick-lime in the ditch. The world order which we seek is the cooperation of free countries, working together in a friendly, civilized society.

This nation has placed its destiny in the hands and heads and hearts of its millions of free men and women; and its faith in freedom under the guidance of God. Freedom means the supremacy of human rights everywhere. Our support goes to those who struggle to gain those rights or keep them. Our strength is in our unity of purpose.

To that high concept there can be no end save victory.

Excerpts from Presidential Inaugurals

JOHN ADAMS' INAUGURAL ADDRESS

March 4, 1797

The shadow of Washington's example is very much over this Address. Both Houses of Congress had by specific resolution commended this example to the imitation of his successors.

When it was first perceived, in early times, that no middle course for America remained between unlimited submission to a foreign legislature and a total independence of its claims, men of reflection were less apprehensive of danger from the formidable power of fleets and armies they must determine to resist than from those contests and dissensions which would certainly arise concerning the forms of government to be instituted over the whole and over the parts of this extensive country. Relying, however, on the purity of their intentions, the justice of their cause, and the integrity and intelligence of the

people, under an overruling Providence which had so signally
protected this country from the first, the representatives of this
nation, then consisting of little more than half its present number,
not only broke to pieces the chains which were forging the rod
of iron that was lifted up, but frankly cut asunder the ties which
had bound them, and launched into an ocean of uncertainty.

The zeal and ardor of the people during the Revolutionary
war supplying the place of government, commanded a degree of
order sufficient at least for the temporary preservation of society. The Confederation which was early felt to be necessary
was prepared from the models of the Batavian and Helvetic
confederacies, the only examples which remain with any detail
and precision in history, and certainly the only ones which the
people at large had ever considered. But reflecting on the striking difference in so many particulars between this country and
those where a courier may go from the seat of government to
the frontier in a single day, it was then certainly foreseen by
some who assisted in Congress at the formation of it that it
could not be durable. . . .

. . . if elevated ideas of the high destinies of this country and
of my own duties toward it, founded on a knowledge of the
moral principles and intellectual improvements of the people
deeply engraven on my mind in early life, and not obscured
but exalted by experience and age; and, with humble reverence,
I feel it to be my duty to add, if a veneration for the religion of
a people who profess and call themselves Christians, and a fixed
resolution to consider a decent respect for Christianity among
the best recommendations for the public service, can enable me
in any degree to comply with your wishes, it shall be my
strenuous endeavor that this sagacious injunction of the two
Houses shall not be without effect.

With this great example before me, with the sense and spirit,
the faith and honor, the duty and interest, of the same American people pledged to support the Constitution of the United
States, I entertain no doubt of its continuance in all its energy,
and my mind is prepared without hesitation to lay myself under
the most solemn obligations to support it to the utmost of my
power.

And may that Being who is supreme over all, the Patron of

Order, the Fountain of Justice, and the Protector in all ages of the world of virtuous liberty, continue His blessing upon this nation and its Government and give it all possible success and duration consistent with the ends of His providence.

JEFFERSON'S FIRST INAUGURAL

March 4, 1801

Let us, then, with courage and confidence pursue our own Federal and Republican principles, our attachment to union and representative government. Kindly separated by nature and a wide ocean from the exterminating havoc of one quarter of the globe; too high-minded to endure the degradations of the others; possessing a chosen country, with room enough for our descendants to the thousandth and thousandth generation; entertaining a due sense of our equal right to the use of our own faculties, to the acquisitions of our own industry, to honor and confidence from our fellow-citizens, resulting not from birth, but from our actions and their sense of them; enlightened by a benign religion, professed, indeed, and practiced in various forms, yet all of them inculcating honesty, truth, temperance, gratitude, and the love of man; acknowledging and adoring an overruling Providence, which by all its dispensations proves that it delights in the happiness of man here and his greater happiness hereafter—with all these blessings, what more is necessary to make us a happy and a prosperous people? Still one thing more, fellow-citizens—a wise and frugal Government, which shall restrain men from injuring one another, shall leave them otherwise free to regulate their own pursuits of industry and improvement, and shall not take from the mouth of labor the bread it has earned. This is the sum of good government, and this is necessary to close the circle of our felicities. . . .

Relying, then, on the patronage of your good will, I advance with obedience to the work, ready to retire from it whenever you become sensible how much better choice it is in your power to make. And may that Infinite Power which rules the destinies of the universe lead our councils to what is best, and give them a favorable issue for your peace and prosperity.

JEFFERSON'S SECOND INAUGURAL

March 4, 1805

. . . I shall now enter on the duties to which my fellow-citizens have again called me, and shall proceed in the spirit of those principles which they have approved. I fear not that any motives of interest may lead me astray; I am sensible of no passion which could seduce me knowingly from the path of justice, but the weaknesses of human nature and the limits of my own understanding will produce errors of judgment sometimes injurious to your interests. I shall need, therefore, all the indulgence which I have heretofore experienced from my constituents; the want of it will certainly not lessen with increasing years. I shall need, too, the favor of that Being in whose hands we are, who led our fathers, as Israel of old, from their native land and planted them in a country flowing with all the necessaries and comforts of life; who has covered our infancy with His providence and our riper years with His wisdom and power, and to whose goodness I ask you to join in supplications with me that He will so enlighten the minds of your servants, guide their councils, and prosper their measures that whatsoever they do shall result in your good, and shall secure to you the peace, friendship, and approbation of all nations.

MADISON'S FIRST INAUGURAL

March 4, 1809

. . . But the source to which I look or the aids which alone can supply my deficiencies is in the well-tried intelligence and virtue of my fellow-citizens, and in the counsels of those representing them in the other departments associated in the care of the national interests. In these my confidence will under every difficulty be best placed, next to that which we have all been encouraged to feel in the guardianship and guidance of that Almighty Being whose power regulates the destiny of nations, whose blessings have been so conspicuously dispensed to this rising Republic, and to whom we are bound to address our devout gratitude for the past, as well as our fervent supplications and best hopes for the future.

JOHN QUINCY ADAMS' INAUGURAL ADDRESS
March 4, 1825

. . . To the guidance of the legislative councils, to the assistance of the executive and subordinate departments, to the friendly cooperation of the respective State governments, to the candid and liberal support of the people so far as it may be deserved by honest industry and zeal, I shall look for whatever success may attend my public service; and knowing that "except the Lord keep the city the watchman waketh but in vain," with fervent supplications for His favor, to His overruling providence I commit with humble but fearless confidence my own fate and the future destinies of my country.

JACKSON'S FIRST INAUGURAL
March 4, 1829

. . . A diffidence, perhaps too just, in my own qualifications will teach me to look with reverence to the examples of public virtue left by my illustrious predecessors, and with veneration to the lights that flow from the mind that founded and the mind that reformed our system. The same diffidence induces me to hope for instruction and aid from the coordinate branches of the Government, and for the indulgence and support of my fellow-citizens generally. And a firm reliance on the goodness of that Power whose providence mercifully protected our national infancy, and has since upheld our liberties in various vicissitudes, encourages me to offer up my ardent supplications that He will continue to make our beloved country the object of His divine care and gracious benediction.

VAN BUREN'S INAUGURAL ADDRESS
March 4, 1837

. . . In receiving from the people the sacred trust twice confided to my illustrious predecessor, and which he has discharged so faithfully and so well, I know that I can not expect to perform the arduous task with equal ability and success. But united as I have been in his counsels, a daily witness of his exclusive

and unsurpassed devotion to his country's welfare, agreeing with
him in sentiments which his countrymen have warmly supported,
and permitted to partake largely of his confidence, I may hope
that somewhat of the same cheering approbation will be found
to attend upon my path. For him I but express with my own
the wishes of all, that he may yet long live to enjoy the brilliant
evening of his well-spent life; and for myself, conscious of but
one desire, faithfully to serve my country, I throw myself without fear on its justice and its kindness. Beyond that I only look
to the gracious protection of the Divine Being whose strengthening support I humbly solicit, and whom I fervently pray to look
down upon us all. May it be among the dispensations of His
providence to bless our beloved country with honors and with
length of days. May her ways be ways of pleasantness and all
her paths be peace!

WILLIAM HENRY HARRISON'S INAUGURAL ADDRESS

March 4, 1841

This is the longest of all the Presidential Inaugurals, running to 17
pages. The religious profession and summation, given below, is short but is
one of the more interesting passages of the kind in the Inaugurals.

. . . I deem the present occasion sufficiently important and
solemn to justify me in expressing to my fellow-citizens a profound reverence for the Christian religion and a thorough
conviction that sound morals, religious liberty, and a just sense
of religious responsibility are essentially connected with all
true and lasting happiness; and to that good Being who has
blessed us by the gifts of civil and religious freedom, who
watched over and prospered the labors of our fathers and has
hitherto preserved to us institutions far exceeding in excellence
those of any other people, let us unite in fervently commending
every interest of our beloved country in all future time. . . .

PIERCE'S INAUGURAL ADDRESS

March 4, 1853

. . . We have been carried in safety through a perilous crisis.
Wise counsels, like those which gave us the Constitution, pre-

vailed to uphold it. Let the period be remembered as an admonition and not as an encouragement, in any section of the Union, to make experiments where experiments are fraught with such fearful hazard. Let it be impressed upon all hearts that, beautiful as our fabric is, no earthly power or wisdom could ever reunite its broken fragments. Standing, as I do, almost within view of the green slopes of Monticello, and, as it were, within reach of the tomb of Washington, with all the cherished memories of the past gathering around me like so many eloquent voices of exhortation from heaven, I can express no better hope for my country than that the kind Providence which smiled upon our fathers may enable their children to preserve the blessings they have inherited.

GRANT'S SECOND INAUGURAL

March 4, 1873

The unusual excerpt below refers to the constitutional rejection in Grant's first administration and against the President's recommendation of the admission of Santo Domingo as a Territory of the Union.

. . . In future, while I hold my present office, the subject of acquisition of territory must have the support of the people before I will recommend any proposition looking to such acquisition. I say here, however, that I do not share in the apprehension held by so many as to the danger of governments becoming weakened and destroyed by reason of their extension of territory. Commerce, education, and rapid transit of thought and matter by telegraph and steam have changed all this. Rather do I believe that our Great Maker is preparing the world, in His own good time, to become one nation, speaking one language, and when armies and navies will be no longer required. . . .

HAYES' INAUGURAL ADDRESS

March 5, 1877

The words quoted by President Hayes in the excerpt below are from A Prayer for Congress found under Prayers and Thanksgivings in the Book of Common Prayer of the Protestant Episcopal Church.

. . . Looking for the guidance of that Divine Hand by which

the destinies of nations and individuals are shaped, I call upon you, Senators, Representatives, Judges, fellow-citizens, here and everywhere, to unite with me in an earnest effort to secure to our country the blessings, not only of material prosperity, but of justice, peace, and union—a union depending not upon the constraint of force, but upon the loving devotion of a free people; "and that all things may be so ordered and settled upon the best and surest foundations that peace and happiness, truth and justice, religion and piety, may be established among us for all generations."

GARFIELD'S INAUGURAL ADDRESS

March 4, 1881

It is hard for us today, when we know and admire so much individual Mormons and the great Mormon Choir, to realize what a scandal and furore was created by the insistence of the Mormon Church on the practice of polygamy. The excerpt below is of exceptional relevance to the concern of this book.

. . . The Constitution guarantees absolute religious freedom. Congress is prohibited from making any law respecting an establishment of religion or prohibiting the free exercise thereof. The Territories of the United States are subject to the direct legislative authority of Congress, and hence the General Government is responsible for any violation of the Constitution in any of them. It is therefore a reproach to the Government that in the most populous of the Territories the constitutional guaranty is not enjoyed by the people and the authority of Congress is set at naught. The Mormon Church not only offends the moral sense of manhood by sanctioning polygamy, but prevents the administration of justice through ordinary instrumentalities of law.

In my judgment it is the duty of Congress, while respecting to the uttermost the conscientious convictions and religious scruples of every citizen, to prohibit within its jurisdiction all criminal practices, especially of that class which destroy the family relations and endanger social order. Nor can any ecclesiastical organization be safely permitted to usurp in the smallest degree the functions and powers of the National Government. . . .

BENJAMIN HARRISON'S INAUGURAL ADDRESS

March 4, 1889

. . . My promise is spoken; yours unspoken, but not the less real and solemn. The people of every State have here their representatives. Surely I do not misinterpret the spirit of the occasion when I assume that the whole body of the people covenant with me and with each other today to support and defend the Constitution and the Union of the States, to yield willing obedience to all the laws and each to every other citizen his equal civil and political rights. Entering thus solemnly into covenant with each other, we may reverently invoke and confidently expect the favor and help of Almighty God—that He will give to me wisdom, strength, and fidelity, and to our people a spirit of fraternity and a love of righteousness and peace. . . .

Let us exalt patriotism and moderate our party contentions. Let those who would die for the flag on the field of battle give a better proof of their patriotism and a higher glory to their country by promoting fraternity and justice. A party success that is achieved by unfair methods or by practices that partake of revolution is hurtful and evanescent even from a party standpoint. We should hold our differing opinions in mutual respect, and, having submitted them to the arbitrament of the ballot, should accept an adverse judgment with the same respect that we would have demanded of our opponents if the decision had been in our favor.

No other people have a government more worthy of their respect and love or a land so magnificent in extent, so pleasant to look upon, and so full of generous suggestion to enterprise and labor. God has placed upon our head a diadem and has laid at our feet power and wealth beyond definition or calculation. But we must not forget that we take these gifts upon the condition that justice and mercy shall hold the reins of power and that the upward avenues of hope shall be free to all the people. . . .

CLEVELAND'S INAUGURAL ADDRESS II

March 4, 1893

. . . Above all, I know there is a Supreme Being who rules the affairs of men and whose goodness and mercy have always followed the American people, and I know He will not turn from us now if we humbly and reverently seek His powerful aid.

McKINLEY'S INAUGURAL ADDRESS

March 4, 1897

Fellow-Citizens:

In obedience to the will of the people, and in their presence, by the authority vested in me by this oath, I assume the arduous and responsible duties of President of the United States, relying upon the support of my countrymen and invoking the guidance of Almighty God. Our faith teaches that there is no safer reliance than upon the God of our fathers, who has so singularly favored the American people in every national trial, and who will not forsake us so long as we obey His commandments and walk humbly in His footsteps. . . .

THEODORE ROOSEVELT'S INAUGURAL ADDRESS

March 4, 1905

My fellow-citizens, no people on earth have more cause to be thankful than ours, and this is said reverently, in no spirit of boastfulness in our own strength, but with gratitude to the Giver of Good who has blessed us with the conditions which have enabled us to achieve so large a measure of well-being and of happiness. To us as a people it has been granted to lay the foundations of our national life in a new continent. We are the heirs of the ages, and yet we have had to pay few of the penalties which in old countries are exacted by the dead hand of a bygone civilization. . . .

Much has been given us, and much will rightfully be expected from us. We have duties to others and duties to ourselves; and we can shirk neither. We have become a great nation, forced by the fact of its greatness into relations with the other nations of the earth, and we must behave as beseems a people with such responsibilities. Toward all other nations, large and small, our attitude must be one of cordial and sincere friendship. We must show not only in our words, but in our deeds, that we are earnestly desirous of securing their good will by acting toward them in a spirit of just and generous recognition of all their rights. But justice and generosity in a nation, as in an individual, count most when shown not by the weak but by the strong. While ever careful to refrain from wrongdoing others, we must be no less insistent that we are not wronged ourselves. We wish peace, but we wish the peace of justice, the peace of righteousness. We wish it because we think it is right and not because we are afraid. No weak nation that acts manfully and justly should ever have cause to fear us, and no strong power should ever be able to single us out as a subject for insolent aggression. . . .

COOLIDGE'S INAUGURAL ADDRESS
March 4, 1925

. . . Because of what America is and what America has done, a firmer courage, a higher hope, inspires the heart of all humanity.

These results have not occurred by mere chance. They have been secured by a constant and enlightened effort marked by many sacrifices and extending over many generations. We can not continue these brilliant successes in the future, unless we continue to learn from the past. It is necessary to keep the former experiences of our country both at home and abroad continually before us, if we are to have any science of government. If we wish to erect new structures, we must have a definite knowledge of the old foundations. We must realize that human nature is about the most constant thing in the universe and that the essentials of human relationship do not change. We must frequently take our bearings from these fixed stars of our political firmament if we expect to hold a true course. . . .

TRUMAN'S INAUGURAL ADDRESS
January 20, 1949

. . . The American people stand firm in the faith which has inspired this Nation from the beginning. We believe that all men have a right to equal justice under law and equal opportunity to share in the common good. We believe that all men have the right to freedom of thought and expression. We believe that all men are created equal because they are created in the image of God.

From this faith we will not be moved. . . .

EISENHOWER'S FIRST INAUGURAL

January 20, 1953

President Eisenhower broke all precedents when he prefaced his First Inaugural Address by asking the dignitaries and others present to bow their heads while he uttered a "little private prayer of my own." This prayer is reproduced below. The President told friends that he was moved to write it after attending an earlier Service of Dedication at the National Presbyterian Church. The second paragraph of the prayer evidently echoes I Kings 3:5-15, one of the Lessons read at this Service. As the writer recommended to the Pastor, Dr. Edward L. R. Elson, this Lesson and got the reference for him a second time after it had been mislaid, he feels a slight proprietary interest in this small but significant episode of contemporary history.

Almighty God, as we stand here at this moment my future associates in the executive branch of government join me in beseeching that Thou will make full and complete our dedication to the service of the people in this throng, and their fellow citizens everywhere.

Give us, we pray, the power to discern clearly right from wrong, and allow all our words and actions to be governed thereby, and by the laws of this land. Especially we pray that our concern shall be for all the people regardless of station, race, or calling.

May cooperation be permitted and be the mutual aim of those who, under the concepts of our Constitution, hold to differing political faiths; so that all may work for the good of our beloved country and Thy glory. Amen.

PRESIDENT KENNEDY'S INAUGURAL ADDRESS

January 20, 1961

. . . The world is very different now. For man holds in his mortal hands the power to abolish all forms of human poverty and all forms of human life. And yet the same revolutionary beliefs for which our forbears fought are still at issue around the globe—the belief that the rights of man come not from the generosity of the state but from the hand of God. . . .

Appendix C

Franklin's Plea for Prayer

The aged Benjamin Franklin arose at a moment of tension and discouragement in the Convention assembled in Philadelphia to draft a Constitution for the new nation, the United States of America. The time was late June, not long before the 4th of July. His purpose was to make a motion that the Convention have recourse to prayer and he read from a paper, we are told, with a quavering voice. After Franklin finished, Dr. Hugh Williamson of North Carolina said that the reason for lack of prayers was that the Convention had no funds to hire a minister. Edmund Pendleton, Governor of Virginia, suggested that on the 4th of July they could all go to Church.

The small progress we have made after 4 or 5 weeks close attention . . . is methinks a melancholy proof of the imperfection of the Human Understanding. We indeed seem to feel our want of political wisdom since we have been running about in search of it. We have gone back to ancient history for models of Government, and examined the different forms of those republics which, having been formed with the seeds of their own dissolution now no longer exist. And we have viewed Modern States all round Europe, but find none of their Constitutions suitable to our circumstances . . . how has it happened, sir that we have not hitherto once thought of applying to the Father of Lights to illuminate our understandings?

226

Chapter 9

What Is the Remedy?

We have before us in the preceding pages of this book the heart of many decisions handed down by the Supreme Court of the United States over numerous decades in the field of Church and State, religion and government. This is an essential and vital strand in the American tradition, both legally and religiously. It shows, especially when considered and understood in the light of the large and central place devoted to religion in American State Papers, that there has been of recent date a sharp and accelerated evolution in the trend of Court opinion. This trend has been in the direction of innovation and radicalism, if not absolutely, at least as tested by the main current of the past and the certain understanding and practices of the Founding Fathers of the Republic.

This evolution reached what seemed to the writer, as well as to literally millions of Americans, to be a culmination in the decision handed down by the highest Court on June 25, 1962, in the case of *Engel v. Vitale.* The implications of the opinion of the Court, written by Mr. Justice Black, author of the official opinions in the two earlier cases of *McCollum* and *Everson,* seemed to be sweeping and to bode ill for the future of prayer in any form and the reading of the Bible in the public schools, to say nothing of the fate of various religious customs and practices embedded in the rituals, institutions, and laws of the Nation.

Yet there was a passage in the *Engel* decision which arrested nearly universal attention and seemed to many to prove that the Court was far from having burned its bridges and pulled out all the stops in the direction of a radical break with the past and its principal precedents. This passage, as we have indicated more than once before in this book played a crucial role in the moderation and pacification of outraged public opinion. It was most widely quoted and on all sides appealed to in the days of controversy following the promulgation of the Court's verdict in *Engel*.

The crucial and—as the sequel proved—highly misleading passage in the opinion of the Court in *Engel* reads as follows: "The petitioners contend among other things that the state laws requiring or permitting use of the Regents' prayer must be struck down as a violation of the Establishment Clause because that prayer was composed by government officials as a part of a government program to further religious beliefs. . . . We agree with this contention since we think that the Constitutional prohibition against laws respecting an establishment of religion must at least mean that in this country it is no business of government to compose official prayers for any group of the American people to recite as part of a religious program carried on by government."

An arresting example of the kind of thing that happened all over the country, as a result of this language and the propaganda to which it understandably gave rise, has come to my attention through the perusal of government documents—in this case *Hearings* before the Senate Committee on the Judiciary. A distinguished Baptist divine of my native State of Oklahoma, the Rev. Dr. Herschel H. Hobbs, Pastor of the First Baptist Church, Oklahoma City and President of the important and powerful Southern Baptist Convention, appeared at his own request before this Committee. In the course of this statement he said:

> Following the recent decision of the Supreme Court relating to prayer in the public schools much misunderstanding and concern have prevailed throughout the Nation. . . . The immediate occasion stems from proposed amendments to the Constitution designed to clarify the issue.
>
> It is my sincere judgment that such an amendment is unnecessary. This does not mean that I am opposed to prayer in public schools or to any other religious exercise which does not involve the establishment of one religious faith over others. It is my conviction that the first amendment as it now stands is a sufficient safeguard

both to the state and to the church. My position may be outlined in the following affirmations:

First, the first amendment has stood the test of time.

. . .

Second, the recent Supreme Court ruling does not forbid prayer in the public schools. It does rule that it is unlawful for any government agency to compose a prayer and require that it be used in public schools.

My first acquaintance with this decision was a newspaper headline "Supreme Court Outlaws Prayer in Public Schools." This greatly disturbed me. But when later I read an analysis of the decision it was quite clear that what appeared, at first glance, to be a blow at religious freedom was in reality a blow in its favor. I then declared it to be the greatest single decision for the separation of church and state since the adoption of the first amendment. (Italics supplied)

Dr. Hobbs proceeds to quote a portion of the key-passage in Mr. Justice Black's opinion cited above. He then continues:

The Supreme Court cited specific history, such as the Book of Common Prayer, to indicate that prayers officially composed or sanctioned lead to malfunctions in both the state and religion. It pointed out that such a history was the occasion for the first amendment being included in the Constitution. . . .

It is to strain the meaning of the first amendment beyond reasonable measure to say that the Court's ruling would forbid teachers to lead their pupils in prayer. This does not comprise a government agent or agency composing a prayer. It is the expression of one soul to God as he or she leads others to a like expression. The language of the Court's decision clearly implies that a prayer by a teacher, pupil, or minister is a "purely religious function" of "the people themselves" and/or of "those the people chose to look to for religious guidance."

In the light of further decisions by the highest Court there is a certain element of humor in this testimony of one of the most eminent pastors in the country. One cannot help hoping that Mr. Justice Black and Mr. Justice Clark and their colleagues happened to see the construction put on *Engel* by Dr. Hobbs. One who is not a Baptist and is used to Prayer Book prayers though by no means opposed to impromptu praying, is tempted to say to the Baptist leader: "A good try, Doctor; you almost had the Supreme Court behind free prayer in the public schools and even a little evangelism."

And speaking of the Prayer Book and different forms of prayer, there is the charming story, which I hope Dr. Hobbs may read here and enjoy, of the colloquy between the Baptist and the Episcopalian on precisely this subject. "I do not believe in prayers read from a book," said the Baptist firmly; "I believe in prayer that comes from the heart."

"Are you sure about this?" replied the Episcopalian. "You believe in the Bible, don't you?" "Indeed I do. I believe it is God's Word and I accept every word in it," rejoined the Baptist. "You do," continued the follower of the Prayer Book; "that's surely very interesting. And you believe only in prayer from the heart. Well in my Bible it says: 'The heart of man is deceitful, and desperately wicked.'"

The final sequel to this is not recorded.

Readers of earlier portions of this book know that I was skeptical in the extreme of the apologia for *Engel* which developed with such spontaneity and swept over the entire country. I continued doubtful that the Supreme Court would or could halt in its headlong plunge toward radical libertarianism. I did by the winter of 1963 weaken in my suspicions based on logic to the extent of hoping and possibly even believing that one or two of the Justices, in addition to Mr. Justice Stewart, might take advantage of the "out" possibly and even apparently left in the *Engel* opinion and appear on the dissenting side.

Obviously, this was wishful thinking from start to finish. It is not conceivable that the well informed Justices including Mr. Justice Clark were unaware of the interpretation placed upon the *Engel* opinion throughout the Nation. But logic was not really on the side of viewing the Regents' composition of a prayer as an establishment of religion while the official use of the Lord's Prayer or even a spontaneous prayer by a teacher, also a State official in some sense, was an expression of the free exercise of religion. It may be presumed that the Justices saw this and did not seriously consider splitting such a hair, even though distinctions quite as superfine are not unknown in the history of the Court.

There is abundant evidence that the Justices realized the crucial and drastic character of the issues before them in the twin cases of *School District* and *Murray*. They faced, I believe with courage and candor, the moment of truth which had finally arrived. I say this even though I differ sharply from their conclusion. The decision of the Court in its fulness, with all the concurrences and the second and longer dissent of Mr. Justice Stewart, bears on its face the realization on the part of the Justices that a step of the utmost gravity was being taken. All nine members of the Court participated. Of these only three simply accepted the opinion of the Court delivered by Mr. Justice Clark. There were three concurring opinions, with four members participating in them, and one dissenting opinion. Mr. Justice Brennan presented one of the longest and most involved opinions in the history of the Court. It runs to 77 pages. All the opinions in the decision run to 121 pages, as compared with 30 pages in *Engel* a year earlier.

The undercurrent of concern in these opinions was made explicit in one of the concurring statements, that of Mr. Justice Goldberg with Mr. Justice Harlan joining him. The caveat thus entered is gentle rather than strident and there is no backing away from firm agreement with the opinion of the Court. Still it is entirely possible that the cautionary qualification made by Mr. Justice Goldberg will be repeated and may assume a larger significance in future cases. He says:

> It is said, and I agree, that the attitude of the state toward religion must be one of neutrality. But untutored devotion to the concept of neutrality can lead to invocation or approval of results which partake not simply of that noninterference and noninvolvement with the religious which the Constitution commands, but of a brooding and pervasive devotion to the secular and a passive, or even active, hostility to the religious. Such results are not only not compelled by the Constitution, but, it seems to me, are prohibited by it.

This is a very slight crack, and it is not certain how appreciably it leaves the door ajar. It does seem clear that the present Court is nearly unanimous in regarding the issue of prayer and devotional Bible-reading in public schools as settled. The repercussions on state schools, already sore beset with strains and complications deriving from *Brown v. Board of Education* (1954) do not seem to have troubled the Court unduly.

This raises the sixty-four dollar question—the one that arose and was voiced insistently and earnestly after *Engel* but then dropped: *What is to be done?*

One answer of course is, Nothing. This is the reply that many are giving, not out of conviction we believe, but because it is easy to drift and because we are in a society that is relatively affluent with many absorbing avocations and pastimes and because we are becoming, in contrast to our forbears of the wilderness and the frontier, a conformist people.

But we do not have to lie down and see our inheritance as Americans dissipated or partially liquidated even by Guardians as sincere and devoted as the nine Justices of the Supreme Court. We do not have to abandon a major doctrine of the Bible and of the Judeo-Christian tradition, that God is the Lord of nations quite as much as of individuals. We do not have to behave like a nation of sheep. The doctrines of the sovereignty of the people and the consent of the governed, even of the division of governmental powers, underlie our Federal Constitution and represent our indefeasible rights as free men

I am, of course, not counselling disobedience to any ruling of the highest Court or hostility toward that eminent tribunal. What is done in criticism or opposition must be done in decency and order; it must be in accordance with the Constitution; and there must be in any advocacy and agitation an appeal to reason and right, not a blind emotionalism or the impulse of a heady fanaticism.

In the American past the Supreme Court has inevitably embroiled itself in deep and bitter controversy. This is almost a staple of the American past. Presidents have been enraged by the Court's decisions and have spoken their mind in public and in private. Thomas Jefferson employed strong language. So did Andrew Jackson. Abraham Lincoln in his First Inaugural, in words quoted earlier in this book, did not hesitate to criticize the Court and to wonder about its future. Franklin D. Roosevelt, in the heyday of the New Deal, sounded off sharply and threatened to pack the Court. He thought better of this but his first appointment of a Supreme Court Justice was that of Senator Hugo La Fayette Black.

At any rate we are in no way acting disloyally but are in good American company when we say: No, we intend to fight even against the opinion of the Supreme Court for the American tradition and the American way!

The question is, How? What do we work for? What do we try to accomplish? What is the remedy?

> For every evil done
> Under the sun,
> There is a remedy.

Our first problem is to decide what it is.

Several proposals have been made. Mr. L. Brent Bozell says: Let the Congress employ "the simple expedient of a Resolution affirming its own understanding of the Establishment Clause, and encouraging states that share its views to deal with religion thenceforth in accordance with that understanding. . . . The confrontation would not have seemed strange to the authors of the *Federalist*."

The last statement of Mr. Bozell might well be true. The difficulty is that a lot has happened since the first discussions of the proposed Constitution. We cannot return to 1788. Then there is the little matter of the minds and wills of the members of the Congress. Can any one seriously imagine the Senate and House of Representatives in 1964 calling on the 50 States to defy the Supreme Court of the United States? Finally, instead of solving the problem in an orderly manner, this could be to provoke disorder, piling Pelion on Ossa with a vengeance, and making confusion worse confounded.

The same difficulties are in the path of another drastic answer, which is to impeach the members of the highest Court. This sounds very wild today and really quite outrageous. Yet this was widely advocated in the lifetime of Thomas Jefferson, who advanced his solution for "curbing the Judiciary in their enterprises on the Constitution," namely appointment for six years with reappointability by the President with the approval of both

Houses of Congress, because impeachment had been shown by experience to be impracticable and was no longer feared by the Justices.[1]

Professor Sidney Hook is my authority for the curious fact that in 1804 Chief Justice John Marshall wrote a letter to Associate Justice Samuel Chase, then under trial in impeachment proceedings, in which he said: "I think the modern doctrine of impeachment should yield to an appellate jurisdiction in our legislature." Dr. Hook himself, in his University of California lectures *The Paradoxes of Freedom* (University of California Press, 1962) advocates the latter as a solution unless the opinion of the Supreme Court in nullifying Congressional legislation is unanimous. He would not however apply the unanimity rule to the States, and his discussion is not in a Church-State context.

The remedy most widely proposed, after the *Engel* decision and since, is a clarifying constitutional amendment. Bishop James A. Pike of California advocated this before the Senate Judiciary Committee and many Senators and Congressmen have indicated their approval of such a solution. This trend in Congressional opinion seems, however, to have been less pronounced since the latest edict of the Supreme Court than it was after *Engel* in 1962.

A weighty endorsement of the amendment answer to the problem came in a nearly unanimous resolution of the Governors of our 50 States at their 54th Annual Meeting, Hershey, Pennsylvania, on July 3, 1962. The position of this resolution was reaffirmed a year later by the Governors meeting at Miami, Florida. When it is remembered that the Governors are directly elected by the people in their respective States and are in extraordinarily close and constant touch with school systems and the pupils, parents, teachers, and administrators constituting them, these actions of the Governors Conference in successive years are most notable. The tone and content of the 1962 resolution are especially fine, making this document a message to the whole American people which rings out clear and strong, yet with the persuasiveness of reverence and reason.

[1] Letters to Ritchie and Pleasants (1820, 1821).

This is the Resolution of the Governors:

> Whereas the recent majority opinion of the U. S. Supreme Court in the New York School Prayer case has created far-reaching misunderstanding as to the Nation's faith and dependence in God: and
>
> Whereas the Governors assembled at the 54th annual Governors' conference acknowledge their dependence upon God and the power of prayer to Him; and
>
> Whereas the power of prayer has sustained man throughout our history and provided the moral foundation for our great Nation: Now, therefore, be it
>
> *Resolved,* That the Governors' conference urge the Congress of the United States to propose an amendment to the Constitution of the United States that will make clear and beyond challenge the acknowledgment by our Nation and people of their faith in God and permit the free and voluntary participation in prayer in our public schools.

What form should a clarifying amendment to the Constitution take? Several resolutions were presented in the Congress in 1962 and the subject is still before that body though we hear less about its deliberations in this context than we did a year ago. Here are examples of proposed amendments:

> SECTION 1. No provision of this Constitution or any article of amendment thereto shall be construed to prohibit nondenominational religious observance through the invocation of the blessing of God or the recitation of prayer, as a part of the activities of any school or other educational institution supported in whole or in part from public revenues, if participation therein is not made compulsory. (S. J. Res. 206, 87th Cong., 2nd Sess.)
>
> SECTION 1. Nothing in this Constitution shall prohibit the offering of prayers or the reading of the Bible as part of the program of any public school or other public place in the United States.
>
> SECTION 2. The right of each State to decide on the basis of its own public policy questions of decency and morality, and to enact legislation with respect thereto, shall not be abridged. (S. J. Res. 207, 87th Cong., 2nd Sess.)

The above examples are in proposed Senate Resolutions. Here is one from the House:

> SECTION 1. Prayers may be offered in the course of any program in any public school or other public place in the United States. (H. J. Res. 752, 87th Cong., 2nd Sess.)

There is a problem about amending the Constitution to create specific exceptions. If only prayer and Bible-reading are mentioned, other issues may arise at a later time. If numerous usages and customs developed in our American life over the decades and centuries are spelled out, as some have proposed, the result is likely to be a monstrosity. A Constitution is not an encyclopedia.

Also, as Bishop Pike has observed, the enumeration of any exceptions implies that the Supreme Court is right and that we wish now to change the American tradition. To solve all these problems, the Bishop, who was a highly trained jurist before he entered the Church, proposes that the First Amendment be reaffirmed with a restatement of the present phrase "an establishment of religion" to read: "the recognition as an established church of any denomination, sect, or organized religious association."

This proposal is ingenious and I personally would welcome it. It would however arouse much more determined and bitter opposition than the suggestions for an amendment already put forward in the Congress. It involves very complex questions of history and would be interpreted as leaving the door wide open on pending legislative issues respecting Federal support of school systems which at present are universally conceived to have constitutional overtones. The simple, concrete issue of prayer and Bible-reading raises no other questions and has considerable emotional appeal. An amendment excepting them would seem to have the best chance of passage by two-thirds of both Houses of Congress and three-fourths of the State Legislatures.

Even so, the way ahead for a clarifying amendment in the Church-State, religion-and-government area is likely to be long and hard. Is there an alternative?

The only alternative—and fortunately it is not an exclusive one but could supplement handily a drive for a constitutional amendment—is education and the mobilization of public opinion.

This, it seems to me, must be undertaken without delay and with a strong sense of mission by all Americans who value our religious inheritance in its fulness and feel that such phrases as "one Nation, under God" and "In God We Trust" are not empty words but true declarations of national dedication and a people's faith.

It is with a view to assisting such a movement of education, reason, and worthy sentiment in our country that this Handbook for study and thought has been prepared and is submitted to my fellow Americans.

I may add that as a lover of tradition and a moderate conservative who happens to believe that every Christian and right-thinking man or woman must have in his mental make-up a certain liberal element, for after all *liber* means free, I would be happy if the American "establishment" including the Supreme Court could recover the common sense and middle way we have known through nearly all of our history and thereby avoid the need to pursue officially revising the First Amendment. The great men, many of them still young, who drew up the Constitution and Bill of Rights, had much intuitive wisdom. They knew that it is often best to refrain from spelling out the ultimate directives of a free society too precisely. Some principles and even prohibitions will serve best if they are phrased with a certain roominess, the apostolic injunction being borne in mind: "For the letter killeth, but the spirit giveth life."

We have one other counsel, which we address especially to young people in our public high schools and junior high schools. On our elementary school teachers a particularly difficult burden has been placed by recent decisions of the highest Court. Certainly they will need guidance and no doubt this will be very much on the minds of our State officials and School authorities at various levels.

Above the elementary level and certainly in our high schools, subject to the policy formulated in a State or by particular School authorities, there can be no objection to purely voluntary religious activities undertaken by young people themselves. The contrary of this would surely be a violation of the free exercise clause of the same First Amendment.

This necessity to emphasize voluntarism and personal respon-

sibility could be a blessing in disguise for our young people,
galvanizing for them the meaning of religious faith and reverence for God, and producing in their lives and relations with
one another a deeper power. Possibly also as such voluntarism
develops, teachers and even principals and other administrators
may be asked to act as advisors of particular groups, with a
new opportunity to play a creative role in spiritual counsel
and character guidance.

The premier strength of religion in the United States has
come out of a situation of liberty fostering freedom of individual
choice and group voluntarism. Who knows that this may not be
due for a new birth as a result of recent sweeping decisions of
the Supreme Court? Yet one thing is sure. It is wholly contrary
to the spirit and power of religion to accept domestication and
confinement to narrow compartments, whether in the home, the
church, the temple, or elsewhere. "The wind bloweth where it
listeth, and thou hearest the sound thereof, but canst not tell
whence it cometh, and whither it goeth: so is every one that
is born of the Spirit."

So we can predict infallibly that any and all attempts to
sterilize spiritually and religiously the public school systems of
this country will fail. And they will deserve to fail. For this is
contrary to our history, our traditions, and our deepest instincts
both as religious persons and as Americans. It is to go against
the sternest and noblest imperatives alike of Judaism and of
Christianity.

> I am the Lord thy God, which have brought thee out
> of the land of Egypt, out of the house of bondage.
> Thou shalt have none other gods but me.
> Thou shalt not make to thyself any graven image. . . .
> Thou shalt not bow down to them, nor worship them.

> And Jesus answered (the scribe), The first of all the
> commandments is, Hear, O Israel, the Lord our God is
> one Lord:
> And thou shalt love the Lord thy God with all thy
> heart, and with all thy soul, and with all thy mind,
> and with all thy strength. This is the first commandment.
> And the second is like, namely this, Thou shalt love
> thy neighbor as thyself. There is none other command-
> ment greater than these.

Epilogue: Two Witnesses

I propose in taking leave of the reader, which I do with happy salutations and good wishes from the heart, to summon two witnesses. They happen to be both of the female sex. The testimony of each one was unknown to me even after I was deep in the preparation of this book. One of the fascinating things about the enterprise of authorship is the manner in which ideas, experiences, and materials converge and to some extent arrange and assemble themselves.

The first witness is the woman, Mrs. Madalyn J. Murray, formerly of Baltimore, Maryland, who brought the lawsuit against the Board of School Commissioners of Baltimore City which was carried up to the Supreme Court and ended in the overturn, on the ground of the establishment clause of the first Amendment to the Constitution, of the practice of having an Opening Exercise in public school in which either a chapter of the Bible was read or the Lord's Prayer said or both. The successful petition of this woman and her son William J. Murray, III, alleged that the rule of the State of Maryland respecting an Opening Exercise in school violated their rights "in that it threatens their religious liberty by placing a premium on belief as against non-belief and subjects their freedom of conscience to the rule of the majority; it pronounces belief in God as the source of all moral and spiritual values, equating these values with religious values and thereby renders sinister, alien and suspect the beliefs and ideals" of the said petitioners.

One could conceivably have real sympathy with the problems of a family convinced of the truth of atheism. There is no reason to doubt that this was the attitude of the School Commissioners. The rule of the State was immediately adjusted to excuse any child from the Opening Exercise upon the written request of a parent or guardian. Also, it was directed that the

Douay version of the Bible might be used by those pupils who preferred it.

This was not enough and so we have the wishes and religious preferences not only of a majority but an overwhelming majority —certainly not less than ten to one—of the citizens of Maryland arbitrarily denied and prohibited by the Supreme Court of the United States.

What was the mentality of this petitioner who proved to be one of the most successful non-violent revolutionaries of the age? It would not have occurred to me, normally, to ask such a question. I would not, for one thing, have supposed that enough information would be available for the inquiry to be worthwhile. Mrs. Murray, however, is not given to hiding her light under a bushel. She likes to talk and is apparently extremely uninhibited and spontaneous in imparting to the public revelations of herself.

So it comes about that we have not only this case and its far-reaching results. We have also a personal testimony from Mrs. Murray so unusual and expressive that it deserves to be known by Americans generally. It has become inevitably a part of the case and an aspect of the data that people throughout the land must know, consider, ponder, and finally render their judgment on. Regretfully but in this solemn spirit it is recorded as she gave it in an interview to *The Realist* shortly before the verdict of the Supreme Court was handed down:

> If I can't come through this case the same offensive, unlovable, bull-headed, defiant, aggressive slob that I was when I started it, then I'll give up now. My own identity is more important to me. They can keep their gawd-damn prayers in the public schools, in public outhouses, in public H-bomb shelters, and in public whore-houses.

We understand that Mrs. Murray is now in the state of Kansas, editing a magazine called the *Free Humanist* and trying to found near the town of Stockton an atheists' colony, for which 80 acres of land has been donated by former Kansas Senator Carl Brown and over $100,000.00 has presently been pledged. We have also just seen an account of another interview with Mrs. Murray in which she says that "within 24 hours after Garth (her son aged 8) starts school" in Hays, Kansas, this fall, she "will file a suit challenging the practice" of Catholic nuns, in uniform, teaching in public schools.

So having saved the children of all of us from the menace of the Bible and the Lord's Prayer in the public schools, Mrs. Murray has, it seems, in addition to farflung schemes and dreams of establishment of a kind, other pressing reforms for the Supreme Court to enact.

The second witness is a girl of seventeen. She lives in the State of Florida and is a high school Senior. She had been elected Chaplain of the Honor Society of her High School when the decision of the Supreme Court in *School District* and *Murray* was handed down. This disturbed her deeply, and aroused penetrating reactions also in a circle of extremely gifted students in which she moved. Among these is a boy leaving in the fall (of 1963) for M.I.T. who is a brilliant mathematician and is fascinated with the philosophical and theological implications of the concept of infinity. A paper of his on this profound and somewhat esoteric subject has been sent me.

The reason this young lady is in this book is that she saw one of my letters to the press on the Prayer and Bible-reading decision of the Supreme Court and wrote me a letter. This letter is not only remarkably articulate. It is a document charged with conviction. It is a testament of youth, typical of thousands of the young people of the United States who have been reading the Bible and leading in prayer in school assemblies. These young Americans have a right to be heard. It is their rights, their beliefs, their destiny which the highest Court has seen fit to take very summarily and dogmatically into its hands.

I predict that we have not heard the end of the convictions of young America typified by this communication from a seventeen-year-old Florida girl. I am of course not endorsing every expression in this letter. The youth, ardor, and femininity of the author must be borne in mind. Nevertheless this message gave me real stimulus and encouraged me to persevere in the labor and travail of bringing to birth this Handbook, TO PRAY OR NOT TO PRAY! My fondest hope is that it may reach and be helpful both intellectually and religiously to many, many young people like the author of the epistle below. They are our hope. On them the cause and the glory of the Republic rest.

This then is our second witness:

July 24th, 1963

Charles Wesley Lowry
Dear Mr. Lowry:

As Chaplain of Honor Society and Secretary of Student Government Association in my school I am obliged to keep faith with my God and the students who elected me by their majority votes to fulfill those duties, including the leading of Devotions.

Without other support, knowing my duty is not excused by mistakes of any secular court on earth, I should have done my best alone with my God when the students expected it, next Fall. You have helped me, as our own Legislators of this wonderful free State with the motto "In God We Trust" have helped me, by showing that others realize how wrongfully distortions of the truths in our Declaration of Independence and Constitution of the United States have been used for destruction of our very foundations.

I know the wonder for children who may be of many different opinions about everything else, of different races, religions, nationalities—almost any kind of difference imaginable in our "melting pot." I know how one feels as a little child when the moment comes for joining our minds, hearts and souls quietly together for a little prayer to our one "Our Father." I remember my first day as a strange "Yankee," here, very well. I want other children to be blessed, too.

Most that I have read in the Decision 119-142 and in the newspapers appears to come from the father of lies. A few wonderful and truthful gems like yours telling the truth are like those little prayers that only the children can really appreciate. I do not know how long our country may stand once the soul has been killed. I have read of how Greece rotted away from the inside, Rome crumbled, Israel was scattered, Russia was enslaved, and even the religious and political leaders of the poor and innocent victims of Hitler betrayed them. Yet, people having the strongest propaganda and political machines cannot seem to see that they destroy themselves by imitating those who persecuted them in other times and other places. What is wrong with adult Christians? After 2,000 years can only a few like you and children understand? Can or won't anyone teach the truth?

Reading about the Justices of the Supreme Court, their temple, their draperies, robes, acolytes, even a blindfolded Greek goddess and knowing the power of the little group of men made high priests by politics is a frightening thing. Their published decision is not scholarly and I find no Justice in it, or Honor.

How can people accept as "neutral" a violation of Amendment I, . . . the overruling of the Constitution and the Declaration of Independence? How neutral are the heavy feet of judges who stamp off legal paths onto the beds of spirit, crushing blooms and buds? How can this court censor the Holy Bible?

A lawyer friend said I was tilting at windmills if I tried to get any defence against such trespasses. He said that the most immoral Justice could not be made to stop his immorality, and never was. He said that a new Amendment might help restore us from despotism, but odds are against me and all who fight the Law as the Supreme Court now writes and enforces it.

I am only 17 and cannot even vote. I can only write a letter of thanks, and ask questions. I am very sorry that my country is being torn apart by spoilers, that neighbors are being made to hate and hurt neighbors, a church burns, one People is being divided into small hostile groups, locals, clans, tribes, associations, and other divisions easier for opportunists to handle.

When America's body and soul are destroyed, where else in the world may the persecuted peoples go for what we gave them here while they allowed us to? I shall pray for God's blessing on your good work.

Sincerely,

Sheri Ann Small
Seabreeze High School
Daytona Beach, Florida

Appendix D

A Creed for Americans

This Creed is entirely *documentary*. It is taken wholly from Papers of State and National Ordinances or Shrines. It was prepared for FRASCO (Foundation for Religious Action in the Social and Civil Order)[1] by Kevin Corrigan and Charles Wesley Lowry in September, 1959, at the time of Chairman Khrushchev's visit to the United States. It is intended as a prayerful Meditation for use on any solemn National occasion.

Dates are an important part of this document. For example, in the last item, the National Motto, they refer respectively to the composition of the Star-Spangled Banner, the first coins so marked by direction of Secretary Chase, the Act of Congress dealing with all currency, and the official enactment of a National Motto. When the Pledge of Allegiance was altered in 1954, President Eisenhower in signing the bill said: "In this way we are reaffirming the transcendence of religious faith in America's heritage and future."

[1] This nonsectarian, all-faith organization was founded by a number of distinguished religious leaders representing the major faiths in this country in November, 1953. It is incorporated as a nonprofit religious and educational foundation under the laws of the District of Columbia. The *Third* of its Articles of Incorporation reads: "The particular objects of this corporation shall be to do and perform every lawful act necessary and incident to be done and performed in furtherance of uniting all people who believe in a Supreme Being into a movement having as its avowed aim and purpose the promotion of confidence of people everywhere in religious truth as the prime support of human freedom; of promoting and encouraging resistance to all attempts which may tend to destroy confidence in religion, or which may aim at enslaving the minds of men to totalitarianism in any form; of creating an awareness of the forces bent on the destruction of religion; and of having every participant in this movement endeavor to make religious truth an effective force for the promotion of ordered freedom and the common good in every nation and in the family of nations; and employing every legitimate educational and informational means of carrying out the aims and purposes herein enumerated."

A Creed for Americans

*** In the name of God, Amen. (MAYFLOWER COMPACT, PLYMOUTH ROCK, MASSACHUSETTS, 1620)

*** Proclaim liberty throughout all the land unto all the inhabitants thereof. (LEVITICUS 25, 10: INSCRIPTION ON LIBERTY BELL AT INDEPENDENCE HALL, PHILADELPHIA, PENNSYLVANIA, 1752)

*** We hold these Truths to be self-evident, that all Men are created equal, that they are endowed by their Creator with certain unalienable Rights, that among these are Life, Liberty, and the Pursuit of Happiness—

*** That to secure these Rights, Governments are instituted among Men, deriving their just Powers from the Consent of the Governed, that whenever any Form of Government becomes destructive of these Ends, it is the Right of the People to alter or to abolish it, and to institute a new Government. (DECLARATION OF INDEPENDENCE, PHILADELPHIA, PENNSYLVANIA, 1776)

*** No people can be bound to acknowledge and adore the Invisible Hand which conducts the affairs of men more than the people of the United States. Every step by which they have advanced to the character of an independent nation seems to have been distinguished by some token of providential agency. (WASHINGTON, FIRST INAUGURAL ADDRESS, NEW YORK, NEW YORK, 1789)

*** Our reliance is in the love of liberty which God has planted in our bosoms. Our defense is in the preservation of the spirit which prizes liberty as the heritage of all men, in all lands, everywhere. (LINCOLN, SPEECH AT EDWARDSVILLE, ILLINOIS, 1858)

*** We cannot escape history. . . . No personal significance, or insignificance, can spare one or another of us. The fiery trial through which we pass, will light us down, in honor or dishonor, to the latest generation. (LINCOLN, MESSAGE TO CONGRESS, WASHINGTON, D. C., 1862)

*** We here highly resolve that these dead shall not have died in vain—that this nation, under God, shall have a new birth of freedom—and that government of the people, by the people, for the people, shall not perish from the earth. (LINCOLN, ADDRESS AT GETTYSBURG, PENNSYLVANIA, 1863)

*** One Nation under God, indivisible, with liberty and justice for all. (PLEDGE OF ALLEGIANCE, 1892, 1954)

*** In God We Trust. (NATIONAL MOTTO, 1814, 1864, 1955, 1956)

A Select Bibliography

This Bibliography is not for display purposes and is not intended to be necessarily comprehensive or at all exhaustive. It is meant to serve the alert student who wants to go further, in a practical way.

The Bibliography is arranged in three parts in an order of descending relevance and immediate importance from the standpoint of pursuing further the study objectives of this book, dealing as it does with the Supreme Court, Church and State, and the place of religion in American history and tradition.

PART I

COUSINS, NORMAN: 'In God We Trust': The Religious Beliefs and Ideas of the American Founding Fathers, New York, Harper & Bros., 1958.

HALL, THOMAS CUMING: The Religious Background of American Culture, Boston, Little, Brown & Co., 1930.

HEALEY, ROBERT M.: Jefferson on Religion in Public Education, New Haven, Yale University Press, 1962.

STOKES, ANSON PHELPS: Church and State in the United States (3 vols.), New York, Harper & Bros., 1950.

SWEET, WILLIAM WARREN: Religion in Colonial America, New York, Charles Scribner's Sons, 1942.

TUSSMAN, JOSEPH: The Supreme Court on Church and State, New York, Oxford University Press, 1962.

PART II

BENNETT, JOHN C.: Christians and the State, New York, Charles Scribner's Sons, 1958.

COOLEY, T. M.: Principles of Constitutional Law, Boston, Little, Brown & Co., 1898 (3rd Ed.).

CORWIN, EDWARD S.: The Constitution—What It Means Today, Princeton University Press, 1920 (12th ed., 1958).

HERBERG, WILL: Protestant-Catholic-Jew: An Essay in American Religious Sociology, Garden City, Doubleday & Co., 1955.

HUSZAR AND LITTLEFIELD, EDITORS: Basic American Documents, Ames, Iowa, Littlefield, Adams & Co., 1953.

LITTELL, FRANKLIN H.: From State Church to Pluralism: A Protestant Interpretation of Religion in American History, A Doubleday Anchor Original, 1962.

O'NEILL, JAMES M.: *Religion and Education Under the Constitution,* New York, Harper & Bros., 1949.

PFEFFER, LEO: *Church, State, and Freedom,* Boston, Beacon Press, 1953.

TEMPLE, WILLIAM: *Church and Nation,* London, Macmillan & Co., 1915.

TOCQUEVILLE, ALEXIS DE: *Democracy in America,* New York, Oxford University Press, 1947 (New American Library Paperbound, 1956).

WEIGEL, GUSTAVE, S.J.: *The Modern God: Faith in a Secular Culture,* New York, Macmillan Co., 1963.

PART III

BRYCE, JAMES: *The American Commonwealth,* London & New York, 1st ed., 1889 (Macmillan, 1920).

Constitutions of the States and United States, New York (State) Constitutional Convention Committee, Albany, 1938.

CULVER, RAYMOND B.: *Horace Mann and Religion in the Massachusetts Public Schools,* New Haven, Yale University Press, 1929.

DRINAN, ROBERT F., S.J.: *Religion, the Courts, and Public Policy,* New York, McGraw-Hill Book Co., 1963.

GREENE, EVARTS B.: *Religion and the State: The Making and Testing of an American Tradition,* New York, University Press, 1941.

HERTZBERG, A., MARTY, M. E. AND MOODY, J. N.: *Outbursts That Await Us: Three Essays On Religion and Culture in the United States,* New York, Macmillan Co., 1963.

JOHNSON, A. W. AND YOST, F. H.: *Separation of Church and State in the United States,* Minneapolis, University of Minnesota Press, 1948.

MOEHLMAN, CONRAD H.: *The Wall of Separation Between Church and State,* Boston, Beacon Press, 1951.

MURRAY, JOHN COURTNEY, S.J.: *We Hold These Truths; Catholic Reflections on the American Proposition,* New York, Sheed & Ward, 1960.

PADOVER, SAUL K., EDITOR: *The Complete Jefferson,* New York, Duell, Sloan & Pearce, 1943.

SCHAFF, PHILIP: *Church and State in the United States or the American Idea of Religious Liberty and Its Practical Effect,* New York and London, 1888.